EDDIE MURPHY

EDDIE MURPHY

. . . .

The Life and Times of a Comic on the Edge

FRANK SANELLO

A BIRCH LANE PRESS BOOK
Published by Carol Publishing Group

A Birch Lane Press Book
Published by Carol Publishing Group
Birch Lane Press is a registered trademark of Carol Communications, Inc.

Editorial, sales and distribution, rights and permissions inquiries should be
addressed to Carol Publishing Group, 120 Enterprise Avenue, Secaucus, NJ
07094.

In Canada: Canadian Manda Group, One Atlantic Avenue, Suite 105,
Toronto, Ontario, M6K 3E7

Carol Publishing Group books may be purchased in bulk at special
discounts for sales promotion, fund-raising, or educational purposes.
Special editions can be created to specifications. For details, contact
Special Sales Department, Carol Publishing Group, 120 Enterprise Avenue,
Secaucus, N.J. 07094.

Manufactured in the United States of America
10 9 8 7 6 5 4 3 2 1

Library of Congress Cataloging-in-Publication Data

Sanello, Frank.
    Eddie Murphy : the life and times of a comic on the edge / Frank
Sanello.
        p.   cm.
    "A Birch Lane Press book."
    Includes index.
    ISBN 1–55972–437–4
    1. Murphy, Eddie.   2. Entertainers—United States—Biography.
I. Title.
PN2287.M815S26   1997
792.7′028′092—dc21   97–33224
    [B]   CIP

For Don Myers

"Few in Hollywood have ever achieved domination so quickly and completely."

—Playboy

"He's a genius."

DIRECTOR MARTIN BREST
—Beverly Hills Cop

"I'm here to talk about my real comedy, which is about dicks, farts, and boogers."

—EDDIE MURPHY

Contents

......

Preface

......

Close Encounters of the Weird Kind

"Put Your Mouth on Me"
            —a single off of Eddie Murphy's 1989 album,
            So Happy

ALTHOUGH THE "SCRIPT" is still being written, Eddie Murphy's life has had as much drama and laughs as any of his $200 million movies. "Right now, I'm in a really good place," he said in 1996. Before he reached that location, however, he was called a racist, misogynist, and homophobe. But this future Movie of the Week has a happy ending that continues. On national television, he publicly apologized for previous comments and films that minorities found offensive. "I deeply regret the pain all this has caused," he said on David Letterman's talk show.

At thirty-five, Murphy has finally settled down in a monogamous relationship with the mother of his three children, a supernally lovely model who worships the ground the superstar floats above. His career also prospered with a huge comeback film, *The Nutty Professor*. "Everything just got beautiful," he says. "Now my priorities are my art and my family. Those two things can't be taken away." The once angry young man has mellowed; his career is turbo-charged.

*   *   *

That was how I planned to end my biography of Eddie
Murphy. I even tried to sell the publisher on the title, *Big
Eddie, Happy at Last,* in homage to another public figure who
survived a horrific childhood and prospered as an adult. But
then, in the early morning hours of May 2, 1997, an incident
occurred that required a rapid rewrite of my rosey
conclusion.

From the triple X files of the Los Angeles County Sheriff's
Headquarters Bureau in West Hollywood, this real-life police
story:

"At 4:45 A.M. on 05-02-97, West Hollywood Deputies were
working in an unmarked patrol car in a prostitution-abate-
ment zone. The Deputies saw a male in a [Toyota] Land
Cruiser pick up a known transsexual [sic] prostitute at the
corner of Santa Monica Boulevard and Formosa Avenue,
West Hollywood. The Deputies followed the vehicle two miles
to Van Ness Avenue and Raleigh Avenue, where they stopped
it to investigate possible prostitution activity. The investiga-
tion revealed that no illegal activity had occurred. However,
the passenger in the vehicle had a warrant for prostitution.
The passenger (Atisone Seiuli) was arrested and booked at
West Hollywood Sheriff's Station with a bail of $15,000. Mr.
Murphy was apparently not involved in any criminal activity
and was not detained."

Eddie Murphy's account: "This is an act of kindness that
got turned into a fucking horror show." In the early morning
of May 2, the actor had finished the day's shooting on his $70-
million movie *Dr. Dolittle.* His wife and kids were in Sacramento, visiting his mother-in-law. Battling insomnia and
loneliness, he decided to drive to a newsstand for something
to read. Passing through a red-light district on Santa Monica
Boulevard frequented by male prostitutes, Murphy says, "I
saw this Hawaiian-looking woman and said, 'What are you

doing out here?' She said, 'I'm working.'" As he had many times in the past with streetwalkers, the actor gave the woman a stern lecture. "It's very dangerous. You shouldn't be out here. She said, 'I know, I'm going home, would you give me a ride?' I said, 'Where do you live? She said, 'I live on Willoughby.' That's where I made my mistake."

Murphy and his passenger traveled about two miles before an unmarked cop car pulled the Toyota over. The "Hawaiian-looking woman" turned out to be a male transvestite prostitute, Atisone Seiuli, twenty, with a prior conviction for prostitution. As part of Seiuli's probation after the arrest a few months before, he had been ordered to undergo an AIDS test, which he failed to do. A warrant was issued for his arrest on a probation violation.

E. L. Woody, a freelance paparazzo, happened to be driving by and caught the incident on videotape. Woody said, "[Murphy] wasn't real happy about it. He kept begging the police, 'Don't take me in. Don't arrest me.'" While Woody rolled tape, a visibly agitated Murphy explained his actions to the photographer. The impromptu interview aired on national television.

After ten minutes, the deputies let the driver go but arrested his passenger. Seiuli, a biological male, not a transsexual, as the Sheriff's report erroneously stated, was booked for probation violation and sent to a protective wing of Los Angeles County Jail reserved for transvestites. He pleaded guilty to the probation violation and received a ninety-day sentence. A judge also ordered him to take an AIDS test.

Murphy was shocked to learn the sexual identity of his passenger. "I thought Atisone was a girl. That's not even the issue. It wasn't like I was looking for someone. It was a person I assumed was a girl at the corner."

Press reports noted that Murphy was some distance past Seiuli's residence when the police pulled them over. Sgt. Robert Harms at the West Hollywood Sheriff's Station said,

"For the most part, Santa Monica Boulevard is known for its homosexual prostitute trade. Transvestites, transsexuals, and other males work those areas." Females work a few blocks north on Sunset Boulevard, where actor Hugh Grant and prostitute Divine Mae Brown were arrested in 1996.

Don Crutchfield, a Los Angeles private eye, said, "Eddie had to know that stretch of Santa Monica Boulevard is known for gay hustlers and cross-dressing prostitutes. You don't pick up anybody there. You don't even stop there. That's a drive-by, a look, and a laugh. That's all it is, unless you're serious and want to do some business there."

Murphy said he was in the business of being a Good Samaritan. "What people don't know is, for years and years at night, I'd get in my car, I'd drive all over Manhattan, I'd give derelicts money. I'd stop and talk to homeless people. I'd go to corners where there were prostitutes and give them $5,000 and $10,000 to go home and get off the street.... I'm not doing it for publicity. When I do something, it's out of the goodness of my heart." In fact, just prior to giving Seiuli a lift home, Murphy said he had given $1,000 to a homeless man.

The actor hadn't pulled his Good Samaritan story out of thin air. He was on record as going out among society's unfortunates and lending a helping hand in the form of cash and counseling. In 1990, he told *Playboy* in an interview at his New Jersey estate, "I've got to keep in touch with reality. If I stayed here at Bubble Hill, I wouldn't know what the fuck was going on. That's why I go out and drive around. I see people on crack." His incredulous interviewer asked, "You drive through crack neighborhoods?" As he would with Atisone Seiuli seven years later, Murphy lectured street people to get off the streets and get off crack. "Yeah, I stop and ask addicts, 'What the fuck are you doing?' I used to give them money. I used to say, 'You've got to get your life together.' I'd lecture them and say, 'Get off the street.'" His largesse ended when he suspected his cash gifts were being spent on crack. "I realized I was doing more harm than good."

After the story about Murphy's encounter with Seiuli broke, I called the star's publicist, Arnold Robinson, at Rogers and Cowan for a statement. Mr. Murphy's only comments would be made that evening on *Entertainment Tonight*, Robinson's secretary said. That wasn't quite true. Murphy also talked to the *Star*, which corroborated his version of events, and did a phone interview with *People* magazine while his attorney listened in and frequently told his client not to answer certain questions. Murphy ignored his attorney.

Entertainment Tonight has been called a "publicist's dream" because of its gentle coverage of celebrity news. The infotainment show is produced by Paramount on a sound-stage a few hundred feet away from the Eddie Murphy Productions building. *ET* reporter and one-time game show host Bob Goen conducted the interview in a hotel suite. Murphy wore pajamas.

Agitated as he sipped a bottle of apple juice, the actor recapped what he had told the *Star* and *People*. His wife Nicole's reaction caused him the most distress. "My wife is embarrassed, her heart is broken, and I feel horrible. My wife asked, 'Why would you pick up...' I wash my hands one hundred times a day. She couldn't believe this. 'You gave a prostitute a ride home?' It was a split-second dumb decision. My wife knows I help people out. Usually, I just give my lecture through the window, give them money through a window." Murphy said he thoroughly washed the interior of his Toyota after Seiuli left.

Jeff Gorsuch, a clinical psychologist who watched the segment on *Entertainment Tonight*, said, "You could tell this man is obviously lying."

Goen was in turn interviewed by the local CBS station's anchor, Michael Tuck. Goen said of Murphy's decision to appear on *ET,* "He wanted to set the record straight. It's a pretty smart move because this thing could really get out of control." Anchor Tuck asked Goen a question the *ET* reporter never asked Murphy. "Are we supposed to believe he drives through red light districts and empties his wallet for prostitutes?"

As sensational as the incident on Santa Monica Boulevard was, the mainstream press largely ignored it. The *L.A. Times* failed to report the story in either its Metro or entertainment sections.

The print and electronic tabloids, however, went berserk. The *National Enquirer* ran a purportedly exclusive interview with Seiuli, whose street and stage name is Shalimar. The *Star,* which claimed Murphy was a huge fan of the magazine, supported the actor's story. The tab reported it had been inundated with calls from transsexuals and transvestites who said Murphy had also given them money and advice but never asked for or received sex in return.

One transvestite, though, a former gay porn star, had a different experience with Murphy, in 1990. Geoff Gann, a 30-year-old native of Ozark, Missouri, has appeared on stage and in approximately one hundred porn videos under the stage name of Karen Dior. His guest-starring role on *Xena: Warrior Princess* recently earned the TV series its highest ratings ever. As a woman and a man, he's done TV commercials, a TV-movie with Loni Anderson, and he worked with Richard Chamberlain on an upcoming made-for-TV film. He's also done runway modeling in haute couture drag. After retiring from porn films, he went behind the camera and has directed "hundreds" of gay videos, he says.

According to Gann, whom I interviewed in his apartment near the Hollywood Hills, Eddie Murphy was a big fan of his work in front of the camera.

In the summer of 1990, Gann had just left a gay disco, The Four Star, on Santa Monica Boulevard, where he per-

formed his cabaret act in drag. Walking with friends down a
side street, he heard someone shout from a parked limousine,
"KAREN!" Gann peeked inside and saw Eddie Murphy.

His friends discreetly left them alone. Murphy said to
Gann, "Are you Karen Dior?" Gann said he was. Murphy
replied, "I've seen your movies." Gann said, "I've seen *your*
movies."

Gann had only appeared in two adult films at the time,
and he says Murphy mentioned both by name. The movie star
asked the porn star if he would like to go for a ride. New to
town, Gann said he was shy and "susceptible to flattery."

He got into the limo, and they chatted for a while. "He
was very polite and very nice and, um, asked if I was on
hormones. All the questions people typically ask. He said,
'You look really feminine. Do you want to get a sex change?' I
said no to all those things. And then we had sex."

While they rode through West Hollywood's gay ghetto,
Murphy fellated Gann first. Then Gann performed oral sex
on Murphy. Gann says they both ejaculated. Their time
together totaled about half an hour, he estimates.

The two men never saw each other again. Since then,
Gann has been diagnosed with AIDS. He's had bouts with
Kaposi's sarcoma, an AIDS-related skin cancer, and several
opportunistic infections, including microsporidia, a parasite
which causes wasting syndrome and is incurable. The parasite caused a thirty-pound weight loss, but the new generation of AIDS drugs has partially restored Gann's damaged
immune system. "I was really sick for a year and then
protease inhibitors came along, and I started taking them and
I've been totally fine. Technically, I have AIDS, but I'm really
doing fine now," he said, sprawled on a chaise lounge in his
apartment decorated in '50s kitsch. When I interviewed him
in June 1997, he felt strong enough to direct a transvestite-
themed porn film, *I Dream of Queenie*.

AIDS experts now recommend that drug treatment

begin early with those infected with the virus, even if they are asymptomatic. Gann believes Murphy should be tested for AIDS. "Anyone who's had sex with multiple partners or is picking people up off the street and having sex with them—yes, I would urge them to get an AIDS test."

Just as the Hugh Grant scandal soon become old news after the tabs had finished their feeding frenzy, Murphy's encounter with Seiuli also faded away as new celebrity scandals broke. Tim Allen's DWI arrest, Frank Gifford's hotel hug, and Farrah Fawcett's shoplifting convictions and alleged theft of a romantic rival's wardrobe bumped Murphy's travails off the page and the TV screen.

Then the actor did something extraordinary: He breathed new life into the two-week old story by filing two lawsuits in Los Angeles Superior Court against the *National Enquirer* and the *Globe* for $10 million, claiming the tabs had harmed his reputation and caused him "severe emotional and physical distress" which required medical treatment. Murphy also sued Gann and a cousin of Seiuli, who told the *New York Post* Murphy had known Seiuli before the incident and had promised him a role in one of his movies.

Since Murphy had not been arrested, the *L.A. Times* chose to ignore the original incident. After a nationally known figure filed suit, the paper was forced to report the story along with details of the encounter on Santa Monica Boulevard. If and when the case goes to court, it will make national news all over again, with the mainstream press obligated to cover a distasteful story it would rather leave to the tabloids.

An unidentified business colleague felt Murphy was his own worst enemy, and the lawsuit reinforced the feeling. "I believe we all know what he was doing, and what he wanted to do," the associate said. "I think he could be a self-destructive guy reaching out for help and about to blow up."

Others attributed the star's appearance on *Entertain-*

ment Tonight—like the later lawsuit, both of which kept the story fresh long after its shelf life should have expired—to panic on Murphy's part. Sources predict cooler heads, his attorneys' and handlers'—will ultimately prevail, and Murphy will quietly drop the lawsuits.

If he doesn't, the tabloids' army of libel lawyers, who get a lot of practice, will vigorously fight the case. The *Enquirer* responded to the suit by saying it stood by its story and would not "tolerate this legal attack....Mr. Murphy is attempting to rehabilitate himself at our expense. We intend to prove our case in open court."

Geoff Gann was also hanging tough. "It's just a scare tactic and being a bully and to keep me from talking or to scare other people off." He noted that he didn't have any assets Murphy could seize "except my dresses."

Besides, "I'll probably die of AIDS before it ever gets to court."

Author's note: My sources who predicted cooler heads would prevail and Murphy would drop his lawsuits against the tabs proved prophetic. Less than two months after filing, Murphy quietly dropped his action against the *Enquirer* and settled with the *Globe*. Geoff Gann was never even served. Murphy, however, did more than drop his *Enquirer* suit. Mike Glynn, a reporter for the tab, told me the star also agreed to pay the magazine's legal fees. The *Enquirer* is represented by the blue-chip Washington-based firm of Williams & Connolly, the nation's premier First Amendment-rights law firm. Glynn said, "Williams & Connolly charge a fortune. They flew out two lawyers from D.C. to L.A. That had never happened before." The legal fees, of course, were pin money for Murphy, but his willingness to pay them suggests his bargaining position may have been weak.

No matter what it cost him, the star was wise to drop the lawsuits which would have prolonged the shelf life of the original scandal. Marketing executive Henry Shafer believes the longer a celebrity hangs and twists in the wind, the greater the damage. "It [could seriously tarnish an image] depending on how much press and coverage it gets nation-wide and how long it stays in front of the American public," Shafer said. A major movie star, Murphy couldn't escape international press attention, but he could put closure to the story by staying out of court. Another variable Murphy had no control over, however, was the contrast between his public image and his private behavior. "How [a scandal] impacts image varies from where they're coming from in terms of what they had already established with the public...If they're kind of an off-center personality versus someone who's straight and narrow, it'll be judged differently," Shafer said. Murphy's image as both a ladies' man and famous homo-phobe (see chapter 9) didn't jibe with picking up a male prostitute. The irony made the story more sensational and damaging to this particular celebrity than if, say, Rupert Everett, an openly gay actor, had been pulled over for the same behavior. If Hugh Grant, another famous ladykiller, had been caught with a streetwalker named Divine "Mo" rather than Divine Mae Brown, the story might not have vanished so quickly after Grant's public apology. And you can be sure Grant would not have done the talk show circuit and charmed the scandal away if there had been a homosexual component.

PROLOGUE
......
The Up Side of Pain

A TRAUMATIC CHILDHOOD. It's hell on the child; great for the development of an artist: Every *Bildungsroman* seems to have this sad but enriching ingredient. Awful memories of youth fuel the artistic imagination of the adult. Childhood abuse, like a scabrous chrysalis, turns into the monarch of great art. To paraphrase Gordon Gecko's meditation on greed, pain is good.

Not too much of the stuff, of course. Horrific childhood experiences can paralyze the grownup. Self-medicating with licit and illicit substances dulls painful memories, but it also wipes out the razor-sharp consciousness needed to crank out ten pages a day of the Great American Novel or cover enough canvases to wallpaper a gallery exhibit.

Hemingway and Dorothy Parker come to mind as exemplars of the delicate balance between paralysis and productivity: both brilliant talents deluded and diluted by too much liquid anesthetic, one dying a slow death by whiskey sour, the other graceless under pressure with a shotgun in his mouth. Overwhelming childhoods can overwhelm the adult, capsizing the fragile skiff of creativity in tsunamis of self-destructive behavior.

A little childhood pain, preferably of short duration, works wonders on a budding artist. Dickens is paradigmatic. A sunny upper-class childhood suddenly rained on by an improvident father's trip to debtor's prison. Yanked out of boarding school at eight and dumped in a shoe polish factory, Dickens was harassed by the memory for the rest of his life even though he had spent less than a year pasting labels on bottles of bootblack. A bestselling author lionized on both sides of the Atlantic, the most eminent Victorian found himself bursting into tears whenever he passed by his former place of employment. But life on the assembly line lasted only eight months before his father's revived fortunes liberated him from day camp in hell. Long enough to create a tortured artist; not too long to produce a dysfunctional adult lost to opiates (Coleridge) or distilled grains (the list of artistic sots is too long to record here).

Eddie Murphy had the good kind of childhood pain. A few horrific incidents in an otherwise charmed upbringing. Abandonment, physical and substance abuse and a tabloidish murder molded his formative years without smothering the child or crippling the adult. There was even a foster mother wicked enough to fire a child's imagination but not so abusive as to immolate it.

Like greed, pain can indeed be good. Too much and you have Lenin avenging his brother's execution with the murder of five million Ukrainian peasants by artificial famine. One man's vendetta is another man's forced collectivization. Instead, with just enough torture you get *David Copperfield* or Mary McCarthy's *Memories of a Catholic Girlhood*.

While childhood trauma enriches the artist's creative life, it can be hell on his private relationships. Abandonment in youth infects adult-life bonding with uncertainty and distrust. Spurned by a parent who has decamped—or in Murphy's case the absence of both mom and dad—the child grows up dreading repetition of the original betrayal. Why commit to another person when she's likely to up and leave? Better not to get involved in the first place. And if you're rich and famous, you can have your pick of the groupie harem without all the little *douceurs* we mere mortals have to employ to capture and keep a loved one. Instead of "I love you," it's "Next..."

The demons of childhood can reemerge as devilish behavior in adulthood. Murphy has battled his share of demons. Tantrums on stage and CD, politically incorrect pronouncements everywhere, self-indulgent behavior on movie sets, and most recently the unfortunate carpool on Santa Monica Boulevard have punctuated a seemingly perfect life. Approaching middle age, back on top as a nine-hundred-pound box-office gorilla, Murphy has slain or at least suppressed his demons. The battle was largely won with the love of a selfless woman who also happened to be spectacularly beautiful. The three children of this union mellowed Murphy even more and turned any residual demons into the red anticherub Hot Stuff of the comic books, a devil in a diaper.

When Murphy revisits his childhood, the occasional horrors become virtually opaque, the glasses are so rose-colored. Forgotten, apparently, are the alcoholism, the late night whuppings in the basement by stepdad, mom's excusable absence, and dad's permanent departure by the hand of a knife-wielding inamorata.

The rose tint seemed more like a blackout when Murphy at twenty-one said, "I had a real good home life. I never wanted for anything, emotionally or materially."

We'll see about that.

EDDIE MURPHY

Chapter 1

......

Bildungsroman

So much of Eddie Murphy's life and career can be divided into good news and bad news, starting with his birth and continuing through a career of ups and downs that could make roller coaster fans nauseous.

To start with the bad news, Edward Regan Murphy was born in the slums. On April 3, 1961, in the Bushwick section of Brooklyn. In public housing. The outside world of pushers and hookers, stabbings and muggings, was much less nightmarish for the youngster than what was going on at home.

The good news: Eddie didn't suffer long enough for this early environment to leave troubling memories. The family was prosperous enough by his eleventh birthday to move to the tidy, all-black suburb of Roosevelt, Long Island.

At the time of his birth, despite the surroundings, Murphy had a big advantage over many of his peers. In the ghetto, single mothers are endemic, but Murphy was blessed with both a mom and a dad on the premises, however modest those premises were. His mother Lillian was a telephone operator. His father, Charles Lee Murphy, worked as a policeman for the New York City Transit Authority. Eddie had a sibling, Charles Jr., two years his senior.

This nuclear family imploded early, before Eddie's consciousness could appreciate the benefits of a stable, two-parent household. "My parents broke up when I was

3

three....After the divorce, [dad] and I used to go out on weekends to movies, but I don't have a really clear memory of him. People tell me I walk like my father, hold my head like my father, but I don't have a 'Once my father did this' story," Murphy said.

It got worse. A few years later, his mother became gravely ill and spent a year in a hospital. At this point, Murphy's childhood hits horrific depths. The fairy tale sounds like the grimmest of Grimm's. While mom convalesced in a hospital bed, Eddie and Charles Jr. were placed in foster care. The usual rose-colored glasses of childhood happiness come off when Murphy describes his version of Dickens' trip to the shoeshine shop.

Recalling the year-long ordeal, Murphy called his foster mother a "black Nazi. One day she gave us pigs' tails for dinner, and then, when I told my grandmother that we were being fed *snakes,* the woman grabbed Charles and whipped him. Those were *baaad* days. Staying with her was probably the reason I became a comedian." Shoe polish accomplished a similar feat for the author of *Great Expectations.* A "black Nazi" led to three *Beverly Hills Cop*s. The importance of childhood pain in the creation of an artist was brilliantly described by Mary McCarthy in her memoir of growing up Catholic with abusive foster parents, her great-aunt and -uncle. McCarthy's period of foster care, like Murphy's, didn't last long, and soon she was returned to the loving care of Currier & Ives grandparents. McCarthy speculated that if it hadn't been for this interlude of beatings and starving, she might have become a Junior League country-clubber rather than the respected best-selling novelist she was. What price art? Pain.

Murphy's personal fairy tale had an evil foster mother, but like all fairy tales, it also had a happy ending—sort of. Happiness came from an unlikely source, a stepfather who was anything but wicked. Okay, Vernon Lynch boozed a bit and gave life lessons wearing boxing gloves, but Lynch was good enough for Murphy as an adult to say, "I love the guy."

Like Prince Charming, Vernon Lynch rescued Mrs. Murphy and her boys from the bane of sociologists of ghetto life, the single-mother home, the alleged cause of *all* the inner city's problems.

Lynch was a retired prizefighter, a featherweight with a 17-4 record, who drove a truck and worked as a foreman at a Breyer's Ice Cream plant. He was a dominant enough figure to wipe out any vestigial memory of Eddie's biological father. "I don't remember having a father figure, because my mother married the father I have now," Murphy has said.

Lynch was a strong father figure and a role model who inculcated his boys with the work ethic by his own example. Sometimes, though, he instilled discipline with his fists. When the boys misbehaved, they'd join their stepfather in the basement and go a few rounds. Years later, Lynch recalled his philosophy of child-rearing with no apologies: "I could still whip Eddie. Eddie respects his parents. I used to be a professional fighter. And I believed in me; I believed nobody could whip me. Eddie always had that; he always believed in himself, even from a little kid." The message seems to be that your child lacks self-confidence, beat it into him. Perhaps this comes from one of the chapters Dr. Spock deleted.

It's easy to see where Eddie's in-yo'-face attitude came from. Lynch to this day continues his basement tutorials. "I will still take Charlie or Eddie downstairs and put on the gloves with them. Toughen them up a little bit, show them how tough they can be. If he wanted to, I think he'd be a dynamite middleweight boxer. He don't like to be hit, but he's quick to learn. His reflexes are good, terrific. But he said, 'Pop, no good. Don't want to fight nobody.' But he can defend himself."

Not all Lynch's lessons were delivered with an uppercut. The Murphy brothers and their half brother, Vernon Jr., learned from their father that an adult male goes to work in the morning and comes home at night. He doesn't laze about and hide on the day the social worker from ADC drops in to make sure mom is indeed a single mother with dependent children. Actually, Lynch went to work at Breyer's at night and came home at dawn, but the kids still learned the circadian rhythms of the eight-hour workday from dad.

Lynch's behavior also provided material for the future comedian's standup act, although at the time it seemed anything but funny. On stage, the adult Murphy did a bit called "Drinking Fathers."

The short joke speaks volumes about successful coping. While child abuse leaves some adults among the walking wounded the rest of their lives, others rise from the ashes and give phoenixes competition. That which does not destroy us makes us stronger, Nietzsche said. Eddie obviously wasn't destroyed; he used his stepfather's obstreperousness as a punch line in a sold-out concert tour.

One morning, home from Breyer's after a stop at a bar that opened early, Lynch woke up the boys and began to give them a rambling lecture about life. The kids weren't in the mood for guidance from a souse, so Lynch challenged them to a fight. Murphy, revealing more than necessary for a simple gag, recalled that their rebuff of Lynch's drunken soliloquy infuriated their stepfather even more. To get his sons to take him up on the challenge, he laid down his paycheck, winner take all. On stage, Murphy delivered a punch line as sleek as a one-two. "We beat the shit out of the motherfucker." In the comedian's retelling of the incident, a potential trauma is transmuted into a lucrative reward. Nietzsche might have added, that which does not kill us makes us laugh.

Murphy may have embroidered—punched up if you will—the episode, but Lynch concedes that while the details are exaggerated, the facts are basically correct. "That was me," Lynch said, admitting that he and the hops were not strangers, although bosom buddies would overstate the case. "True, true, true. Maybe I'd stop and have a beer someplace and try to joke with the boys. I'd come in here, three o'clock in the morning, get them up. We're just a normal, everyday family, hardworking. I wanted those boys up and out, working or at school. I don't think I was as bad as he makes out. But I rolled him out: 'Get up, get these dishes washed!'" At three in the morning?

"I always kept two pairs of boxing gloves around. And Eddie doesn't like no kind of violence. All I had to do was tell him, 'Let's go, just you and me, downstairs.' No problem." Lynch's recollection fails to mention who got to cash his paycheck.

Sermons from a boozy stepfather were nothing compared to another childhood incident so traumatic it never made it into the comedian's stand-up act. In fact, the event rarely made it into published interviews because the usually thick-skinned star found it too painful to dredge up. Or, as he put it, "It was really fucked up, man, the worst tragedy ever to happen to me."

In 1969, over the Labor Day weekend, Eddie's biological father was knifed to death by a jealous girlfriend. Eddie was eight. Years later, Murphy giggled nervously when he described the murder. "He was a victim of the Murphy charm. [chuckles] A woman stabbed my father. I never got all the logistics. It was supposed to be one of those crimes of passion: 'If I can't have you, then no one else will' kind of deal."

Journalists, and even friends, would attribute his adult behavior to this childhood trauma. While Murphy conceded its gravity, he refused to believe that the murder turned him into a misogynist. "Someone said to me one day, 'That's why you don't trust women.' Get the fuck outta here. What are you, a fucking psychiatrist?' I don't think the two have anything to do with each other. But I was really fucked up about his death. It was really traumatic. Will some woman take me out? I doubt it. Richard Pryor's father died fucking. That's a good way to go. I'll take that over being hit by a truck."

When an interviewer from *Playboy* asked if the incident had at least made him wary of women, Murphy deadpanned, "Nah, I don't trust anybody."

In 1985, the *National Enquirer* splashed Murphy's childhood tragedy across its front page with the headline, "Eddie Murphy Haunted by Dad's Brutal Murder—He's Afraid He'll Die the Same Horrible Death." In its inimitable, pathological way, the *Enquirer* claimed the superstar had become paranoid and mentally unstable. Murphy sued the magazine in the U.S. District Court in Manhattan for $30 million in compensatory and punitive damages. He claimed the story was "totally false and defamatory." Not quite. His attorney, Leonard Marks, said, "While it is true that his father was murdered in 1969, the rest of the alleged facts in the story are totally false."

His father's murder traumatized him, but it didn't paralyze him. A strong father substitute was already in place when his father died. "The death of my father was a real big disappointment in life, but my stepfather, I love the guy. If I have some kids and should die at an early age, I hope some guy will do as well for them as my stepfather has done for me."

The transformational event of Murphy's formative years, however, was not his father's violent end, but a totally positive development. When Eddie was eleven, the family moved from the Brooklyn ghetto to the lower-middle-class suburb of Roosevelt on the south shore of Long Island. The three-bedroom house was the largest on a quiet street. *Rolling Stone* said, "It was a sheltered, almost protected life, even from the vagaries of casual, everyday American racism."

Another magazine condescendingly added that he was "exposed to middle class values." In fact, while Roosevelt was no Larchmont, it was energetically, upwardly mobile. The Lynch home in particular was always being renovated, repainted, wallpapered. As Lynch said proudly, "We always wanted to go forward. Eddie never knew anything about no ghetto."

Murphy's memories contradict his stepfather's. His are less rosy, but not necessarily more accurate. The comedian may be embroidering his roots because life in the ghetto is a more dramatic story than life behind a white picket fence.

Years later, driving past tin-doored tenements in East Harlem, he claimed, "This looks like where I grew up in Brooklyn." This is definitely autobiographical myth-making. Murphy spent the first decade of his life in public housing, which, however run down, doesn't have tin doors or the bombed out, World-War-II-Berlin look of East Harlem.

More accurately, he added, "We were never rich growing up. We were always working-class. My kids are the first generation of both my wife's and my family that weren't born in project houses. My backstory is project houses, welfare. I stayed in boarding houses during a period when my mother was in the hospital.

"I'm the first person in my family who's been able to do things for the family because of my situation. I've never lost sight of where I've come from or what's going on."

East Harlem's desolation made him ponder his success—and question whether he would have enjoyed any if his formative years had been spent in this American Beirut. "I wonder if the same things would have happened to me if I had stayed in Brooklyn. I would've had more material. 'Hey, I got shot once. Anybody out there ever been shot?'"

Murphy's material would come from a much more prosaic—and safer—source, TV—America's most popular baby-sitter and the medium that would make him a national star.

Instead of drive-by shootings and junkies slamming smack in the hallway, young Eddie was safely lodged in front of the Lynches's TV set, which would turn out to be a major source of creativity and inspiration for the future comic. While other artists might point to Brando in *Streetcar* or David Lean's telescopic long shot of Omar Sharif in *Lawrence of Arabia* as the pivotal aesthetic experience of their youth, Murphy found the roots of his comedy in Bugs Bunny and Tom and Jerry. He learned to imitate anybody or any accent by doing impersonations of his favorite Saturday morning cartoon characters.

The recollections of relatives suggest they felt as though they were living with a male Sybil or the three faces of Adam. Mom Lillian: "You'd never be sitting around with just Eddie, always with some other character. You worry about a child's identity when he's doing Deputy Dawg all the time."

Lillian recalled that her son would lock himself in his room for hours, with the hi-fi blaring Elvis, while he wrote comedy scripts. TV was his teacher in this bedroom-class-room. "When he watched TV, he didn't just watch. He *studied*. I don't think he ever missed *West Side Story* on TV. I'd say his three main influences were *West Side Story*, Elvis Presley, and Bruce Lee," his mother said. These influences are a telling commentary on the lack of positive black role models for youth. Murphy was forced to seek inspiration from ballet-dancing gangs (*West Side Story*), a chopsockey hero (Bruce Lee) and a fat white guy with dreadful fashion sense (Elvis).

Eddie was no athlete. As an adult, he would admit he never watched sports programs because he hated to see people excel at something he couldn't. Also, Murphy was just plain afraid of the rough and tumble. "He didn't like contact sports. He played baseball, but basically he didn't want to get hurt," his mother says. She also suggested he was something of a borderline hypochondriac. Obsessive hand-washing was a childhood trait that lingers to this day.

Instead or risking life and limb to dunk a ball through a steel hoop, Murphy watched reruns of *I Love Lucy, The Honeymooners*, and *Batman*. Years later, one of his funniest and more controversial bits was a homosexual version of Ralph Kramden and Ed Norton as a very odd couple indeed.

Director John Landis summed up the Murphy cosmology: "His world experiences come from the tube."

Murphy described his education via video: "My mother says I never talked in my own voice—always cartoon characters. Dudley Do-Right, Bullwinkle. I used to do Sylvester the Cat ('Thufferin' thucotash') all the time. I could always get my brother Charlie mad by doing Bela Lugosi. Get him in trouble. I was that kind of kid."

When he wasn't surgically attached to the TV set, you could find him in the basement, which his imagination transformed into an auditorium of rapturous fans. After an uncle gave him a gold lamé coat, Murphy recreated Elvis Presley's entire Madison Square Garden act, which he had a recording of. The youngster also studied Elvis's movies and did a dead-on impression of the singer's once notorious pelvic thrusts. Eddie became so engrossed in his shaking, he began baking, drenched in sweat by the end of the "concert."

"Elvis was my idol then—still is. I thought he had more presence and charisma than anybody who ever existed," Murphy has said. Years later, pop psychologists would suggest Murphy had a pathological reverence for the bloated icon whose pharmaceutical lifestyle was an unhealthy and unlikely role model. Others hinted Murphy might come to the same sad end if his infatuation with Elvis overwhelmed common sense. When director Martin Brest (*Beverly Hills Cop*) told him his sixty-one-city concert tour was too back-breaking, Murphy countered that Elvis had done the same. Brest said, "I think it's time somebody told you that Elvis is not the healthiest role model." Murphy refused to smash his idol. He still insists that Presley is "the only entertainer of any kind that I would have liked to trade places with." No doubt before the King's unfortunate Vegas period and damaged kidneys.

Those caveats didn't occur to him back then and don't lessen his admiration now. An early critic was his brother Charlie, who once watched Murphy do his Elvis act for 10 minutes before the performer became aware that he had an audience. His first "fan" was anything but. His brother said, "You're crazy, man. Really crazy." Charlie also asked why he was doing Elvis, of all people, since the Elvis impersonator industry would not boom until after the King's death. Murphy recalled, "I had no answer."

The urge to entertain, even when his only audience was himself or a spying sibling, amounted to a genetic predisposition, Murphy felt. "The Murphys are just funny people. At family reunions, everybody's trying to outjoke everybody else. Uncles, aunts, and cousins—we all got big mouths. We were poor people, but we're a real proud family. We have so much pride we seem arrogant. We're not. I'm not." His mother also blamed it all on DNA: "We never encouraged him to be a comedian. He really did it all on his own. But humor has got to be a trait in the Murphy blood. Eddie's father was a weekend comic and emcee. What's strange is that Eddie never knew him."

Fortunately, for the future of blockbuster movies, Elvis wasn't the only icon Murphy worshiped: Lionel Ritchie, Bill Cosby, and soul-singer Al Green were other objects of study. If imitation is the sincerest form of flattery, Murphy was a suck-up big time.

His performances weren't confined to the family basement. At school, it would be inaccurate to call him the class clown; his behavior was too sophisticated to be described as clowning around. "Class headliner" would better describe the way Murphy commanded his peers' attention and appreciation. His popularity and success were all the more noteworthy since his physical presence was so unprepossessing. "I had a pot belly, brown frame glasses, and a bald head," Murphy said. He was being too hard on himself. A photo from grade school does indeed reveal a shaved head, but the face underneath is cute as a bug's ear. "One day in third grade, Mr. Wunch came into class and said whoever made up the best story would win an Eskimo Pie. I cracked the kids up with a story about rice and Orientals. It was my first performance. And guess who won the pie?" This was his first—but definitely not last—brush with both politically incorrect humor ("rice and Orientals") and an audience's approbation.

The youngster was also a brilliant impressionist and a quick study. He would stand outside the boys' lavatory at school and do a perfect imitation of the principal—so dead-on, his stepfather proudly recalled, that the students would panic and run back to the classes they were cutting. "Eddie could watch you for ten minutes and mimic your mannerisms and vocabulary to a tee. He does a great imitation of Grandma," Vernon Lynch said. Years later, Murphy's performance as Grandma would gross $200 million. It was in a movie called *The Nutty Professor*.

Let's hope his childhood impressions of grandma weren't as cruel as the film's foul-mouthed termagant. His real-life grandmother recognized his potential early on and gave him an easel and canvases. When he wasn't writing scripts in front of the TV, he could be found painting away. He did give up guitar lessons because the strings hurt his fingers; puppet shows were easier on the hands. At eleven, when he asked for a ventriloquist's dummy, it showed up under the Christmas tree. Murphy wasn't spoiled. Vernon was too much the disciplinarian ex-boxer for that. But he was clearly loved by two generations of the family and indulged in all his artistic endeavors. His mother basically let him do whatever he wanted.

It was easy to indulge Eddie. He was a lovable child, endearing with a smile that would later become his trademark on film and TV. "He never got into trouble," his mother said. "He didn't belong to a gang. He had only one or two best friends, and I always knew where he was. Eddie could never understand why kids hung out in the streets." With unabashed favoritism, Mrs. Lynch says her middle son was the most sensitive of her offspring. "He has always been loving and generous, family-oriented. He was such a lovable kid. He'd sit on your lap until you moved him. Your leg would fall asleep, and he'd still be sitting there." Like his humor, lovable but a bit irritating.

Even when the youngster was bad, he was, well, good. "Eddie was always a good child. I'll never forget when he was six or seven and I would spank him. He would just say, 'I know why you spanked me, Mommy. You spanked me because you love me. 'Cause if you didn't care, you wouldn't spank me.'" The Murphy charm was already showing itself at age six.

While charm had fatal results for Murphy Sr., it made Junior the most popular kid in school—even with teachers who weren't crazy about his absenteeism and comic riffs which, while entertaining, were also disruptive.

"For some reason," his mother said, "he would always get passes to leave class. He would go to study hall and entertain the kids practicing his material."

Eddie was not a scholar, to put it mildly. "I wasn't the brain or the great sports star at school. I told jokes and I was the rough guy. But I was always getting lectured about how I was gonna be a failure at school, about how I didn't have a serious attitude. I'd go...yah..."

His grade point average hovered around C-minus. The future entertainment conglomerate could already foresee his stardom and pooh-poohed a temporary setback like a 2.0 GPA. "I used to come home with report cards when I was fifteen with zeroes on them, and fifties and sixties. My mother would say, 'What's wrong with you?' and I'd say, 'I'm going to be famous, Ma.'"

When one high school teacher, a rare nonfan of the class cutup, told him he'd never amount to anything if he didn't apply himself in school, Murphy said with supreme self-confidence, "One day I'm going to me more famous than Bob Hope," a bizarre reference for a black youth in a segregated suburb.

A more serious problem, chronic absenteeism, was handled with the same remedy—disarming wit. He said, "I cut class, and I was a prankster."

A former classmate recalled, "If he was late, he'd say something funny and everybody would laugh and forget he was late. He had a rep as the coolest guy in school. After a while, the teacher stopped expecting us to go to all our classes. We'd just walk by. No one wanted to work. We'd rather be laughing all day than learning geometry."

His strange sartorial affectations didn't alienate the other students. They just added to his cool, although weird sounds more like it. At suburban Roosevelt High, Murphy would show up in a suit, shirt, and tie with a collar pin, a briefcase nestled under his arm. Like some black Sinatra, Murphy also wore a cashmere coat—a gift from an uncle—nonchalantly draped over his shoulder. Murphy needed to be noticed. Instead of getting him beat up, his wardrobe won him sought-after attention—even admiration. A classmate said, "Everybody would say, 'There goes Eddie Murphy.'"

With no sense of modesty, Murphy recalled, "I was voted most popular. I was like a little celebrity. I was hot shit."

Besides a strange fetish for goat wool, Eddie had some other fussy habits that a psychologist might classify as pathological. Murphy has often described himself as a "clean freak" who showers four times a day and washes his hands fifteen times. He washes up after shaking hands because "you don't know where people's hands have been. I shake a lot of hands. I won't take a dump in a public bathroom. I can pee anywhere. I can pee outside."

Vernon recalls his stepson's germ phobia. "He hated to touch anything nasty. He would always wash his hands right after taking out the garbage. I used to tell him that when he grew up he'd better get a degree and sit behind a big desk so other people could do the dirty work." Murphy still refuses to use public restrooms. Once, as he emerged from his Porsche in front of NBC's Rockefeller Center to report to work on *Saturday Night Live,* he stepped into a pile of dog excrement. Without missing a beat, he untied his shoes, slipped out of them and entered the building in his stocking feet. The shoes remained behind on the sidewalk, immortalized in doggie doo like found art.

Personal hygiene wasn't his only preoccupation. Sibling Vernon Jr. described his brother's hypochondria. Every bruise or cut would become a situation worthy of attention in the emergency room. The slightest scratch, "and he would wash it thoroughly, put Mercurochrome on it and Band-Aid after Band-Aid." Although Vernon was his baby brother, he found himself giving Eddie lessons in maturity, telling him it wasn't really necessary to cry over paper cuts. His mother described Eddie's aversion to all contact not of the romantic kind. "Eddie didn't like contact sports. He played baseball." Like her husband, she noticed Eddie's dread of tactile en-counters with all things icky. "I used to cover up for him, clean up after him.... You ever notice how often he washes his hands? He would never take out the garbage; he didn't want his hands to touch the stuff."

Like most successful adults, Murphy knew early on exactly what he wanted to be and believed stardom was inevitable—at least after the age of ten. Before that, his career goal was to drive a Mr. Softee truck in order to have access to all the ice cream he wanted. By junior high, his goals had risen quite a bit. A book report he submitted in eighth grade bore a signature and putative resumé that showed his self-confidence surpassed his spelling ability: "Eddie Murphy, singer, writer, actor, comeidian [sic], impersonist [sic]. boxer, basketball player, football player, genius, and a gift from God to all womenkind [sic]. P.S. I'm not conceided [sic], I'm just not a lier [sic]." The only part of this self-accolade that wasn't prophetic was the boast about athletic prowess. The possibility of a divine hand in all this will be left to theologians.

Mom Lillian felt his self-confidence was more like egotism, bordering on narcissism. "I remember when Eddie started calling himself 'Comedian Eddie Murphy.' He was sixteen, seventeen—the most obnoxious person in the world. I would come home from work and see lip prints on the hall mirror. That boy had some ego!"

Arsenio Hall described Murphy's transcendent belief in himself. "He wanted to be a star. He knew he would be. He'd go to school carrying a briefcase with nothing in it. But he knew that at one point there'd be Paramount contracts in it." Hall said his cashmere coat was worn as though it were a cape, "Clark Gable or a Dark Gable kind of thing. He told people, 'I'm going to be a millionaire.'"

The briefcase wasn't empty, although it didn't contain any $15 million movie studio deals—yet. It did hold a joke book and eight-track cartridges.

Murphy's lackadaisical academic career eventually caught up with him. No amount of gags or impersonations could make up for the fact that he was basically flunking out. In fact, by the tenth grade, that's exactly what happened.

"I was articulate, with a strong vocabulary, but most of the courses bored me. I mean, $E = mc^2$...who gives a damn? My focus was my comedy. You could usually find me in the lunchroom trying out my routines on the kids."

But when the word came down that he would have to repeat his junior year, his sense of humor deserted him.

Murphy panicked, but used his distress as a galvanizing force to get back on track—and out of the eleventh grade. "As vain as I was, I don't have to tell you what that did to me. The real joke was me on report-card day. I messed up real bad. Well, I went to summer school, to night school, doubled up on classes, and I graduated only a couple of months late. I wasn't a slow student. It was just that I was in the lunchroom or hallways telling jokes. I was going to be a star. I still wake up in a sweat sometimes from dreaming that I didn't graduate from high school."

To catch up, Murphy attended summer school every year from grades eight through twelve. Despite the heat, the cashmere coat came along. "I was always the best-dressed guy in summer school."

It's a testament to his strong family environment that Murphy—despite his distaste for academics—didn't simply drop out. You get the feeling that this wasn't an option. Vernon might tolerate a 2.0 grade average, but leaving school without a diploma would have probably meant a trip to the basement boxing ring. His stepfather wouldn't be drunk this time, and Eddie couldn't boast, "I beat the motherfucker up."

Murphy's lackluster performance in high school did not arise from any laziness on his part—as evidenced by the energy he put into catching up once it looked as though he would suffer the ignominy of repeating a grade, the ultimate in uncool for the coolest cat at Roosevelt High. Murphy was simply too busy working on his career.

Dave Better, his ninth-grade history teacher, recalled, "He wasn't stupid. Far from it. But he was absent half the time, working on comedy."

His first public performance, not counting the school lunchroom and study hall, took place on July 9, 1976. Eddie served as master of ceremonies for a talent show at the Roosevelt Youth Center. Attendees remembered a "skinny black kid in a loud green jacket and matching fat necktie."

Between acts, Murphy put a record by soul singer Al Green on the turntable and imitated the performer's Elvis-like hip thrusts. The audience howled. Ominously, however, others in the audience were not amused and complained about the emcee's liberal use of profanity. Eddie didn't care. It was love at first sight, a mutual affair between performer and audience. Describing the look of rapture on the faces of show-goers, he recalled, "I knew that I was in show biz for the rest of my life."

Fifteen was a crucial year for Murphy in other ways. His pelvic thrusts were not reserved for the stage. Nineteen seventy-six was also the year he lost his virginity. According to the usually circumspect *Life* magazine, Murphy was rehearsing the senior class talent show when "a girl in the twelfth grade came up to me, licked my ear, and said, 'It's time,'" according to the star. A year later, Murphy got a bittersweet sixteenth-birthday present, a sexually transmitted disease, which must have been especially hellish for the hygiene-obsessed youth. Murphy came clean in the pages of *Playboy* that he got a case of the crabs [venereal body lice] "from this bitch when I was sixteen."

It was the beginning of a love life Don Juan might have envied. His bedroom closet wall had dozens of girls' names and phone numbers scrawled on it. The indelibleness of the name suggested how indelible an impression the girl had made on the young Lothario—some names were recorded in pencil, others in pen. Major crushes were immortalized with Magic Marker. In 1977, he wrote the name of a so-called fiancée on the closet wall; the lucky girl had her name surrounded by little hearts and flowers. Unfortunately, other names had the same decoration. Eddie was a shameless self-promoter of his career and romantic life. One club owner was so impressed with Murphy's performance, he gave him money to have publicity photos taken to give out to agents and managers. Instead, Eddie distributed his glossies to pretty girls.

Murphy's public career prospered as mightily as his private life. By sixteen, he was headlining at comedy clubs up and down Long Island. His parents backed their boy like Mama and Papa Rose. Before Eddie got his driver's license, Vernon would chauffeur him to gigs. When Lillian attended a club for the first time, she was shocked by her fifteen-year-old's triple-X shtick. Mom always insisted the expletives were a pose. Underneath the smut, he was just a nice boy from suburban Long Island. "That's not the real Eddie. He knows what people want to hear. It's his act. It wasn't as bad then as it is now," she said. Mrs. Lynch also refused to take any genetic credit for her son's talent. She dryly noted that her only influence on his material was to tell him to stop talking dirty.

Vernon backed his wife up. Eddie, he insisted, never used that kind of language at home. "He doesn't talk to me or anybody else in the family that way," Lynch said, perhaps with one eye on the door to the basement. In fact, *New York* magazine said that a horrified Lynch "kicked his son's ass" after catching Eddie's act for the first time.

Lillian was kinder. "Eddie is a firm believer in God and prayer. That's probably why he's so hot today," said his mother, sounding as though *she* had one eye on *Variety*. For all the raunch in his standup routine, offstage Murphy is apparently deeply religious. One Christmas, during a heart-to-heart with Vernon Jr., his brother dissed the value of prayer. Eddie was shocked and said, "You mean you don't pray every night? I do."

While Lynch Sr. was bullish enough on his stepson's prospects to drive him up and down Long Island, he worried what would happen if his career fizzled. Vernon told him, "You better become famous or rich, because, boy, you are the laziest kid I've ever seen."

Actually, Eddie was only lazy about irrelevant things, like grades and day jobs. When it came to his career, he was as driven at fifteen as he would be as an adult, making back-to-back films punctuated by trips to the recording studio and concert halls.

His drive, however, wreaked havoc on the family phone bill. Lillian: "You really couldn't leave him home. He'd be on the phone all day, calling Connecticut, the city, Jersey, trying to find work. I got our phone bill, and I was sitting at the table looking at the long distance sheets, and I said, 'Eddie, look at this. What am I going to do with you?' and he looked at me and said, 'I don't never want to be middle class.'"

Vernon felt his stepson would be lucky to achieve that socioeconomic status. Eddie reluctantly agreed to work at a shoe store in the local mall, even though he performed at clubs like the Richard M. Dixon's White House Inn in Massapequa or the East Side Comedy Club in Huntington almost every night. His mother said, "Eddie was funny as a child, but we wanted him to have something to fall back on."

Vernon was not impressed by his stepson's day job *or* night job. Even though Eddie had worked late into the night at clubs, Vernon couldn't bear to come home from the ice cream mill and find his kid sleeping in. Murphy recalled climbing into bed in the early hours, exhausted. Back home from the night shift, just as Eddie was drifting into REM sleep, Vernon would behave like a drill sergeant or bugler whose reveille was verbal. "Get up, son! Got to go! Got to hit the streets," he'd yell in Eddie's ear, more obnoxious than an alarm clock in a cooking pot. Eddie didn't even bother to argue. He would dutifully get out of bed and go over to a friend's house and crash while the parents were away at work. Waking up in mid-afternoon, Murphy either hit the mall's shoe store or punched up his comedy sketches for his night job.

In addition to this killer work schedule, Murphy had all those catch-up classes to avoid flunking. As it turned out, his mediocre academic record didn't cut into his big-man-on-campus status. Classmates voted him most popular. His yearbook bio revealed a poetic touch and a youth whose career seemed preordained. Underneath his photo, Eddie wrote, "All men are sculptors, constantly chipping away the unwanted parts of their lives, trying to create their idea of a masterpiece. Future plans: comedian."

By this time, Eddie's adoration of Elvis had devolved into mere infatuation. Maybe it was the King's premature death that made Eddie decide a bloated, drug-habituated joke was not exactly the kind of person to pattern your career after. For whatever reason, Murphy adopted two very different comics as his new role models: the ultra-foul-mouthed Richard Pryor and Bill Cosby, the avatar of black respectability and achievement. Although at opposite ends of the humor and lifestyle spectrums, the two older men reflected Eddie's aspirations and inspirations. He explained why such polar opposites guided him: "Pryor on an artistic level. Cosby on a moral level. Cosby was this cool guy and Pryor was brilliant. I wanted to combine the two. Be funny *and* have a clean life." Indeed, Murphy would out-profane Pryor's stand-up style, while avoiding his self-destructive behavior. Eddie wanted to burn brightly on stage, not self-immolate in his bedroom while sucking on a crack pipe. "As a teenager when I watched Richard Pryor for the first time, I realized what I was—a comedian. He paints pictures with words. He can tell you a story and you can see the whole thing. He was a genius," Eddie added tellingly, using the past tense to describe the burned-out case his idol had become.

It's not going out on a limb to say that Cosby had no aesthetic influence on Murphy's comedy. The elder statesman of stand-up and sitcom told interminable shaggy dog stories about raising teenagers and placating the wife. Eddie's humor existed in an alternate, scatalogical universe. Cosby had the credibility to make Jell-O seem delicious. Murphy was selling something else that couldn't even be mentioned on TV. The Cos served as a super-successful example of clean living, hard work, and clear goals, the very traits punched into Eddie at home in the basement. You can almost imagine the young man visualizing the door to the boxing ring downstairs when he explained why he always turned down offers to do cocaine. "I was afraid I might like it too much." The cross-addicted Pryor was his creative inspiration, but Murphy made it clear the comic was not his alter ego. When a psychodynamic-oriented reporter tried to draw parallels between the two men's upbringing, Murphy cut him off quickly. "Richard's had a tough life. He's been through a lot of shit I've never had to face." Like growing up in a whorehouse in Peoria, Pryor's childhood address.

When he was seventeen, Eddie teamed up with two white comics: Rob Bartlett and Bob Nelson. They billed themselves as "The Identical Triplets." Get it? The audience got it but wasn't amused. Eddie suffered one of his rare career setbacks when the trio lost a "laugh-off" contest in Manhattan. But his self-confidence had a prophetic, even messianic flavor. One night, the Triplets were bombing in front of an audience at a teacher's convention. Gradually, the teachers began to ignore the show and chat among themselves. Eddie grabbed the mike and announced, "Listen up. We're going to be on the *Tonight Show* in two years." He told his parents, "I'm going to be a millionaire by the time I'm twenty-two." Both predictions turned out to be conservative.

On his way to Johnny Carson's couch and the bank, Eddie first had to attend to a little career essential known as the big break. He achieved it early, at age seventeen and just out of high school. Confined by the insular limitations of Long Island, Murphy decided to try his luck across the waters in Manhattan. His partners may not have been funny, but one of them, Bob Nelson, provided a crucial connection. Nelson asked the owners of Manhattan's Comic Strip, Bob Wachs and Richie Tienken, to audition Murphy. For once, Murphy's brash self-confidence almost killed his career before it got off the ground.

Supremely arrogant, the adolescent showed up at the Comic Strip and said, "I'm Eddie Murphy. I'm ready to go on." Wachs, a Harvard-educated attorney, reined him in immediately. "Wait a minute. We have systems around here, procedures. You don't just walk in and say, 'I'm here and I'm going on.' Get the hell out," Wachs said to the youngster, who would later enrich the club owner's fortune beyond fantasy. The scrappy attorney-turned-barkeep threw Eddie out of the club. Chastened, Eddie returned two weeks later and agreed to go on late in the evening, not prime time for a comic or a drunken, tired audience.

Murphy was lucky the club owners hired him because the proprietor of the other big standup venue in New York, the Improv's Silva Friedman, found the comic "appalling" and turned him down flat. In Friedman's case, however, it wasn't the young man's brashness but his obscenity-laced routine that scared her off. Murphy's brashness did earn him a lifetime friend who would be instrumental in his career. Before *In Living Color* and *I'm Gonna Get You, Sucka* turned him into a star, talk show host Keenen Ivory Wayans paid his dues at the Improv. One night after the show, Murphy crashed Wayans' dressing room and said, "Hi, I'm Eddie Murphy. I thought I was the only funny black guy in New York. Now I see there are two."

During a break from his new syndicated talk show, Wayans confirmed that the legendary story was true. Unlike Wachs and Tienken, Wayans found the seventeen-year-old's supreme self-confidence endearing rather than off-putting. "We immediately bonded. It was kinda like two gunslingers meeting actually," Wayans told me. "It was fun meeting because we had heard about each other. I tried to help him get into clubs in the city. He wound up at the Comic Strip. I was at the Improv. We didn't have much success there because

Silva Friedman was appalled by his act. She wouldn't put him on."

Despite their bond, Wayans shared Wachs and Tienken's estimation of Murphy's material and his stage presence. "Everybody talked about his presence. He had an amazing amount of confidence on stage. His stage presence was years beyond his material. At fourteen, fifteen, your material is limited in terms of what you've experienced, so it's juvenile. But Eddie had a command of stage and audience that people ten years his senior could only wish for."

The young comic's lack of etiquette wasn't the only thing that turned off the club owners. Wachs in particular was not impressed with his material; he found the jokes flat and unoriginal. But there was something in the young man's enthusiasm and energy that convinced the men not only to hire him but to provide a more valuable service as well. Wachs and Tienken had a sideline managing talent. Their decision to represent the obnoxious but lively seventeen-year-old would be instrumental in the Murphy march to super-stardom. It was quite a coup for a teen who wasn't legally old enough to sign a management contract. Wachs and Tienken met hundreds of hungry comics in search of a gig at their club; the fact that they not only loaned Murphy their stage but invited him to join their exclusive stable of clients showed just what a stand-out the unproven stand-up comedian was even at that time. Soon they had booked their protégé into comedy clubs up and down the East Coast. At one venue in Florida, Murphy ran into Rodney Dangerfield in the men's room. Even at seventeen, the comic heeded his own counsel, not his elders'. Dangerfield avuncularly told Murphy to clean up his standup act. "You're funny, but where you gonna go with that shit?" Dangerfield asked him—not because of any quibbles, but because he questioned the commercial value of Murphy's material. The only route to stardom for a comedian was through TV, which in those pre-*NYPD Blue* days considered toilets flushing risqué and cutting-edge. Forget about using toilet humor on the tube. After Dangerfield told him to avoid profanity, Murphy said, "I ain't takin' his mother-fuckin' advice. Dangerfield is a funny guy, but how old was he when he got famous? In his fifties?" Murphy had a dramatically faster timetable for achieving fame—age nineteen—which he would meet promptly and spectacularly.

Wachs and Tienken's prophetic confidence would be repaid in spades. Eventually the partners would dump all their other clients to service their discovery exclusively.

Chapter 2

......

Saturday Night Revives

In the fall of 1980, *Saturday Night Live*, the highest-rated late-night show, found itself at a turning point. Industry observers felt a precipice was a more accurate analogy. During its first four years, the skitcom had breathed life into the oh-so-stale variety show format that had fossilized into the TV equivalent of the Borscht Belt. Ed Sullivan and Sonny and Cher were as hip as variety got on TV.

Postmodern is a term that has been overused to describe everything from architecture to toaster design, but when *Saturday Night Live* debuted on October 11, 1975, the gestalt of variety found a very different kind of pie flung in its face. *SNL's* comedy was truly postmodern in that it took the staples of variety shows and relocated them in a completely novel environment. Instead of "take my wife, please," or well-scrubbed Beatles in suits and ties, *SNL* featured the punked out Rolling Stones and sexually voracious bumble bees. It did the unthinkable: make fun of the handicapped and dramatize bathroom odors. Literal toilet humor was raised to a low art form. A hard-of-hearing editorialist asked questions like, "What's all this fuss about *violins on TV?*" (The need to save "Soviet jewelry" also confounded the pundit, played by the late Gilda Radner.)

The cast of unknowns, archly called The Not Ready for Prime Time Players, became the only cliché no one objects

27

to—overnight stars. Primus inter pares, Chevy Chase turned into a movie star after only one year in the salt mines of weekly TV. John Belushi and Dan Aykroyd took a bit longer to conquer films, but they did in money machines like *Animal House* and *Ghostbusters*. Gilda Radner would get her own show on Broadway. And Jane Curtin proved she was more than a Not Ready for Prime Time Player by starring in two huge prime-time sitcoms.

Unfortunately for the network, after four years the stars' contracts expired, and by then they were too busy earning money from more prestigious venues to stay in the wee-hours ghetto of 11:30, 10:30 Central.

Along with the founding cast, the executive producer who had hired them, Lorne Michaels, also departed. NBC wasn't ready to panic. There were more where they came from—the bottom. The original cast had been less than unknowns; Chase, in fact, had been a mere staff writer who landed in front of the camera at the last moment. In 1980, NBC discovered that comic genius isn't easily replaceable. Brilliant producers were an equally rare commodity. The replacements in front of and behind the camera were disastrous. While the seventies cast—except for the much-missed Radner—remain household names, if not box office champs, who remembers their replacements at the beginning of the Decade of Greed: Denny Dillon, Gilbert Gottfried, Gail Matthius, Ann Risley, Charles Rocket? Oh, and two other unknowns: Joe Piscopo and a black teenager by the name of Eddie Murphy.

Lorne Michaels's replacement was Jean Doumanian, whose only qualification seemed to be that she was a friend of Woody Allen's. To say the first season under the new executive producer was catastrophic is like calling Bhopal a gas leak. Years later, Murphy would perform this postmortem on Doumanian's reign of terrible. "She had never produced before. Giving her a show of this magnitude was a joke. She'd make us watch a tape of the show and say, 'What was wrong?' We'd say it wasn't funny. She'd say, 'Okay, now you know what's wrong. Now go and knock 'em dead.' Real depth and direction there, right?"

Doumanian was even less impressed with the emaciated black kid who looked barely pubescent. She hated his audition, which consisted of Joe Piscopo, who had already been hired, doing free association with Murphy pretending they were Chevy Chase and Richard Pryor. Although ten years older than the nineteen-year-old stripling, Piscopo realized he had been outclassed during their very first pairing. "Eddie took charge of [the audition]. So I said, 'This guy is great.'" Doumanian wasn't listening. Perhaps as an omen of her ill-fated tenure, the neophyte producer was the only person on the set not laughing. The writers and the rest of the cast busted a collective gut. *TV Guide* claimed Doumanian was flat-out forced to hire Murphy because the show needed a black guy. In fact, Eddie's manager, Bob Wachs, had heard through the standup grapevine that the network was desperate that the whiter-than-white bread new cast include a comedian of color.

According to Eddie's mother, Eddie wasn't just fighting Doumanian's disdain but competition from much more established black performers in this show business variation on affirmative action. "He auditioned three times," Mrs. Lynch said. "He competed against every black face you ever saw on TV and film. He confided in no one but me and Vernon."

Murphy could smell tokenism in the air, although it seemed amusing rather than malodorous. "I figured they'd hired me so that if someone wrote a letter asking, 'How come you ain't got no brothers on the show?' they could point to me."

The original troupe had the luckless Garrett Morris, not a good role model for Murphy. He was a harbinger of bad things to come. Morris, a classically trained opera singer and off-off Broadway playwright, was shamelessly neglected by the writers and producers during the seventies. In an era before politically correct had even been uttered on college campuses, the writers blithely gave Morris bit parts as a waiter, busboy, or handyman while the rest of the cast became national icons in bumblebee suits and coned heads. It didn't help that Morris frequently flubbed his lines on the live telecast and often seemed to be staring at cue cards rather than at his costars. The neglect had a toxic effect on the rest of his career. While his colleagues went on to prime time and features, Morris, when he was lucky, got to play tenth banana on syndicated cop shows.

To his horror, Murphy during his first season also found himself being ghettoized in the white-flight suburbia of the new cast. Fifteen years after the fact, the memory still irritated the star. "Jean tried to 'Garrett-Morris' me, push me into the background, be the little token nigger. Unlike Morris, I complained and said, 'Do my stuff.' Some got in too, but I was still unnoticed."

Murphy's second-class status even had a name. While unknowns like Anne Risley and Charlie Rocket succeeded to the title of Not Ready for Prime Time Player, Murphy got the credit "featured player." "They told me I was a featured player—that meant an extra, really. I should have been happy even to be part of the show, but I looked at the rest of the cast and—I'm not saying I was better—I just knew I was as good as any of the regulars," he said. During the first year, he wasn't even featured very much, and when he was, more often than not his sketches were a personal humiliation and a public insult to blacks. The actor wasn't imagining the slights. A white costar patronized him with a left-handed compliment that was more like a right hook: "'You know it's good you're not educated,'" Murphy recalled his colleague saying. "As if what made me funny was my ignorance."

The Ivy League writing staff wasn't ignorant, just cosmically insensitive. "Every bit used to open with me strutting in with my baggy suit, wide hat, and a loud radio. I didn't want to be a pimp *all* the time. Now nobody would dare write a piece that's demeaning to me," he said, during the second season. "In fact, some of the writers are intimidated now, so they just stay away." Except when he was writing the material, Murphy found playing a pimp so repellent he never portrayed one in films.

Murphy's "Invisible Man" status turned out to be a blessing in disguise, even if the disguise consisted of pimpwear. He wasn't blamed for the show's Nielsen freefall and a critical reception more appropriate for a representational art exhibit entitled, "A. Hitler: The Early Years." Or, as Murphy said in happy hindsight, "It worked out good. When all the bad press came up, and everyone was getting their heads chopped off, nobody noticed me." At the end of the first season, Doumanian and the cast, it was decided, were not only not ready for prime time, they were unwatchable at 11:30 P.M. All except for Piscopo, whose talent stood out like Michael Jordan's in a pickup basketball game, and the skinny black kid, who had had one moment of glory. He was noticed, but it wasn't a fatal distraction. *Saturday Night Live* was indeed live, and at the end of one show, Doumanian found herself with four extra minutes of unscripted airtime to kill. She sent Murphy in as her hit man, pushing him on stage with the helpful direction, "Do five minutes of your stand-up act." In the wings, manager Wachs marveled as Murphy happily emasculated himself, lopping off the triple-X, ultra-blue staples of his club material and morphing into a Not Ready For an FCC Fine Player. "Remember simultaneous translation? Eddie did simultaneous editing. He edited his routine as he did it live," Wachs said.

The teenager's wilderness year (1980–81) had one happy side effect. He and Piscopo formed a lifelong friendship, with the senior comic briefly serving as mentor to the youngster from Long Island until it became clear that Murphy didn't need any mentoring.

For the second season, a veteran producer, Dick Ebersol, who had worked on the show during its first year in 1975, assumed the Augean task left behind by Doumanian's stable of Peter Principled Players. For Murphy, it was the beginning of a prickly love-hate affair, with Ebersol doing most of the loving while the star going supernova got his revenge for the first season's indignities.

After only a few shows the second year, Murphy had clearly become a lot more than first among equals. The *New York Times* wrote, "Eddie Murphy has stolen the show." The teenager was first, but he didn't have any equals among the rest of the cast, who to a man (and woman) have all fallen into the "Whatever happened to..." Trivial Pursuit box. Ebersol proved no savvier a handicapper than the dread Doumanian when he hired Robin Duke, Tim Kazurinsky, Tony Rosato, Christine Ebersol and Brian Doyle-Murray (Bill's sibling with none of Bill's charisma.) Their bad luck was Murphy's gain, since his considerable talent seemed all the more spectacular in contrast. Murphy used his new star status to make a few changes around the set. The first season, when writers gave him dross, he gamely tried to turn their sketches into gold. Where he had been happy to get a few minutes exposure his first year, it was now a different story. Murphy just said no to stale gags and sketches that seemed to drag on longer than an Andy Warhol documentary.

Murphy would literally toss scripts into Ebersol's waste-basket with the critique, "It's got no whoosh." The producer didn't complain. He didn't want to kill the goose that laid the golden gags, although sometimes he implied he would have liked to strangle the bird. "I put up with Eddie's excesses, realizing the bonus I've got," Ebersol said.

Another problem was the lily-white composition of the

writing staff. The writers, many fresh from the "Hahvuhd Yahrd" and *Lampoon,* were not exactly what you would call color-blind when it came to creating roles for a black man. Murphy found this Ivy-League white ethnocentrism excruciating. "We've got really good writers," he claimed, "but they tend to write in archetypes, and I'm always the black guy. It's hard for them to give me a straight role in a sketch. If I'm playing the husband and my wife is white, the audience is waiting for a black joke." As a result, a pop critic wrote, Murphy got a lot of scenes playing with…himself.

With Murphy as point man, critics and Arbitron alike agreed that the show had returned to the golden days of Chevy and Gilda, possibly even better. The comedian, despairing of the writers and costars, began to generate his own material, writing an entire repertory of characters still fondly remembered nearly two decades later. Most of his creations were also controversial and enraged special-interest groups, like half the population—the female half. As much as he resented being ghettoized by other writers in the role of pimp, when he created his own Easy Rider it was another matter. Now at the millennium, when Dennis Franz's tush seems to be a separate character on his cop show, it's hard to fathom the fact that you couldn't say "whore" on national television in 1981. (A drag-biker band, the Cycle Sluts, were also rejected as musical guests because *TV Guide* refused to print their name in its listings.) As he did during his four minutes of fame the first season, Murphy bowdlerized his raunchy style. He played a G-rated pimp, Velvet Jones, who hawked his bestselling self-help book *I Wanna Be a Ho* in a proto-infomercial. "Are you an unemployed female?" he asked, peering out from under five pounds of processed hair. "I can teach you to be a high-payin' ho." Feminists and blacks were outraged, but Velvet kept popping up on the show, bringing Madison Avenue marketing techniques to the business of peddling flesh.

His Tyrone Green, a prison poet, lampooned Norman Mailer and other glitteratis' lionization of ex-con Jack Henry Abbot. Green's best iamb contained the line, "Kill my landlord. C-I-L-L." In another sketch Green declaimed, "Kill de white people," during a poetry reading—at the VFW!

The comic dressed up like a giant green piece of chewing gum for his riff on Gumby, whom he envisioned as a bitter, never-was Borscht Belt comic. Mister Robinson wore a cardigan sweater just like his more famous Rogerian avatar, but Robinson's neighborhood was set in a burned-out tenement where Murphy asked his audience of preschoolers, "Can you say 'scumbucket,' boys and girls?" Mr. Robinson would say to the white children in his audience, "I'd love to move to your neighborhood someday—only trouble is, when I move, y'all move away."

His adult Buckwheat, who had the I.Q. of a geranium and the enunciation of Demosthenes before he began gargling with pebbles, didn't delight black activists either, although liberal *Playboy* gave him absolution: "As a child of TV, Eddie's version of Buckwheat was no more dangerous than Robert Klein's had been in his Little Rascals sketch ten years before."

Ditto Raheem Abdul Muhammad, the film critic host of *Angry Talk*, who saw racism when J.J. Walker ("Dyn-O-Mite!") wasn't offered the title role in *The Elephant Man*. Raheem also claimed that Jerry Falwell's Moral Majority contained closet porno freaks. "The next time I see one of them in a movie line I'm gonna put the majority of my foot up his moral butt."

Murphy could do white people with a variety of accents that suggested Meryl Streep on steroids. His Philadelphia Main Line impersonation was straight out of *Town and Country*. One critic said his Irish priest brogue was so localized, he could place it in County Clare.

Murphy was an equal-opportunity offender, although when it came to lampooning Jews, his touch was as gentle as an arthritic masseur's. Or, as he elegantly described his modus operandi, "I fuck with everybody. I don't give a fuck." A white person could never get away with black face—at least not since Rosa Parks hijacked a bus—but Murphy frequently did sketches in white face. Just as years earlier he nailed Tweety-Bird and Deputy Dawg, the brilliant impressionist did a dead-on Yiddish accent for his Alzheimer's-afflicted Solomon, a retired barber.

His repertoire included several stereotypical gay characters, the beginning of a feud with activists that would percolate for years before boiling over on stage and film. There was his Dion, a gay hairdresser, and an effeminate Little Richard Simmons, which managed to offend both gays and fans of "Tutti-Frutti." Murphy even dared to use the H-word for a send-up called "The Homo-mooners" with Ralph Kramden and Ed Norton as homosexual lovers. When Murphy said, "Norton, come down here, I've got something to show you," he left what it was to the audience's imagination. His homosexual Mr. T was just unfunny, although Eddie *jokingly* implied the *A-Team*er swung both ways. Murphy rubbed a Brooke Shields doll up against a Mr. T doll and speculated, "I know Brooke's mom is at home right now having a heart attack watching Brookie kiss this tremendous Negro on television." Then, imitating Mr. T's guttural inflection, he added, "Ah love you, woman. Mmmmm."

Murphy's charm and talent allowed him to offend without being terminally offensive. Ebersol and an eighteenth-century epigrammatist both had explanations for the comedian's ability to walk a fine line between funny and infuriating. Rochefoucauld: "Wit sometimes enables us to act rudely with impunity." Ebersol believed the "smile dancing in his brown eyes" allowed him to get away with beating up white people, blacks, gays, women, even mocking a blind man, Stevie Wonder. (Eddie: "If Stevie complains, I'll kick his ass.") The *New York Times* bought Ebersol's philosophy: "No matter how bizarre or fatuous the characters he plays, he manages to send them up with affection and exuberance."

Ebersol was on to something. Murphy even got away with poking fun at Muhammad Ali's Parkinson's tremor and slurred speech. That's impunity.

Any complaints were drowned out by notices that were orgasmic. The usually curmudgeonly *New York* magazine said, "He has carried *SNL* virtually by himself since the show lost the entire original cast." That was an overstatement since, during his first season as a featured player, he rarely carried a scene, let alone a whole show. But by Year Two A.M. (*Anno Murphy*), all the heavy lifting seemed to be done by the omnipotent twenty-year-old. On the bulletin board describing sketches, some index cards said simply, "Eddie." Ebersol explained, "That card means that he does whatever he wants to in that spot." Amazingly, Ebersol admitted the writing on *SNL* was substandard. Murphy performed the levitation act that kept the leaden writing airborne. "He's always had to rise above the material," Ebersol conceded. "He just believes anything he does is going to work."

His single-handed resuscitation of a show critics had nicknamed "Saturday Night Dead" didn't go unrewarded or unremunerated. For his first season, *SNL* paid him a measly $750 per episode. Since he had very little work, on an hourly basis, that wasn't a bad wage. The second year, the network forked over $4,500 per show—until mid season, when it upped his salary to a whopping $8,700 per.

Refreshingly, Murphy didn't let the money or the adulation go to his head. The first year of the show, he continued to live at home; the second, he moved to a one-bedroom apartment ten minutes away from mom and step-dad.

"I'm childish when it comes to Mommy," he said in a rare moment when machismo deserted him. "She's still gotta be nearby. I've got nothing to complain about. I'm young. I got two cars, a happy home life. Last year, my biggest problem was that I had a cavity. Right now, my biggest problem is that it's 4:40, and I gotta pick my mother up at work by five." Indeed, he was such a devoted son that at the request of his mother, who feared his success would be ephemeral, he enrolled in Nassau Community College as a theater major— after he had been hired by *Saturday Night Live*. He wasn't that filial, however, and dropped out after three weeks.

His only extravagance involved loved ones. He began to bestow game show-quality gifts on friends and family. His mother described her son's latest impersonation, Santa Claus. "He was the most generous of my children, and his success has brought us all closer. He has always been very loving and generous, more so now that he can afford to be. We never ask for anything. Eddie is a giver."

His stepfather got a Lincoln with six stereo speakers; his mother a Datsun 200SX, and for his sixteenth birthday, half-brother Vernon Jr. inherited Eddie's Datsun 280ZX. In 1985, the Lynches, courtesy of their generous son, moved out of Eddie's modest childhood home into a spacious place in Alpine, New Jersey, less than a mile from his mansion. It must have seemed anticlimactic later that year when Eddie gave his mother his first Grammy. With understatement, Piscopo said, "He's very close to his mom and step-dad; all the people he hangs out with are old friends, school buddies, and relatives."

Family members weren't the only beneficiaries of Murphy largesse. Eddie was an easy touch. "I'd pick up the check at a restaurant for ten people." He was even generous to strangers a continent away. In 1984, a snowstorm prevented him from performing at a fund-raiser for the Children's Federation's Ethiopian Food Fund at his home base, the Comic Strip, in Manhattan. Instead, Murphy wrote a check to the charity for $20,000, double the amount ticket sales had raised.

While still an obedient son, his newfound wealth allowed him to, uh, delegate pesky household chores. When his mother

told her superstar son to take out the garbage, he'd hand her a
$100 bill and she'd say, "Okay, your little brother can throw out
the garbage." Considering his income, his one major indul-
gence was fiscally conservative: a Pontiac Trans Am. Murphy
defended the purchase as an emblem of pride. It may have been
personally extravagant, but it was politically correct. "If I
drove a beat up Chevy, people would say, 'He's an ignorant
black man. He doesn't know how to manage his money.'"

But even in 1981, $750 a week didn't last long when you
were spending $100 a pop on garbage disposal. Murphy said
after his first year on the show, "Then one day I woke up, and
I didn't have any more money."

The *L.A. Times* didn't consider Eddie's second year a
renaissance for the show. It claimed the '81–'82 season "was
so bad" that when Murphy sat on the window ledge of the
seventeenth floor, a horrified pedestrian thought he was
suicidal and screamed up at him, "Don't do it!" Murphy said.
"They've got no sense of humor. What'd they think I was
gonna do, kill myself before I do my first movie?"

His sophomore success on *SNL* didn't go unnoticed by
Hollywood. The original cast had practically been a farm
team for feature films, with Chevy Chase first out of the box
with *Foul Play* in 1978, followed by John Belushi's epic turn as
a frat boy who seemed educably retarded in *Animal House*.
The *Los Angeles Herald-Examiner* said at this time, "*SNL*
seems to be this generation's Actors' Studio because so many
alumni go on to movie careers."

By the spring of Year Two, 1982, the movie offers began
to pour in. Murphy wasn't starstruck. Summoned to Los
Angeles by a studio executive, the young man wasn't impressed by the honcho's extravagant praise. You can't buy
your mother a house with adulation; Eddie wanted the
executive to show him the money. If he wanted praise, he'd
pick up the *New York Times*. Finally, Murphy turned to his
manager, Bob Wachs, and said, "If they're not going to offer

us a deal, let's go." Then the star stood up and walked out on Hollywood—temporarily.

The comic was clear—not starry-eyed—about a movie career, and even when money was offered, he wasn't about to take any role just because it meant a transition to a more prestigious medium. One offer that particularly irked him involved costarring with then-superhot Henry Winkler. Murphy described it as "a nigger role, some irate black guy."

While in Los Angeles, his self-possession also led him to reject an offer that any other comic would have crawled over broken Baccarat for. In 1981, before the proliferation of other late-night talk shows, an appearance on Johnny Carson guaranteed a comic stardom. Joan Rivers was an unknown, unemployed comedian when she got her big break on Johnny's couch in 1965. The next day her agent was able to book her on a nationwide club tour.

In 1981, Murphy was hardly unemployed; he was even an embryonic star. Unfortunately, Carson's bookers didn't think so. The pecking order on the *Tonight Show* rivaled a Mandarin's court. If you were big, Johnny would motion you over to sit on his couch for some rehearsed ad-libbing after you did your three minutes of shtick. Murphy was told there was standing room only for him on Carson. After his routine, he would get the hook. At the age of nineteen, Murphy had the courage to tell Johnny to buzz off. "They wouldn't let me sit down with the panel. I wasn't going to do my stand-up routine, leave, and then have some foot doctor come out and talk about his book. I'm not a star," Murphy said inaccurately, "but I'm not just another stand-up comic either."

He wouldn't play Henry Winkler's Steppin Fetchit or Carson's mime.

Murphy had good management and even better taste—as well as a terrific business sense. When he finally stuck his toe in the Hollywood swamp, it would be for $1 million per picture, and he wouldn't be playing anybody's "nigger."

Chapter 3

......

Home Run in Hollywood

In NOVEMBER 1982, managers Wachs and Tienken really earned their 10 percent when they negotiated a minimum of $1 million per film for Murphy, *to be paid in advance* by Paramount Pictures, plus 10 percent of the gross for their twenty-one-year-old client. Even savvier than the numbers was the trio's script choice. So many other major TV stars have let their film debut turn into a swan song by starring in a mindless comedy whose lack of wit is only surpassed by its lackluster box office.

For his first time out, Murphy and his gang of two picked a well-crafted action adventure that capitalized on the star's smart-aleck TV persona without requiring too much acting skill. Countless prime time leviathans have found themselves getting lost in the bigger seas of 35 mm; their serviceable talent gets them by on the small canvas of the cathode ray tube, but the wide-screen format magnifies their weaknesses. (Remember Ellen De Generes in *Mr. Right?* Or Tom Selleck in anything?) If the film flopped, Murphy's handlers had an escape hatch ready. "My managers said do the first movie. If it's no good, people will blame Nolte," the neophyte film actor recalled.

48 HRS. was a high-concept buddy movie with a twist: One buddy was a cop (Nick Nolte), the other (Murphy) was a prison inmate let out of the can for two days to help Nolte

40

track down stock sociopaths armed with Uzis. Murphy's Reggie Hammond seems tailor-made for the wisecracking star of *Saturday Night Live*—except that it wasn't written with Murphy in mind. Engaging in a bit of Orwellian revisionism, director Walter Hill claimed he hired Murphy after he saw him on *SNL*. "We never sent the script to any other actor," Hill said, despite earlier press reports that *48 HRS.* was conceived as a vehicle for Richard Pryor, who had to drop out for health reasons.

Murphy picked up Pryor's sow's ear and turned Hammond into a silk purse. If you can point to the moment in his career when it became obvious that he would become a major movie star, it had to be the iconic scene in a redneck bar in San Francisco that made *Star Wars'* cantina look like La Grenouille. Murphy borrows Nolte's gun and police I.D. before entering the bar in search of information on their quarry. *Cosmopolitan* magazine overstated the case when it said the redneck sequence became a classic of American cinema, but it was the funniest scene in a funny movie. When the bar patrons are less than forthcoming on the bad guys' whereabouts, Murphy whips out his borrowed badge and slams one of them up against the bar with the taunt, "I'm your worst fucking nightmare. I'm a nigger with a badge. That means I got permission to kick your fucking ass whenever I feel like it."

Usually, forceful black men make white audiences squirm. It's not a coincidence that most of the blacks on TV play clowns. In films, they are more often than not the likable, non-threatening sidekick to the white protagonist cop. (Think of the not-so-lethal weapon Danny Glover or the ditsy eponymous star of *Martin.*) In the hands of a brasher actor, Murphy's turn in the honky-tonk might have been deeply disturbing to the majority of moviegoers. Instead, *Newsweek* said, "Eddie can tiptoe along the narrow line between anger and laughter in a way that shows everybody how silly we are to imprison ourselves with racial stereo-types. He thinks he can walk that same line in his career."

The *New York Daily News* also recognized his viewer-friendly screen presence. "Murphy livens up *48 HRS.* the minute he struts into view. He is so instantly likable that, although he never looks tough enough to have survived so much as a minute in prison, he has the audience cheering him."

Another reason Reggie Hammond didn't make white America nervous was that he had no basis in reality—at least not in Murphy's world. A product of a middle-class suburb where truancy was his biggest crime, Murphy conceded that *48 HRS.* shouldn't be confused with either documentary or autobiography. "I didn't research my role by hanging out with slick convicts in Harlem to see how they act, because it's dangerous—you can get killed. I just did my interpretation of what those guys are like." One of the real-life cowboy extras in the redneck bar questioned the film's authenticity. "If this were for real," he allegedly told the star, "you wouldn't last two seconds in here."

On-screen, his Reggie Hammond was likable. Offscreen, Murphy displayed the prickly temperament that would wax and wane throughout his career. During his first season on *SNL,* he shut up and did what he was told. But he refused to play the humble acolyte on the set of his first film because he came to it with the clout of a major TV star.

Murphy's reputation as being "difficult," career death unless your movies gross $100 million, began early in shooting when he often showed up late and, even worse, didn't know his lines. Martinet director Walter Hill, who specializes in movies with the testosterone level of a competitive bodybuilder, was no Dick Ebersol. "In the beginning, I had to kick his ass, but God, he did great work for me," said the director.

Hill grossly misattributed Murphy's bad-boy behavior to

a charmed upbringing followed by instant success. The director played armchair psychologist—one who should have his state license revoked—and showed how unaware he was of Murphy's traumatic formative years, which included his father's murder and a "black Nazi" foster mom. Hill said, "The thing about Eddie is that he's never gone through the normal ups and downs like the rest of us[!] He's never really experienced any pain in his life[!!]. But he's smart enough to know that some day, there'll be a bad point, and he keeps wondering when it's going to come."

Although he hid it beautifully under a cocky facade, Murphy's behavior on the set probably came from a terrifying sense of being way out of his depth. The big screen seemed to dwarf his usual self-confidence. Much later, on top of the box office heap, he would admit to an anxiety that bordered on a panic attack. "Every day I called my manager and said, 'My career is *ruined*. It's over. I'm twenty-one and I'm all washed up.' I didn't know what a reaction shot was, and I'd never filmed anything out of continuity, so every morning Nick [Nolte] had to tell me where we were in the story and how our characters were supposed to be getting along." Where's the script girl when you need her? Murphy also got support from his stepfather, the ex-boxer, who helped choreograph the fist fight sequences.

Some higher-ups at the studio shared Murphy's misgivings and actively lobbied to replace him on the picture. Then Paramount production chief Jeffrey Katzenberg displayed the foresight bordering on clairvoyance that led to his hegemony over Disney's Magic Kingdom, then partnership with the box-office Croesus, Steven Spielberg. By rejecting his subordinates' pleas to replace the overweening newcomer, Katzenberg deserved every penny—all 10 trillion of them—he made at Paramount, since Murphy eventually earned the studio $2 billion in less than a decade.

As he had on *SNL,* Murphy immediately began tinkering

with the script. Some of the changes he demanded seemed arbitrary, like rejecting his character's original name, Willie Biggs. Other changes were what today are called "politically correct." In 1982, Murphy had already had enough of playing a white person's concept of black people during his first year on TV. He took a cleaver to the script and hacked off every instance of TV blacktalk like "jive turkey" and "Watch it, sucker."

He didn't go to Harlem for research, but he refused to impersonate a sitcom star on the big screen. "I gave the character some black dialogue," he explained, "so he'd be believable."

Even before *48 HRS.* debuted in late 1982, the heat, as Kenny Loggins would sing in a later Murphy hit, was on. Heat is industry-speak for great word of mouth. Paramount was salivating after it saw the rough cut of *48 HRS.* Three weeks before the premiere, an army of agents and attorneys who had flown in from L.A. invaded Murphy's *SNL* dressing room in Rockefeller Center, waving contracts and a check at the twenty-two-year-old.

Eddie, however, happened to be watching a rerun of his favorite show, *Star Trek.* With the delicious power that comes from box-office clout, Murphy said to the suits, "Wait till the show's over." The big guns sat down with the top gun and watched William Shatner overact for sixty minutes. Only then did the star deign to sign the contract. Based on the rough cut alone, the studio offered him a two-film deal, at a million dollars per film, along with a quarter million advance to set up Eddie Murphy Productions on Paramount's backlot. On top of that, the studio treated him like a Heisman Trophy winner, throwing in a $1 million signing bonus. Murphy at this time began to give hints of the anhedonia that intermittently plagued his life. For him, the glass was not always but often half-empty. Or, as he said of the precedent-setting million-dollar bonus, "After taxes, it was more like $475,000."

Paramount's ardor was not misplaced. *48 HRS.* grossed $5 million in its first three days of release, major money in 1982. The film became one of the top-five moneymakers of the year, grossing $75 million in the U.S. and Canada alone.

The critics were more hypertensive with praise than the suits. NBC's Gene Shalit paid him the ultimate compliment, changing his job description from comic to actor: "Murphy makes a sensational movie debut, leaving behind the fun of *Saturday Night Live* and revealing himself to be a comic actor who can illuminate a character. This twenty-two-year-old is the real goods."

A London magazine, *Time Out,* praised the maturity of his performance. *48 HRS.* "seemed like his fifty-first, not his first" film, the magazine said. Murphy deflected the praise, explaining that his two years on *SNL* made him feel like a veteran. Or, as he put it, "I didn't get freaked out."

New York magazine predicted what by now was obvious. "Murphy is going to be a very big star."

Although TV stars rarely make the successful transition to film, Eddie felt he had an advantage because of his background. Prophetically describing the trend of standup comedians getting sitcoms which led to movies, Murphy said, "People that can do stand-up have to be able to write, have to be funny, have to be able to act, hold an audience's attention. You have to be able to do a whole bunch of things. This is why stand-up comedians get tremendous chops and explode on the movie scene."

Murphy didn't let his instantaneous movie stardom go to his head. He didn't even let it persuade him to abandon the suddenly less glamorous life of a television star. In the fall of 1982, just as *48 HRS.* turned him into an instant movie star, he dutifully reported to the set of *SNL* for his third season.

Chapter 4

......

Portrait of the Artist as a Young Manic-Depressive

BE CAREFUL WHAT YOU WISH FOR; it may come true. Eddie Murphy had predicted he'd be famous by the time he was nineteen—he was. He predicted he'd be a millionaire by twenty-two. His prophecy was too conservative, since he entered the millionaire's club a year earlier, courtesy of a grateful Paramount.

"I don't want to sound like some Zen Buddhist fool, but I think you do a lot to create your own reality," he said. His reality—wealth and fame—might be a wonderful fantasy to everyone else, but it left him frightened and confused.

The speed of his ascent in the movie business particularly unnerved him. In mid 1982, he told *TV Guide*, "Hey, this is happening too fast. It scares me sometimes....I'm getting old when I don't have to. And I'm a cocky kid, too. I know I'm going to be a millionaire when I'm twenty-two, maybe sooner." Apparently he had not looked at his bank balance when he made that prediction.

Super-successful people often live with the fear that their success is ephemeral—that it can all be taken away as quickly as it's been bestowed. Eddie was no exception to this fear, which amounts to a phobia, since superstars may fall out of favor, but they never end up on welfare. They can slip off

46

the mountaintop, but the valley they land in is typically cushioned with stocks and bonds and prime real estate. Still, Murphy worried. "Stardom is kind of scary because this star stuff isn't constant. Your taste for certain things becomes more elaborate, and you can get used to that stuff real quick. So thinking about not having those things you've become accustomed to is real scary."

There were other stresses. *Saturday Night Live* maintained a grueling schedule. He appeared on five shows in as many weeks. "There's just been a lot of pressure. All the press, the movie offers, concerts, and the album deal. I've had to draw back a little."

Success had its little and big pleasures, however. His clout on the big screen allowed him to commandeer the little screen. None of the writers would have dared by the third season to put him in a pimp sketch, although the producer always welcomed a visit by Velvet Jones, Eddie's empowered panderer. Before *48 HRS.* landed in the Top Five, Murphy basically did what he was told, even if it meant donning baggy pants, a Panama hat, and a white person's transliteration of jive Caucasian-onics. Before movie stardom, when he complained about the material, the writers said, "Just do it." He grumbled, but he did it. Afterward, it was the writers who grumbled. "They'd say, 'Oh, so you think you're hot shit now,'" Murphy recalled. Actually, he was. Murphy insisted he wasn't being temperamental or arbitrary; it was simply that when a sketch didn't work, he had the clout to say so and make his criticism stick. "I wasn't an asshole. I just didn't do anything I didn't think was funny. And then people started expecting me to get conceited and my head to swell."

Producer Ebersol was afraid it would burst. He began to ask guest hosts to have a word with the performer. Murphy was amused when Ebersol asked Jerry Lewis, not exactly a poster boy for good career moves, to counsel him. Ebersol said to the crankiest man in show biz, "Jerry, do you think you could talk to Eddie, because I don't think he's handling his fame well?" Lewis declined to mentor Murphy and Ebersol was getting desperate. *SNL* had to crank out ninety minutes of material every week, and Murphy was rejecting much of it. Ebersol called Larry Holmes and asked for a bro'-to-bro' summit meeting with the star. Holmes felt it was the producer, not his protégé, who needed a remedial lesson on career management. Ebersol quoted Holmes's advice: "Well, you gotta remember where he came from." When Eddie heard about this exchange, he said, "I don't know where [Ebersol] comes from."

While privately begging veterans to admonish Murphy, publicly Ebersol insisted they were one happy, bickering couple. The producer denied that movie stardom had turned Murphy into a prima donna. "Has it changed him in terms of his dealings with us? Not really. It might be harder to get him on the telephone, but other than that, he doesn't give us any more shit *than he used to*. He never cared how many pieces he was in," Ebersol claimed, unaware of Murphy's bitterness over his first season as a featured player-pimp. "If he felt he was good, that's all he cared about. Eddie wouldn't let us put him a position of doing something that he felt was shaky. He has a pretty good shit detector."

Whatever tension exited between the two men, it was camouflaged with an affectionate, if scatological, camaraderie. Once, as Murphy stood backstage just before opening the show, Ebersol said, "Your butt's getting big." Murphy, an X-rated Oscar Wilde, riposted, "That's cause I get fucked in it every night."

Perhaps the material on *SNL* was so unsatisfying because Murphy had stopped contributing sketches. At the end of the second season, he complained that he hadn't received a writer's credit. He laid down the gauntlet. "If I don't get a writer's credit, I'm not going to do any writing." The accredidation rule on *SNL* was simple: if you only wrote your own material, you didn't get a writer's credit, even if you were creating the best moments on the show. If you wrote for other performers, you got listed as a writer.

The third season Murphy more than made good on his threats. Not only did he stop writing, he stopped attending story meetings. While the writers and other cast members were desperately trying to come up with an a hour and a half of gags, Murphy was either tooling around in his Trans Am, going to a movie, or just hanging out with friends who did appreciate him. Was this temperamental behavior or a writer-star justifiably demanding his due? Either way, the producer was crazy to alienate the show's biggest asset over inclusion in a very quick screen crawl that said, "written by..."

Interviews from this period suggest his disenchantment with the show and his sudden movie fame didn't really represent ungrateful whining. An armchair psychologist, Murphy diagnosed his problem and even knew the clinical name for it, along with its pathological symptoms. For someone who had barely managed to graduate from high school, Murphy displayed an intimate knowledge of the ups and downs of the emotional roller coaster known as bipolar disorder. "The year *48 HRS.* hit and I was hot shit on the show, I was going crazy. It was happening too fast; my ego was all fucked up. I'd go from being the happiest guy in the world to being depressed. I was manic-depressive."

A few years later, his malaise hadn't lessened. "I'm still manic-depressive. I still go up and down. Everybody does. But sometimes I'll wake up, and my manager'll say, 'This is wrong, that's wrong, this is wrong, that's wrong, and I'll say, 'Ah, so what? I'm happy to be alive.'"

Another symptom of manic-depression, or bipolar disorder as it's now known, is excessive promiscuity. He admitted to that behavior when he said, "I'm in my sexual prime. I fuck, man. These are the years to fuck. This is where you do your best fuckin'." He also liked to grope himself on stage and

say, "Suck my dick." That's the fun, manic part of manic-
depression; its ugly twin is the blues. "Sometimes I'll wake up
and want to cry. And not really have any reason: just a bunch
of small stuff, wondering about my career. Or sometimes I'll
get depressed about certain places I can't go anymore, like
the park." That last complaint encapsulates the despair of
bipolar depression—obsessing about quality park time when
the backyard of your New Jersey estate is lovelier than any
part of crime and dog-ridden Central Park. Plus, squirrels
and coyotes don't pester you for autographs.

Murphy used the stage as self-medication the way an
alcoholic grabs a bottle to banish the blues. "It's like medi-
cine. Used to be, if I was depressed, I'd just go somewhere and
do a show and try to work really hard, and they clap at the
end, and you feel yourself worth it again. Now, I just walk
into a club and people start clapping. I feel like saying,
'Thanks, I was really depressed, but I'm not now, so I'm
leaving.'" Punchlines instead of Prozac for a celebrity who
was famous for *not* using drugs.

As he approached thirty, the balance between mania and
depression tipped in favor of depressive episodes that he
found maddening because of their inexplicability. As a creative person, the manic episodes fueled his writing and
performing; depression paralyzed him. "I get depressed a
lot," he said in 1989. "I was depressed this morning. It's just
natural; it's human. My depressions are even more frustrating because I think, 'Why the fuck am *I* depressed?' But more
entertainers are like that. Michael Jackson and Stallone tell
me they feel the same way."

Perhaps in a manic mood, Murphy once denied having a
depressive personality. Forgetting the blues he once sang, he
claimed, "I'm not a brooder. I'm always looking at the big
picture. I'm happy, and I have options, and I have love around
me, and I can do as an artist what I want to do. The only thing I
want from the public is to know, Was it funny? Do you like it?"

In the fall of 1982, Murphy's bipolar disorder was in full swing(s); like Dickens' twin cities, Murphy's tale encompassed the best and worst of times. His film career just kept getting better—and more lucrative. At twenty-two, not only had he surpassed his dream of becoming a millionaire by that age, but Edward Regan Murphy was in love. The emotion, however, couldn't hide the profound anomie he felt toward his TV work. In the depressive corner of bipolar hell, Murphy began to experience the three-year itch at his home base, *Saturday Night Live.*

"I'm a cocky kid," he said, sounding as though he were trying to convince himself more than the *TV Guide* reporter interrogating him. "I know I'm just scratching the surface. This show is no place, it's $4,500 a week." Actually, by then a grateful and nervous NBC had nearly doubled his salary, but, as we've seen, Eddie didn't pay a whole lot of attention to his bank account or little bookkeeping irrelevancies like a near 100 percent raise in weekly salary.

While his career failed to satisfy him, his love life more than compensated for dissatisfaction in the workplace. For a while at least, fame, as the novelist Graham Greene once dryly noted, was a powerful aphrodisiac. And though Murphy was not traditionally good looking, the superstar seemed to be the human equivalent of the mythical love potion Spanish Fly. Women gathered around him like moths to his brightly burning flame. A costar, Jamie Lee Curtis, described the Murphy Experience, "I love it that despite all his success, Eddie acts like he's twenty-two years old. His life is cars and girls, girls and cars. More cars. More girls." Eddie may have acted like a twenty-two-year-old because that's how old he was when Curtis described his love life. Director Walter Hill said, "Eddie can hear the rustle of nylon stockings at fifty yards."

If the actor turned into something of a sybarite at this time, it was excusable. Women sent him five hundred letters a

week. His head swelled proportionate to the volume of mail.
One woman, however, suggested that his dating etiquette was
overbearing. Patricia Matthews recalled their first meeting,
which turned into a three-month affair. They met at a bar on
the Sunset Strip. Eddie by this time was using intermediaries
to trawl for the catch of the night. Matthews recalled, "A guy
came over and said, 'Eddie wants to talk to you.' I said, 'He
knows where I'm sitting.' He said, 'He wants to ask you to
dance.' I said, 'Can't he talk?' So Eddie came over and asked
me to dance." While his technique for meeting women was
primitive, his pickup lines were positively Neanderthal. Matthews quoted his opening line: "Where'd you get the square
chin? Did you fall on the cement when you were a kid?" Still,
after they broke up, Matthews remembers him with affection, saying, "He's very smart, very sensitive, a perfect
gentleman."

Sometimes. At other times, he stopped just short of
letting it all hang out. During one concert, a woman in the
audience screamed out, "Eddie, will you marry me?" Murphy
declined the offer, but let the fan down gently with a counter-
offer: "You can give me a blow job." Murphy amazed himself
at his ability to offend without being offensive. "What could
be worse than what I said to her? And they laughed. Sometimes I wonder if the audience is going to get mad, but they
never do." That would come with time as his act evolved from
crudity to cruelty. While the audience laughed loudly, Murphy's mom was laughing nervously. The first time she caught
her son's act she wondered out loud where he had picked up
such language. Years later, proud but still a bit embarrassed,
Mrs. Lynch began telling friends not to bring their children
to Eddie's shows. Murphy didn't feel his mother overreacted.
He admitted, "I'd go on stage and do disgusting things."

Murphy felt his attractiveness was a case of mind over
matter. Fame wasn't the aphrodisiac, despite Greene; it was
positive thinking. Murphy was the Norman Vincent Peale of

career management. "I think that even the ugliest bitch in the world can say, 'I want to be a model'—and be one," he said, sounding like a cross between Peale and Larry Flynt. While he didn't make any canine comparisons with himself, his good looks were also a case of mental projection. "Girls think I'm handsome because I act handsome. I tell jokes." But on other occasions his self-assurance proved evanescent, giving way to self-doubt and even self-loathing. "Sometimes I'm insecure about everything. I wonder if I'm good-looking, if I'm talented, if I can sing. I wonder how funny people really think I am, or if it's a fluke."

But more often, Murphy believed in Eddie Murphy. Comanager Tienken described his client's stage strategy. "Haven't you figured it out yet? He wants to be the first comic who can get up on stage and throw scarves to women. He wants to be Elvis Presley."

Arsenio Hall described Murphy's charisma with a voluptuousness that sounds either envious or homoerotic. "He has natural charm and black good looks. Eddie has the thing women like—this sexy thing, this charm. White America had Rob Lowe. But the girls in the 'hood didn't have their Rob Lowe. All of a sudden, here comes a classically handsome black man without white features, with a black man's nose, lips, saying, 'I'm not buying the bullshit, here I am.' Everyone finds Eddie attractive. You know why? Because Eddie finds himself attractive. He has tremendous self-esteem." Later revelations and events would show that, like everyone else, Hall, his closest friend, had been blinded by a shiny patina that hid deep self-loathing.

To his credit, Murphy seemed to value brains over beauty. His dating preferences could be called upwardly mobile. Coeds turned him on. For a couple of years in the early eighties, he had an on-again, off-again affair with Robin Givens, a premed student at Harvard. "We were children then. I was nineteen or twenty; she was seventeen. I remember she spoke like a white person, very mannered and aloof. Every sentence was an exercise in linguistic propriety. She was very bossy. A powerful girl."

Although the romance was short-lived, their friendship endured and, a decade later, they remained on terms good enough for Murphy to give her a big role in one of his films. Despite the professional and personal ties, Murphy felt Givens wasn't marriage material, not only for himself but for anyone else who asked. He tried to scare off Mike Tyson. "When she and Mike Tyson hooked up, I thought, 'Shit, they're exact opposites!' I tried to pull Mike's cards on it, because he and I were close. I told him, 'Mike, please, *please!*' Mike said, 'Hey, man, I don't give a shit 'bout no girl, I just want some pussy!' Next thing I knew, he was married!...I guess he really wanted that pussy!"

A year post-Givens, Eddie fell in love with another brainy woman, Shirley Fowler, who was studying to be a social worker at the University of Pittsburgh. The star's attraction to women with high I.Q.s and no show-biz aspirations may not mean that Murphy valued brains over bosom. Supremely insecure about his attractiveness to women—as opposed to his attractiveness to TV and movie audiences—Murphy has said in numerous interviews that he feared women wanted him for his money and fame. A future social worker and a physician, like Fowler and Givens, were safe choices. They weren't starlets looking for their big break via Eddie's bed. Murphy explained his vulnerability succinctly: "I have a really low self-image sometimes."

It wasn't surprising then that in 1983, the woman he fell profoundly in love with was yet another college student, Lisa Figueroa, a premed major at Adelphi University on Long Island. Manager Bob Wachs described the first time: "It was immediately a case of 'some enchanted evening.' Soon, Eddie was forking over a diamond ring and announcing their engagement on stage and to any reporter who would listen.

Like a proud parent describing a child who made the honor roll, Murphy announced, "She's a biology major at Adelphi University. She's Puerto Rican. We're gonna have spicy black children. And she's got a straight-A average." The only thing he failed to do was announce his fiancée's SAT scores.

Rolling Stone condescendingly mentioned that Figueroa was "articulate." What did they expect, a tongue-tied honors student? Figueroa, per the *Stone,* also reported she was delicately featured and "resembles a Hispanic Brooke Shields." Figueroa, like her fiancé, had strong family ties: During her junior year at Adelphi she became so homesick she moved back in with her parents in the Bronx.

In many interviews, Murphy has suggested that when it comes to interpersonal relationships, he's no Alan Alda. Figueroa, however, was no doormat, and Murphy loved a woman who stood up to him. For a while at least. "She's a good girl. She engages on every level. I can talk to her, hang out, she's funny. And you know how I say eventually my wife is going to be a submissive woman? She is the exact opposite of that. She's like a female me. Her sense of humor is not as good as mine, but as far as being pigheaded and wanting her own way, Lisa is very much like me. She's great for me. I've had a problem since I was young. If a woman lets me dominate her, I get bored really fast. Lisa won't listen to me if I'm being an asshole. She doesn't go along with the game plan; she questions me. It's *shocking* to me. It's like she'll ask, 'Where are you goin?', and I'm like this, 'Uh, out.' And she'll go, 'Where, why?' It used to be, 'I'm going out.' 'OK, if only you come back.' She's a great girl."

Murphy loved the tug of war, but ultimately he demanded the whole rope. "In the long run, I have to get my way, and with Lisa it just takes me longer to get it. It's a challenge, not at all a boring relationship." Murphy eventually revealed that Figueroa hadn't really changed his Neanderthal mindset. In the endorphin rush of new love, he might be willing to impersonate Alan Alda, but the sensitive-guy charade didn't last long. "I'm pretty old-fashioned. I'm your basic average everyday guy, and I know women don't like to read it, but I feel like a woman can have *some* say in what goes on in the relationship, but the guy is the core of it, and what I say goes. That's the kind of woman I'll wind up with, someone who's willing to let me call most of the shots." This was not a good omen for holding on to an independent, career-oriented woman. However, that was not the kind of woman Murphy usually dated. In an interview at his Paramount office, Murphy was speaking in his trademark soft voice, a contrast to his brash stage locution, which many article writers have commented on. During his chat with one reporter, a beautiful woman quietly sat in the corner, but not quietly enough. Suddenly, Murphy's concentration was broken by the clanging of the woman's earrings. "Take 'em off!" he ordered. Pointing to the reporter, he explained, "He's recording this. You're gonna fuck up the recording." Then, in a rare case of minding his image, if not his manners, he said to his interviewer, "Write that I did that and you'll make me look like an idiot."

Two people who perhaps knew him best—his mother and best friend Arsenio Hall—described an emotionally immature young man who fell in love too quickly and indiscriminately. In a rare moment of criticism, Lillian said, "Eddie gets himself into things quickly. I wish he'd take his time before settling down. I think he will." His mother implied that despite his brash public persona, underneath the profanity and braggadocio lay a vulnerable romantic who presented his heart for vivisection to all female comers. Hall also picked up on this easy emotional availability. "On the first date, Eddie will say, 'Oh, man! Isn't she wonderful? That's the next Miz Murphy.'

"He wants Cinderella so bad. But you can start off with the sweetest, nicest girl in the world, and then she gets caught in being 'Eddie's woman.' I've seen some of them take bows in clubs all on their own." Long before Eddie apparently saw the transformation of Figueroa from student to wannabe star, Hall recognized the metamorphosis. "I saw her change under the pressure. She began to think she was Eddie. The one person he really loved broke his heart. He was very hurt and down in that period."

Murphy would have agreed with Graham Greene about fame's aphrodisiacal effect on the opposite sex. But fame and money were the Spanish Fly in the ointment, poisoning his relationships with distrust and the search for hidden agendas. "Girls cluster to me like moths to a flame, like the old song says," said the *Blue Angel* aficionado, referring to Marlene Dietrich's description of men's fatal attraction to her. "It's tough knowing when they like me for me or they're on some superstar trip. Most girls are just groupies at heart. But it's fun finding out what their real intentions are. I was always popular with girls. Now it's even worse. But if I can tell a girl's blown away by what I do, and not into me, then I stop seeing her."

Other friends fueled Murphy's insecurity. They pulled him aside and said Figueroa was more interested in spending his money on jewelry and furs than in her fiancé. Eddie should have fired these "pals," who were probably on his extensive payroll. If any of them had been ever been on a college campus, they would have known that animal skins and semiprecious stones are not exactly sorority wear. As for money, Figueroa seemed intent on making her own way in the world as a physician; as for gold-digging, Figueroa paid her own way. While a full-time student, she also worked as a receptionist for a midtown Manhattan accounting firm. Maybe that's where she wanted to wear the alleged furs and diamonds.

While Murphy explained his emotional life in solipsistic detail to the press, Figueroa's public access was monitored and controlled. Originally, she agreed to an interview with *US* magazine, then canceled when a Murphy-handler told her "It wouldn't be wise to have Eddie's private life out on the streets," unless of course Murphy cared to disclose it himself.

He unwittingly disclosed a lot about himself in interviews, which he often regretted granting. *Playboy* seems to attach its subjects to a combination lie detector-electric shock machine; when the star lies, the machine lets loose a thousand volts. How else can you explain the following rant that is as shocking for its self-loathing as it is for its lack of circumspection? Sounding more amazed than annoyed, Murphy told *Playboy's* David Rensin about a woman who agreed to spend the night with him—but not in his bed. "She slept on a futon! You should have seen her apartment. She let a hundred million dollars of dick get away and she's sleeping on the floor."

And while he treated Figueroa like a Soviet dissident trying to talk to the Western press, Murphy revealed that he had never had a venereal disease, "except crabs," and that his penis was shaped like the number nine. After that, what could he have possibly feared Figueroa might say about him?

While his private life revolved around fear and loathing of himself and others, Murphy's career continued to thrive. In 1982, he recorded his first comedy album live at a Manhattan club. The record was titled simply, *Eddie Murphy*. Only forty-eight minutes long, it went gold, unheard of for a nonmusical recording. The album also earned two Grammy nominations, despite *Time* magazine's complaint that it was "undisciplined." Ominously, the mostly-talk recording contained two musical numbers that didn't augur well for his aspirations as a singing star. Both cuts parodied disco, which by 1982 was already dead and had degenerated into self-parody. (Remember the Village People?) One song lampooned Streisand and Donna Summer's duet, "Enough Is Enough," a 1979 release too old to be topical and suitable for satire. The other musical selection was a scatological ditty, "Boogie in Your Butt." The title apparently was the only funny thing about it. Years later, Murphy would admit "Boogie in Your Butt" was not his finest moment. In fact, the term he used for the entire album was "garbage." "I think it was a marketing idea that didn't work. It makes me angry when I look at that album," despite the gold and Grammys. A second comedy album also went gold. Its title duplicated the inscription beneath his high school yearbook photo: *Eddie Murphy: Comedian.* This time, his record won a Grammy in the Best Comedy category in 1984. That same year, he released his first single as a vocalist, "Party All the Time," from an album that would come out a year later to much critical derision. *USA Today* said of this first taste: "It reveals a strong baritone voice but little style or control." Murphy himself displayed rare self-doubt about the territory he was invading. "I'm real nervous about the album, because I'm treading unknown ground here." The song included the puzzling lyrics, "My girl wants to party all the time..." The "girl" was Lisa Figueroa, and as a straight-A student at Adelphi, partying "all the time" seemed unlikely, although she did attend every single one of his club dates, sitting in the front row, where Eddie always introduced her to the audience during his act.

At the same time, his film career went platinum, prospering beyond a TV star's wildest fantasy. His day job on the tube, by contrast, was beginning to seem more like a bad dream.

Chapter 5

......

Trading Mediums

In 1983, WITH HUBRIS that was also correct self-assessment, Murphy said, "I still don't have what I want. I want to be more than big. I want to be tremendous. I wanna be like the Beatles, man. Like the Beatles were to music, that's what I want to be like to comedy. That's my goal."

In another man, such self-confidence would be insufferable. But Murphy was just predicting the actual course of his career for the rest of the decade.

In the fall of 1983, a sophisticated comedy, *Trading Places*, starring Murphy and founding-*SNL*-father Dan Aykroyd, proved that Eddie was not a one-hit wonder. *48 HRS.* wasn't a fluke; it was an omen. While his film debut grossed a handsome $75 million, his second try did a gorgeous $90 million. And this was in the days when VCRs and the lucrative video rental market were in their infancy—long before video would outpace theatrical receipts.

Again, the actor did cleanup after Richard Pryor, who dropped out of *Trading Places* to make the disastrous *The Toy* with Jackie Gleason. Gene Wilder had also been attached to the project, but Murphy declined to work with Wilder because he feared being too closely identified with Pryor's screen persona.

One critic claimed, "It seemed as if Murphy had suddenly filled Pryor's job slot: that of a hip, angry but likable

60

black comedian who is a hit with white audiences while retaining a staunch base of black fans." The pundit got it wrong.

Although Pryor was Murphy's idol, he wasn't a fan of the type his idol most often played on screen—victim. He felt Pryor was a comic Monroe or Garland, laughed at instead of pitied while being victimized. Murphy's humor stood with an in-yo'-face posture, not pants-down, caught defecating in the Vietnam jungle as Pryor did in *Sometimes a Hero*. Whereas offstage Pryor would raise his victimization to Medean levels of self-immolation, self-empowerment fueled the Murphy Laugh Factory.

Besotted director John Landis would later compare Murphy to Marilyn Monroe, but if you have to use white women to describe the two black comics, Richard Pryor is Marilyn; Eddie Murphy is Madonna.

Pryor's role in *Trading Places* had to be extensively rewritten to fit Murphy's philosophical funny bone. "It was written for Pryor, and it's funny to see Richard get fucked over in a movie, in the way he reacts. He goes, 'Oh, *shee-it*,' and that's *funny*. And that's Richard's thing. But I'm not funny like that. When I'm being cocky, straightforward, *that's* when I'm the funniest. I'm funniest when I'm a wiseass. This character, I make this pathetic guy still have some guts left."

Murphy lobbied Paramount to hire Aykroyd and dump Pryor's alter id, Gene Wilder. It didn't take a whole lot of lobbying. At this point in his career, the studio would have offered Dame Sybil Thorndike gross points if Murphy wanted to work with her.

The elegant farce was more than a buddy movie and didn't involve any squealing tires or bickering cops. The film represented a comic debate that biopsychologists and psychoanalysts are still wrangling over in *Scientific American* and *Nature:* nature, in fact, versus nurture. Which has the greater influence on the individual, heredity or environment? This arid topic bloomed as Murphy and Aykroyd debated it in human form.

The story took place at the beginning of the Decade of Greed, the era of Ivan Boesky, Michael Milken, and ketchup as a vegetable in school cafeterias. *Trading Places* was as timely as it was courageous, since it attacked the venal epoch a good ten years before it was labeled for what it was—a period of unbridled me-first, you-last ideology, the Decade of Greed. Don Ameche and Ralph Bellamy were dragged out of retirement to play the living embodiments of evil capitalism. They are stockbroker brothers who decide to test the nature-versus-nurture argument with human guinea pigs.

Dan Aykroyd is an up-and-coming executive in their Main Line Philadelphia brokerage. His life is Reagan-era perfect. A beautiful townhouse, hot car, trophy girlfriend. Everything in his world functions as precisely and accurately as his beloved collection of museum-quality clocks. Aykroyd's junior exec is completely anal retentive.

To say Eddie Murphy's Billy Ray Valentine is a member of the underclass is to elevate his position on the socioeconomic ladder. Billy Ray is a homeless con man who panhandles while pretending to be a double amputee. His legs hidden under a blanket, he rolls around on a homemade sled straight out of Buñuel's film *Los Olvidados*. On his knees, he says to a disgusted passerby, "What's the matter? Ain't you seen *Porgy and Bess?*" He hits on another woman with the world's most original pick up line: "Once you have a man with no legs, you never go back."

Through a series of ingenious but believable plot twists worthy of Restoration Comedy, Bellamy and Ameche manage to beggar Aykroyd and put beggar Murphy in his place, his townhouse, his seat on the stock exchange, even in his girlfriend's bed. Aykroyd becomes homeless; Murphy becomes a Buppie. The elderly stockbrokers make an ungentlemanly wager as to whether Aykroyd's inherited intelligence or Murphy's lavish new environment will triumph in these circumstances.

Trading Places is a buddy movie, a revenge caper, and a relationship movie. It also began a tortured love-hate relationship between the larval superstar and the film's director, John Landis. During the next ten years, the two men would quarrel like (platonic) lovers and fight like martial artists.

For Landis, at least, it was love at first take. Using a bizarre analogy best left to Freudian analysts, Landis, when he first set eyes on Murphy, found him "stunning, almost like Marilyn Monroe." Not even a well-paid publicist would make such comparison without blushing, but Landis's infatuation was genuine. The initial bonding would survive a murder trial and two attempts at strangulation—one literal, the other financial. Murphy would accuse the director of calling him a "nigger," Landis would grab Murphy's testicles and squeeze really hard. Sometimes, Landis seemed to be playing Desdemona to Murphy's Moor as the star actually wrapped his hands around the director's throat and squeezed him into unconsciousness. At other times, it was like a kinkier Moe and Curly, with genital torture instead of eye-gouging. Whatever the situation, the relationship was the most tumultuous director-star relationship since von Sternberg made Dietrich straddle a chair or Hitchcock hit on Tippi Hedren. But these tomcat fights were one movie and five years away. During their first teaming, Murphy was a respectful student, Landis the respected auteur of *Animal House.*

His older costar, Ralph Bellamy, had a happy experience with the actor, who treated him with respect, not asphyxiation. "He's like an old-timer," said Bellamy, himself a genuine one. "He has the professional confidence without intruding on the scene or script. I caught him watching Don Ameche and me, not to learn from us—heavens, no—but so as not to take anything away."

Trading Places, on Philly's mean streets and Main Line,

was a happy set, although there was at least one symbolic sign of times to come, of superstar superego and low-level paranoia. *People* magazine snidely noted that an off-duty police officer stood guard outside Murphy's Winnebago, while Aykroyd's remained undefended. The magazine attributed it to the younger man's clout after the success of *48 HRS.* As future events would show, extra security was a wise precaution, not a perk. Or as Henry Kissinger said, "Sometimes even paranoid people have enemies."

Increased security wasn't pretentious, it was a precaution, well-justified by recent events. Less than a year earlier, John Lennon had been murdered on his doorstep at the Dakota. What some criticized as an entourage, Murphy defended as self-preservation: "I'm supposed to be walking down the street alone? In a recession? If you saw Donald Trump walking down the street alone you'd think he was an ass. Somebody would say, 'I know he has crazy money' and put a gun in his back and take him somewhere. All it takes is one asshole. This country loved John Lennon. And they killed him." Eerily, the only book Murphy claimed he ever read in its entirety was *Catcher in the Rye,* both Lennon's and Ronald Reagan's attackers' favorite novel. While the Lennon tragedy scared him from the safe distance of newspaper accounts, Murphy personally learned how a mob of fans can turn simply into a mob. In 1984, while signing copies of his record, *Eddie Murphy: Comedian,* in Washington's pricey Georgetown, two thousand fans tried to force their way into the record store. Some of them pushed a policeman through a plate-glass window.

Press reports commented on his large entourage of hangers-on and bodyguards. Although he rarely played the racist card, Murphy's rebuttal suggests similar complaints would not have been leveled at a white superstar. When five black men get together, he said, it's called a gang or entourage. A group of five white men is called a dinner party.

"As much as we think we're liberals, society has this underlying bed of racism. It's like this thing I keep hearing about my entourage. If Michael J. Fox walks into a restaurant with his friends, it's Michael J. Fox and his guests. When Eddie Murphy walks into a room with his friends, it's like, 'Oh, my, it's Eddie Murphy—and his entourage.' I don't have an entourage. I don't have bodyguards. My cousin Ray, he takes care of all my little stuff. My high school friend is a production assistant. Larry Johnson is my personal assistant. The fact that they're big makes people think they're bodyguards. I walk into a room with my cousin and my brother and Ken Frith, the guy I went to school with, and *one* security person. That's five cats. You tell me where I got the reputation that I have a bunch of bodyguards. There's one bodyguard there, but the rest of the people are relatives or my buddies."

His cohorts became mythical and the stuff of legend, urban division. A famous incident, repeated as gospel, although it was actually apocrypha, allegedly involved his goon squad and a little old lady. Murphy and company got into an elevator and stood next to a nervous woman. Murphy said, "Hit the floor." He was telling a flunky to press the button. The woman thought it was a command and did just that. The next day an abashed Murphy sent the woman flowers and paid her hotel bill. The incident never happened and belongs in the same urban legend file with gerbils and the woman who impaled herself on the stick shift after being drugged with Spanish Fly.

Although Dan Aykroyd didn't have a bodyguard, much less an entourage, he didn't resent his costar's perks. Indeed, he admired Murphy's work ethic and squeaky clean sobriety. No doubt thinking of the loss of his best friend only a year earlier, Aykroyd predicted Murphy was no Marilyn Monroe or John Belushi. "Eddie lives for his work. He's not going to blow his youth and fortune the way so many young performers before him have. Eddie is virtually an untapped reservoir of talent. This guy's going to go on forever."

Eddie declared his life a drug-free zone. There was no need to dull his senses with pharmaceuticals; he wanted to experience every bit of success completely sensate. "I'm a happy guy," he said on the set of *Trading Places*, perhaps during the upswing of a manic cycle. "I'm real secure with myself, and I'm not into drugs and shit like that. My vices are cars and clothes and jewelry. This ring on my finger is *my* cocaine. You can't snort a ring, or else my obituary would be, 'Murphy was found dead with a ring in his nose.'"

In fact, at fifteen, Murphy blew his first paycheck on junk food, cake, candy, but never alcohol or illicit drugs. In 1983, he told Barbara Walters, "I'm funny about narcotics. I don't have to sniff cocaine. I could afford cocaine, but I've never tried it because I'm afraid I might like it."

Nine years later, Murphy had changed his story, although technically he had told the truth when he denied using *narcotics*. Despite what the DEA says, marijuana is not a narcotic, according to a more scientific source, the *Physician's Desk Reference*.

In 1992, Murphy admitted, "I experimented with pot, like everybody when they were kids. That's it. I've never, ever, ever, ever, like even held cocaine. Or seen anyone around me doing it. I'm a pretty drug-free cat."

With *Trading Places*, Murphy aced the transition from big TV star to even bigger film star. None other than Howard Rosenberg, the *L.A. Times*'s Pulitzer Prize–winning John Gotti of TV critics, described the difficulty of the move and announced that Murphy had made it brilliantly. Genius was the actual term the guerrilla critic used: "The movie records of John Belushi, Dan Aykroyd, and Bill Murray indicate that, first, TV is not necessarily a classroom for movie craft. Second, TV genius does not necessarily translate to the big screen...Not unless you're Eddie Murphy."

Maybe it was lack of self-esteem or accurate self-assessment, but Murphy felt profoundly uncomfortable about the Einstein label. When the director of his biggest hit also called him a genius, the genius demurred. "There's no such thing as a comic genius. Geniuses are people who do things with their brains—scientists, people with academic training," said the swain of numerous coeds. "Not guys who play the piano or make people laugh. I'd be the first to admit I'm a very funny guy and last to admit I'm a genius."

Chapter 6

......

Saturday Night's Dead

AFTER *TRADING PLACES*'S critical hosannas and financial haul, Paramount basically had to pay Murphy a $4 million bribe to keep him on board. What perks could a modestly budgeted TV show like *Saturday Night Live* give the movie star to return for a fourth season? During the third, his salary had been upped to eight thousand a week. How could *SNL* compete with Paramount's counteroffer of one million per picture?

Dick Ebersol proved he was an even better psychologist than producer. Instead of big money, he used a little guilt to lure his protégé back for the 1983–1984 season. Okay, Ebersol did offer him $300,000 to appear on only 10 shows, but that wasn't what brought the million-dollar man back to Studio 8H at 30 Rock.

Ebersol said to Murphy, "I know you've got a career, but I've got other people up here who won't have a career if you leave the show. I'm not talking about me—people like secretaries and stuff will be out of a job. *I don't want you to think about that, though...*" If Ebersol's career ever takes a downturn, he should teach a course on how to be a Jewish mother or write a psychological travel book called *Guilt-Tripping.*

It wasn't only guilt that brought Murphy back. Despite the artistic clashes the men had during their two-year collaboration and Murphy's tardiness and no-shows at staff meetings, they genuinely liked each other. One magazine insisted it was neither money nor guilt that made Murphy return to his roots. It was loyalty to Ebersol. Richard Pryor, Murphy once said, had given him the best advice of his career: "Never trust nobody." Murphy made an exception in Ebersol's case. He trusted the producer enough to take a break in his film career, even though a brief hiatus can become permanent retirement in the short-attention-span world of moviegoers. Ali McGraw left the business at the height of her *Love Story* glory when Steve McQueen demanded she become a hausfrau. When McGraw returned to the screen just a few years later, it was a case of Ali Who? followed by public-career death, late-night infomercials. (They're still running.)

Murphy did not enjoy his homecoming at Rockefeller Plaza. He loved the producer and felt the other cast members were more like siblings than costars, but he hated the medium. Television was just too confining, and we're not talking about his ego or the size of the screen. In 1981, when the show had an extra four minutes, and Jean Doumanian told him to go out there and do his stuff, his stuff had to be edited beyond recognition by concert-goers used to hearing the f-word every ten seconds in his act. In the eighties, TV was still G-rated. After experiencing the R-rated freedom of film, Murphy couldn't tolerate this bowdlerization by committee. Battles with the censors were Pyrrhic defeats. His movie star clout might compel studio executives to sit through *Star Trek* reruns, but the network's euphemistic standards and practices controlled content with an absolute power Will Hays would have envied during his twenty-year reign as the movie industry's top censor.

Murphy didn't care to do, in Wachs's phrase, "simultaneous editing" of a raunchy style that was reflexive. "Lately, I've been writing things that TV can't accommodate, so in a creative sense, maybe it's time for me to go." *Ebony* predicted that if Murphy left, so would the audience, and the network would cancel the show. The magazine wasn't indulging in racial favoritism. *Newsweek* was even more bullish on his importance to *SNL*. "For the last two seasons," the magazine said in 1983, "Murphy has been the only reason anybody with a mental age of more than twelve would watch *Saturday Night Live.*"

As much as he hated the medium, Murphy made two more appearances on TV in 1983. One made sense; the other was surreal. In October, HBO aired his one-man show, *Delirious*. Pay cable channels don't employ censors, so Eddie didn't feel confined by the medium. In fact, he apparently spewed more Anglo-Saxonisms than usual—enough to land in *TV Guide*'s "Jeers" column. The magazine complained, "The talented comedian and film star pushed the uncensored limits of cable comedy past blushing point with his gratuitous and non-stop use of four-letter words during his routine." If *TV Guide* had a column for surreal TV fusions of past and present, it would have to include Murphy's appearance on a Bob Hope special in April 1983. Although the young comic had predicted that one day he would be as famous as Hope, fame would be the only thing the two men would have in common. Hope's highly rated annual TV specials were basically turn-of-the-century burlesque—although the show's nurses and bathing beauties have larger breasts, thanks to turn of the millennium silicone and saline. But there on the NBC special, in the middle of G-rated doubles entendres that were already stale when Minsky's was fresh, stood Eddie Murphy, titillating white America and no doubt making Hope's core audience of senior citizens reach for the beta-blockers. Fortunately for the censors, who would have developed carpal tunnel syndrome twisting the bleep-out knobs, Murphy didn't appear live on the show. Very carefully selected snippets from his live stage act, *Delirious*, were pretaped and sanitized into unintelligibility. It remains a mystery how the videotape editors managed to find anything to use besides "the," "and," and "but."

Along with censorship, burnout extinguished his enthusiasm for the weekly grind of TV. Comics have said that "dying" on stage is worse than the real thing. Murphy felt he died during one sketch in which the real-life Mr. Rogers met his ghetto incarnation, Mr. Robinson; Murphy didn't get a single laugh. "I stank tonight," he said at the cast party after the show. "I didn't know my lines. I was reading the cue cards for everything. I'm just burned out. I won't shoot myself. I'll just be depressed." Freddie Prinze, another young comic who enjoyed quick success before blowing his brains out, haunted the even more successful Murphy. In several interviews during those years, you can almost feel him shudder as he invokes the image of Prinze as a cautionary possibility. "When I'm alone, in here thinking about things, feeling the business getting the best of me, that's when I get scared....I figure it's good that I know enough to get away. I won't do no Freddie Prinze deal, pretend the pressures aren't there. I'll never put a bullet in my head."

By the spring of 1984, Murphy had had enough of substituting "doo-doo" for "shit." At the grand old age of twenty-two, he did a Sinatra and prematurely announced his retirement. With the sadness of MacArthur leaving the Philippines, the comic explained his departure with no promise that he would return. "I'm retiring from TV at twenty-two. Never again. No weeklies or specials. I may pop up on a talk show now and then. I don't like feeling restricted. There are things I can't do on TV. Back when this show started, if someone told me I had to do something I didn't want to, they would say, 'Fuck you, you have to.' I don't have to put up with bullshit—anymore. I want to do my concerts and albums and movies. I want to do *my* stuff."

Murphy's departure coincided with that of his best

friend, Joe Piscopo. The two men talked for years about making a film together, but unlike Murphy's other best friend, Arsenio Hall, Piscopo never got the chance to have his big screen career jump-started by Murphy's more powerful box-office engine.

An incident during the last season also suggests that professional rivalry—or perhaps jealousy, considering Piscopo's status vis-á-vis Murphy's—infected the friendship. When guest host Nick Nolte canceled at the last moment, Ebersol diplomatically canvassed every cast member before giving Murphy the job. Only Piscopo objected, urging the producer to let him host as his Frank Sinatra character. The real Ol' Brown Eyes had a higher TVQ than a pale imitation of Ol' Blue Eyes, and Ebersol ignored Piscopo's other imitation, Eve Harrington.

Murphy almost immediately regretted his departure—not from the claustrophobic show but from his fellow inmates. "When I first left *SNL,* I was tired of my work. But now that I'm gone, I realize how much I loved everybody I worked with. I get sad sometimes watching, just reading the names, 'cause I really grew up on that show. The show molded me; everybody big-brothered or big-sistered me, right down to the new people who were there when I left."

He especially missed Ebersol's counsel. It seems Ebersol had other psychological skills besides guilt-tripping Eddie into staying another year; the producer also functioned as therapist and father confessor, a living couch for Eddie to lay his sins and hang-ups on. "When I was fucked up, I could go to Dick." If Ebersol was unavailable, costars played shrink. "Joe Piscopo was the first guy I'd go to," Murphy said, apparently unaware of Piscopo's attempted coup when he replaced Nolte as guest host. "If Joe wasn't there, there was [*SNL'S*] Tim Kazurinsky. If they couldn't help, I was fucked."

Murphy's reliance on professional associates instead of friends or management is sad and ironic. As later court depositions would show, Murphy kept a huge, fifty-man personal staff on the payroll, year-round, whether he was working or not. His generosity inspired fierce loyalty from his entourage. Bodyguard Derrick Lawrence, who amusingly held the title Vice President of Eddie Murphy Productions, called his boss "an old friend. I'd been laid off from my job, and Eddie asked me if I wanted to work for him. I love Eddie for it, and I always will. I'm like his Knight of the Round Table. I'll serve him till the day I die." Unfortunately, while Lawrence was an excellent bodyguard, he was a rotten script reader, a skill the rest of the Murphy Mafia also lacked. Apparently, not a single one of these well-paid yes-men filled the job of compassionate listener. Murphy's comments also anticipate a growing isolation that would become so creepy the press drew comparisons with Elvis and Howard Hughes.

Emotionally adrift, Murphy didn't get good professional advice at this time either. As *SNL* wound down, the high-energy performer found himself unemployed—not that he needed cash to pay the mortgages on the houses he had lavished on family members. But you don't achieve Murphy's kind of success without at least a bit of the excessive drive known as workaholism. Manager Bob Wachs found him a script, but even Murphy's need to work wasn't strong enough to make him ignore the stinker Wachs came up with.

Best Defense was a vehicle for Dudley Moore, still hot three years after his hit comedy about third-stage alcoholism, *Arthur*. The first thing the superstar wanted to know: why Wachs was urging him to play second banana to a dwarfish Oxford graduate? Wachs had one million good reasons for his client—actually, one million *dollars* for just a few weeks' work, since Murphy had only one scene. At his age and even with his lucrative multipicture pact with Paramount, a million dollars was a fairly large sum. Or as Murphy later confessed, "It was greed."

Perhaps greed made him bullish on a script he knew was

beneath him. For public consumption, Murphy described the project with these words: "It'll be like *48 HRS.*, but bigger. We're gonna be in the bush shooting bazookas and shit."

During his brief screen time, Murphy appeared as a wacko military adviser, Dr. Strangelove on a bad day, stationed in Kuwait. The studio marketing department came up with an original billing, "strategic guest star." You wouldn't have known that from the TV and print ads, which made Eddie look like the lead. Or, at worst, one half of a buddy movie, with Moore the other half. In reality, the two men never appeared together in the film. If it seemed as though Murphy had decided to take the money and run, it's because that's exactly what he did.

Fans were outraged when they sat through the film and found this alleged Murphy vehicle was a moped for Moore. One critic, who apparently brought a stopwatch to the theater, said Murphy's screen time lasted thirty-five seconds and consisted of nothing but obscenities. That was hyperbole, but not too much. His actual screen time lasted all of twenty minutes. Maybe Wachs wasn't such a bad manager after all. Calculated on an hourly scale at $1 million per twenty minutes, Murphy earned maximum wage of $3 million an hour.

Theater owners, who are required to book films sight unseen, were outraged that they had been duped into reserving precious midsummer space for faux Eddie Murphy. Their complaints were temporarily forgotten after *Best Defense*'s opening weekend in July 1984 with a then-whopping $8 million. Wachs, who had pressured his client to do the guest bit, proved to be more than a greedy accountant: Despite leprous reviews, *Best Defense* proved that Eddie could "open" a movie. *Time Out,* a London magazine, noted that there were far more talented actors of color who had achieved success, but Murphy remained unique for one reason. "Denzel [Washington], Wesley Snipes, Laurence Fishburne have transcended their color to achieve stardom in an overwhelmingly white film industry. But Eddie Murphy proved you don't have to be white to open a movie. Like Michael Jackson in music or Michael Jordan in sport, Murphy has left the boundaries of race and color behind and achieved status where it doesn't really matter if he's black, white, or red."

As far as Paramount was concerned, the only color that mattered was green. For reasons best left to CPAs and the IRS, studios earn more money during a film's early run than later on, when theater owners' share of the gross increases. For the studio, it's important to be able to get the audience inside the tent right away. It also gives executives bragging rights and a headline in the trades as the purveyor of the weekend's No. 1 film. *Best Defense* quickly descended the box-office list, but it nudged Murphy up the steep gradient toward superstardom.

Unfortunately, word of mouth, as usual, was more powerful than star power or duplicitous ad campaigns. In its second week, as it dawned on fans that they had paid to see a Dudley Moore movie, the box office dropped a calamitous sixty percent. The third week, it fell another fifty percent.

"Word of mouth sells a movie," Murphy said. "The idea of Dudley and me in a film was pleasing to the public, so the movie opened real big. But if a movie sucks, I don't give a fuck who's in it. It'll crash. This movie sucked real bad. I saw a screening at Paramount, and I felt like putting a Band-Aid on my eyes 'cause I'd just been fucked. I was depressed."

When it came to assessing blame, however, Murphy could be his own worst critic, although he once got so riled by critics he quipped, "Siskel and Ebert can stick their thumbs up my ass." Murphy himself gave his third film two thumbs down. "*Best Defense* was a bizarre one. It was the first time I was weak in this business, the first time I did something other than what I wanted to do. I read the script and wasn't nuts about it, or about doing a cameo after two very successful movies, but it was, 'Well, it's not your movie, and they'll give you X amount of dollars.' It was the first time I felt I was whoring myself artistically. It was greed. I can't be condemned for it, 'cause we've all been guilty of it at one time or another." Although he tastefully referred to the amount as "X," the $1 million payday proved irresistible to a young man of his socioeconomic background. A million dollars was a lot of money in those days, Murphy said years later, when his fortune was estimated by *Forbes* magazine at $70 million, a wildly conservative sum.

By the end of the year, Murphy felt comfortable enough to joke about his first flop in front of a national audience on his former stomping ground. Guest-hosting *Saturday Night Live* in December, which turned out to be the highest-rated episode in the show's history, Murphy claimed that he thought he was too big to return to TV, but then *Best Defense* came out, "So here I am."

The star could also console himself with the feeling that the biggest hit of his career, his entree into box-office Valhalla with Stallone and Nicholson, loomed less than half a year away and was already in the can. In the meantime, he could sit tight and hug the NASDAQ report for comfort. Or read the commentary in *Commentary* magazine, which said after his first two films (but before *Best Defense* tarnished his track record), "Murphy's rise was more spectacular than Michael Jackson or Bill Cosby's." The magazine balanced its enthusiasm by wondering if *Trading Places* and *48 HRS.* were "flashes in the pan," flukes like *Three Men and a Love Story* that turned Ted Danson and Ryan O'Neal into one-hit wonders, bankable for a nanosecond.

Commentary's editorial writer need not have lost any REM sleep over Murphy's longevity on the big screen. His next film would secure his title as the No. 1 box-office attraction for the entire decade.

Chapter 7

· · · · · ·

Supernova

BEFORE MURPHY ACHIEVED Olympian heights at the box office, a hellish incident showed that money and fame offer no protection at ground level—the Sunset Strip in West Hollywood to be exact.

In the same month *Best Defense* proved to be a mixed blessing, a fight in a Mexican restaurant on the Strip turned into a curse with Murphy ending up in the emergency room.

On July 14, 1984, a Saturday night, Murphy was knocking back a non-alcoholic drink with friends Alex and Larry and bodyguard Derrick, who should have been fired after what ensued. Accounts of the fight contained more conflicting details than *Rashomon*. One version claimed a patron punched Eddie because the man's girlfriend was staring at him. Eddie, trained by his stepfather in basement boxing, hit the man only after being struck. Manager Bob Wachs, who wasn't there but was totally sympathetic, said another man had tried to grab a woman's hand but touched Murphy's instead. Then, inexplicably, the man shoved Murphy against the wall. Only then did his million-dollar client hit back. In another "explanation," Wachs said his client was trying to break up a fight.

Unfortunately, the jealous beau and the confused patron weren't the only guys the star clobbered that night—or so claimed the restaurant manager, Phillip Shumway, twenty-five. Shumway said he was chatting with a friend when fists started to fly, nor were they the only airborne objects. Shumway said Murphy's five companions started throwing chairs. Murphy then threw a glass, which put a "nice little gash" in Shumway's arm, according to the manager's police report, although he did mention that he thought Murphy had been aiming at someone else.

A spokeswoman for the Los Angeles County Sheriff's Department contradicted Shumway's account. She said, "Shumway held him [Murphy] defenseless while another struck him in the face."

Undeterred, Shumway filed a lawsuit against the star, asking $25,000 in general damages and $1 million punitive. He also asked the District Attorney to charge Murphy with battery. The District Attorney demurred, saying, "Witnesses' statements conflicted concerning who caused injury to victim Phillip Shumway...There is insufficient evidence to convict any of the involved parties."

Murphy's own account of the brawl shows that he did indeed pull the first punch, but he was shoved into action. "What happened was I was talking with a friend, and all of a sudden somebody pushed me. I pushed the guy back, he pushed me again, I hit him, and it turned into a barroom brawl, with everybody punching everybody. At the end of it, because I was Eddie Murphy, somebody said, 'Eddie punched me.' Somebody else said, 'Eddie hit me with a chair.' And somebody else said, 'Eddie threw a glass.' The fight didn't happen because of some violent streak in me. I was just a victim of circumstances. What it boiled down to was some guy was jealous over his girlfriend and came and picked a fight with me, and it turned into a barroom brawl. We tore the place apart."

A witness, who also happened to be an attorney, Joseph Gerbac, concurred. "The place was totally destroyed."

Litigation followed, Murphy speculated, "'Cause Eddie's got money, so let's get paid."

Murphy didn't bother to countersue, even though he suffered cuts on his lower lip severe enough to merit a trip to Cedars-Sinai's ER. The comedian even managed to get a punch line for his act out of the fight. Did he learn a lesson from the incident, a guest asked him. "Yeah, get your ass kicked and you got a whole new routine."

The summer storm on the Strip and *Best Defense*'s failure would be forgotten in the wake of a leviathan called *Beverly Hills Cop*. The movie would have the same effect on his career as *Funny Girl* had on Streisand's or *Butch Cassidy and the Sundance Kid* had on Redford's—instant superstardom. Bankability. Name your next project. You're beautiful, kid; never change.

Made for a song, a melodic $14 million, *Beverly Hills Cop* would do the kind of business that had Paramount's Chief Executive Officer waltzing to the annual stockholders' meeting.

Interestingly, the studio for the third time in a row offered its burgeoning star another hand-me-down. Both *Trading Places* and *48 HRS.* had been written for Richard Pryor. Way back in 1976, the script for *Beverly Hills Cop* had been conceived as another ugh and grunt extravaganza for Sylvester Stallone. The script went through seventeen drafts, including one written by Rocky himself, but Stallone couldn't please even himself, and dropped out. John Travolta was also briefly attached to the script, then Mickey Rourke. The project continued to languish in development hell for eight years. Movie industry jargon calls such a state of disgrace "in turnaround," a euphemism that fools no one and means "this script stinks." Other studios can buy a script that has been "turned around," but they rarely take on another company's leftovers. Turnaround is the Scarlet T for the luckless writer who finds his baby so labeled. There have been some exceptions. Columbia turned down *Star Wars*, which continues to enrich savvier 20th Century–Fox. But Fox turned down *The English Patient* and found itself dateless at the Oscars last spring.

Ultimately, Paramount must have been delighted that no other studio wanted its castoff, because when Murphy adopted the orphaned script, the pariah suddenly became the prodigy.

Beverly Hills Cop's high concept sounds like a Sylvester Stallone romp. A tough Detroit policeman goes to Southern California in search of his best friend's killers. The straight action-adventure had to be turned into an action comedy, since the original version didn't feel the need to supply Rambo with yucks along with the ughs.

According to both the director, Martin Brest, and the writer, Daniel J. Petrie, Murphy himself did the rewrite on the run, between takes. The actor reconceived the film's high concept as "tough Detroit cop goes to Beverly Hills and suffers culture shock." The hunt for the killers became the B-plot, something to pin Murphy's marvelous improvisations on.

But according to one press account, the script remained color-blind. Neither Murphy nor an uncredited professional writer redesigned scenes for a black man. The actor had heard too much "jive turkeys" and "dyn-O-mites" on the small screen to let that jargon follow him to the big screen. In fact, in only one scene in the film does race even come up, when Murphy throws a tantrum at an exclusive men's club that has denied him admission because, he claims, he's a "Negro." The maître d' isn't being racist. Murphy isn't a member. Plus, he's dressed like a street punk in sweats instead of pinstripes.

With the director and writer's encouragement, Murphy threw out all his dialogue for the first scene and wrote a parody of street jive. You want jive turkey, sucker? Murphy gave it to the audience on his terms and argot. With some exaggeration, *Rolling Stone* claimed that Murphy "wrote all his own dialogue for all his films." More accurately, the self-possessed star commandeered the alleged black dialect imagined by white writers. "When white writers write for black actors, they use 'sucker' and 'jive turkey' and all that. When I do a black character, it doesn't offend blacks because I just act normal, which isn't offensive to whites or blacks," Murphy said.

Cop's opening sequence, which Murphy did write, takes place in Detroit, where he goes undercover to bust a cigarette smuggling ring. The filmmakers needed a stenographer on the set to record Murphy's stream of consciousness for the sake of continuity, which turned into an editing-room nightmare. Director Martin Brest was astounded rather than annoyed with Murphy's write-as-you-shoot style: "You couldn't write down all the dialogue Eddie can use in one scene. You'd have a ten-page scene and a two-hundred-page script. If he can invent a line out of whole cloth, you devoutly hope he will."

That's exactly what he did for the tony men's club scene. The director and writer couldn't figure out a way for Murphy to get into the members-only dining room. Desperate, Brest knocked on Murphy's trailer and begged for help. Murphy was sound asleep. The director recalled that the star was still rubbing sleep from his eyes when he ad-libbed the entire scenario. Murphy would get past the maître d' by pretending to be "Ramon," the extravagantly effeminate lover of one of the club members. Ramon had an urgent message for his boyfriend, which he had no qualms about sharing with the host. Ramon just had to talk to him because he had urgent bad news. Ramon had herpes. So, he feared, would the club member eventually.

Brest was delighted he had crashed Murphy's Winnebago. "It couldn't have taken him more than four seconds, and he proceeded to spill the whole scene."

Another bit of improv shows how Murphy honed the
script with every take, adding layer upon layer of ad-libbed
humor which invigorated the tired buddy-cop genre. One
scene had Murphy explain why he followed two suspects into
a strip joint. On the first take, he spoke his lines as scripted:
"I saw bulges in the suspects' jackets." After the umpteenth
take, Murphy got bored and started free-associating: "I saw
bulges in their jackets, and that's a bit bizarre, having bulges
on the way *into* a place like that."

Improv was hardly new territory for the stand-up comedian and *SNL* star, two venues that begged for ad-libs. But
Murphy had already had a chance to flex his verbal agility on
a previous film. *Trading Places*'s complex script was set in
stone, and Murphy was sharp enough to realize that messing
with the dialogue would harm the plot's intricacies, if not
make the story unintelligible. But the generic cop pic, *48
HRS.,* was, in Murphy's words, "very weak. Thank god for
[director] Walter Hill's pencil." And, the star might have
added, his own knack for the snappy rejoinder.

On future projects, Murphy's contributions to the script
would have less salutary effects, but that's several films and a
nervous breakdown away. In 1984, Murphy had a golden gut
and platinum instincts.

The director also felt Eddie's acting abilities were equally
gilded. "He was, whether he liked it or not, a great Method
actor." Brest wasn't the only member of the new Eddie
Murphy fan club. Costar Judge Rheinhold, Murphy's dim-
bulb partner, said, "I kept looking for Eddie's tragic flaw, but I
couldn't find it. He's gifted, a comedic Mozart." Lisa
Eilbacher, the Rodeo Drive art dealer who helps Murphy's
Detroit cop deal with culture shock in Beverly Hills, enjoyed
her leading man's unpretentious attitude: "Eddie's like a kid
who never grew up." Bronson Pinchot, who had a bit part as
an effeminate art gallery employee, also commented on
Murphy's accessibility. "He acted like someone you might

have known in third grade, running around doing Michael Jackson imitations. He was like a happy little kid."

Murphy was a lot of fun on the set, and the occasional flair of temperament, which would turn into tantrums during later films, didn't seem to bother the grateful director or admiring costars. When an assistant director knocked on his trailer to call him to the set, Murphy refused to budge. He was deeply immersed in his headphones. "Call me when you're *ready* ready," he told the A.D.

When he finally made it to the set and another assistant director shouted, "Silence, please!" as the camera was about to roll, Murphy ignored the command and broke out into a loud impersonation of Mario Lanza singing Verdi's greatest hits. Only when the director yelled, "Action," did Murphy stop his impromptu aria.

Murphy could have sung the entire Wagnerian canon and no one would have complained after *Beverly Hills Cop* premiered in December 1984. Less than a month later, it had grossed $64 million and remained the No. 1 film for eleven straight weeks. After three months, the take had climbed to $160 million. Overall box office for 1984 hit an all-time high, more than $4 billion. *Variety* claimed it knew the culprit. "Eddie Murphy almost single-handedly pulled the year's final tally to an all-time record." *Newsweek* hailed him as the "hottest star in the Hollywood heavens, the closest anybody gets to a sure thing in box office terms." ShoWest, the annual frat party thrown by theater owners in Las Vegas, named him "box office star of the year" in 1985. Murphy appeared at the event and showed success hadn't gone to his head, although it had affected his unfortunate fashion sense. He wore a black leather suit and no shirt for his acceptance speech. "I'm not one for speeches, unless I can curse, and they asked me not to. The fact is, we don't know what we're doing. We lucked out on this movie."

With *Beverly Hills Cop*, Murphy became an instant

icon—and a barely tapped merchandising bonanza. In one
scene, he wore a sweatshirt with the logo "Mumford Phys. Ed.
Dept.," named after a real Detroit high school. Bloom-
ingdale's and Macy's sold out of the pullovers quickly, and
Murphy graciously donated his take of merchandising,
$50,000, to the eponymous inner city school. Murphy had
landed in Clark Gable territory, where a bare-chested scene
in *It Happened One Night* caused T-shirt sales to plummet.

Murphy's brand-name recognition created an ancillary
market that was new at the time, now crowded by every
sitcom star with a sob story or substance abuse. In 1984, the
star had become such a cynosure that he signed a six-figure
deal with Simon & Schuster to write his memoirs—at the
ripe old age of twenty-three! With Paramount throwing $25
million checks at him, six figures to write (or have ghost-
written) an entire book must have seemed like coolie wages.
Or perhaps the star feared the self-revelation that an autobiography would require. For whatever reasons, *Eddie Murphy: My Life in the (Movie) Theater,* never made it into print.

A survey conducted by fearful Paramount rivals, MGM,
TriStar, and HBO, showed that Murphy was the most popular
performer in the country, followed by Bill Cosby and Richard
Pryor. The poll also noted another phenomenon which explained his muscular box office but would also cause the star
self-doubts about selling out and playing Uncle Tom in a one-
man minstrel show for white Hollywood. The survey said,
"He's a black comic with tremendous *crossover* appeal among
both white and black audiences."

Crossover is a simple-sounding term that speaks volumes about the racial divide that still bisects this country as
neatly as the Mason-Dixon Line did two centuries ago. Mass
entertainment has to appeal to the masses in order to be
commercially viable. The mass of the masses is white. For a
black entertainer to succeed, he has to cross over from the
black subculture to the white *Überkultur.* At least that's the

theory why stars like Murphy and *Independence Day*'s Will
Smith become top box-office draws, while Spike Lee continues to churn out succès d'estime that fail with white
audiences.

There's just one problem with the concept of crossover
when applied to Eddie Murphy. While geographically he had
to make the transition from a black suburb on Long Island to
an upscale white enclave in New Jersey, cinematically he
didn't have to step over any color-coded Rubicon.

In an essay, "The Deification of the Outlaw in Crossover
American Humor," film critic Kenneth Turan put his finger on
why Richard Pryor makes us squirm, while Murphy makes us
relax and laugh. "Eddie Murphy, though he absorbed Pryor's
attitudes, does not have his background; he grew up not in a
whorehouse but in a middle class suburb. He doesn't have to
strive to become one of us, he is one of us, and consequently his
humor never disturbs, never creates discomfort."

New York magazine also marveled at his ability to insult
without losing his audience: "Most remarkably, Murphy ap-
peals to white audiences while doing routines that border on
antiwhite harangues. He can also play with hated black
stereotypes and keep a black following."

That was in 1985, two years before a very raw concert
film gave white America—not to mention gays and women of
all colors—a case of the hives. Turan conceded "the astonish-
ing amount of hostility, both verbal and physical, he can
project, [but] we know instinctively not to take his threat of
violence seriously. He is nasty but safe, a thrill we can live
with."

Rolling Stone contrasted his happy mindset with
Richard Pryor's act borne of a horrific childhood. Murphy's
material didn't arise out of nightmare or sadness. Pryor was
his idol but not a role model. "Richard's funny as a victim, but
I'm funnier when I try to fight back. Maybe the star of the
'90s will be the funny black guy who runs the show." He could

have been predicting Will Smith's saving the world or what was left of it in *Independence Day*.

Not every press pundit found Murphy's hostility cute. The backlash which hits all successful people began surprisingly early in the star's career. One is hard pressed to find a public disenchantment that started sooner, with the possible exception of the "I Hate Brenda" campaign launched against *Beverly Hills 90210*'s Shannon Dougherty. A year after *Beverly Hills Cop* made him a superstar, the Chicago Tribune's Larry Kart was calling him an Uncle Tom. "Murphy is black, so how can he not be consumed by feelings of rage and righteous indignation when he contemplates our nation's racist past and the present-day plight of so many of his brothers and sisters?"

A self-diagnosed manic-depressive, the comedian tried to hide his depression and stay manic on stage. Mania helped with ad-libbing. "I don't like to do stuff about my father being dead. No tragedy. My comedy's good-time comedy, conversations and fooling around with my friends. That's why I poke fun at everybody 'cause I'm not a racist. I'm not a sexist; I'm just *out* there. I use racial slurs. But I don't hate anybody." *Rolling Stone*, the Bible of hip, agreed that his stage act was just that, an act. "Murphy seems to bear no deep-seated animosities. He's likable without bogus big-star charm."

He was likable and, more important, nonthreatening. It's a telling statistic that in at least seven of his seventeen films, he played cops. One way of domesticating scary black icons is to align them with the law and therefore make them obedient to it. To his credit, Murphy never played a drug addict or a pimp on film.

A British journalist disagreed with his American colleagues that Murphy was "safe" for stardom. London's *Time Out* magazine felt that the threat implicit in his swaggering screen image scared whites, but in a titillating rather than gimme-your-wallet way. "He has fashioned his career," the avant-garde publication said, "by scorning the myths about race. In *48 HRS.* and *Trading Places,* he plays an aggressive black, the one who fights back and wins."

In America, at least, people felt Murphy was fighting on their side, regardless of their color. A survey conducted by *Commentary* a few months after *Beverly Hills.Cop* came out indicated that Murphy's core audience was "overwhelmingly white." The respected magazine also claimed that Murphy's role models were the same color. Elvis was his idol, it reported accurately. *Commentary* also claimed—way off the mark this time—that he had "patterned his career on the *Ur*-Wasp, Bob Hope, whose cheeky confidence Murphy's own style recalls in an eerie way." *Commentary* had apparently based the latter claim on Murphy's famous teenage boast that one day his fame would eclipse Hope's. The older comedian's naughty nurse gags are direct descendants of hundred-year-old vaudeville shtick; Murphy's profanity and scatology come from another universe. No matter how old or venerable Murphy becomes, it's a safe bet he'll never play golf with the president of the United States.

Murphy felt all the sociobabble about crossover appeal didn't explain his success. Strip away the black or white epidermis, and all funny bones respond to a deft tickle. "I know that there are black people and white people, but all funny bones are the same color. If something's funny, it's funny." However, blacks made him work overtime. "It's harder to make a black person laugh. Black people won't give it up as easily as whites. You have to work harder to win them over. I can go out in front of a white crowd and say, 'Do you smell shit?', and they'll laugh, but that would take five minutes with a black crowd."

By 1984, his stage act had become so blue that an even bigger black star was seeing red. America's favorite father and Ob-Gyn, Bill Cosby, felt Murphy had pushed the envelope into the wastebin. In a telephone call that made international headlines, Cosby told Murphy to clean up his act. Murphy remained respectful on the phone. Cosby was a father figure to America, black and white, and Murphy had learned long ago to honor his stepfather—or else. But it seemed that as soon as he got off the phone, Murphy began talking back. He let the press convey his displeasure to Cosby rather than confronting him in person or on the phone. Murphy told his unasked-for mentor via *Rolling Stone* to buzz off. "Times are changing. Go to Vegas and do your old-man shit there. Bill Cosby called me up and said [imitating the Cos], 'You can't get onstage and say fuck you.' That was the most bizarre thing that's happened in my career. Bill Cosby calling me up—wow!—and reprimanding me for being too dirty."

Murphy was profane, but he wasn't blasphemous—a seemingly semantic difference, but not really. Just as he was shocked when his brother told him he didn't pray every night, Murphy showed a respect for religion on and offstage that was reverential, bordering on the superstitious. As he drove past St. Patrick's cathedral in New York with a reporter, he suddenly pushed the eject button on his cassette deck which was playing a raunchy song by Prince. The lyrics were about to launch into a string of expletives, and Murphy explained, "It's a lot of profanity getting ready to come on the stereo. Can't play it in front of a church.

"I'm not a religious fanatic, but I pray. I pray every night. And I respect the Church. I won't have Prince singing, 'I want to fuck you' in front of it."

SNL's Dick Ebersol had already explained Murphy's ability to insult blacks, gays, and women without turning off the audience. He attributed it to the "smile in Eddie's eyes" which seemed to say, "'I'm just kidding.' The whole black and white thing works because of his eyes. He never loses the charm in his eyes. In his eyes he never stops smiling. His eyes tell the audience he's laughing. Eddie's eyes are the eraser for any misunderstanding."

Joe Piscopo also glimpsed the glint in his friend's eyes that made everything all right. Eddie did have a "don't fuck with me attitude," Piscopo said. "I would love to be like that. But you know why he gets away with it? It's because he has enormous vulnerability. When he smiles, you want this kid to be your son."

Commentary attributed his immunity to a "sassy self-assurance, strangely without malice. He gets off the most biting lines in a sunny manner which magically neutralizes any suspicion that he himself is malicious."

Although bitterness would eventually come in the wake of a failed romance and a faltering career, in these early, heady days, Murphy correctly attributed his success to the lack of real bile or bite in his material. "What makes a lot of comics bitter is that they have to pay dues a long time. I got my break when I was nineteen. I've got nothing to be bitter about."

TV Guide also noted the *gemütlich* nature of his jokes. Although some people felt there was anger in his characters, they felt there was no real rage in their creator. Murphy didn't make white folks squirm in their seats. Although their styles were as dissimilar as Hope and Murphy's, Bill Cosby shared one trait that made both men monumentally attractive. Neither derived his gags from white guilt the way, say, comedian and hunger striker Dick Gregory did. There's nothing funny about starving yourself. Murphy didn't condemn racism or even satirize it. He poked fun at liberal stereotypes of racism.

He explained his philosophy: "My comedy is nonpolitical. I want to show that I give a damn, but comedy is the wrong thing to preach with. I don't think entertainers should be heroes or preachers. I'm not very political. I don't even vote. The way I see it, the president does what he wants to do, and if we do what we want, we don't have to be affected." Murphy won't be doing any public service announcements for "Get Out the Vote" on MTV. No one would ever confuse him with Mark Russel either. At the Comic Strip in Manhattan during the Decade of Detachment, he proudly announced his lack of interest in trickle-down theory and in catsup as a vegetable. "I'm not here to talk about Ronald Reagan or politics. Nobody's going to spend their money to come out here on Saturday night to hear a nigger complain about Ronald Reagan. I'm here to talk about my real comedy, which is about dicks, farts, and boogers."

Apolitical, but not oblivious to current events when they provided comedy fodder. Following his nothing-is-sacred rule, Murphy dared to make papal assassination jokes shortly after the attack on John Paul. When a member of the audience clapped after Murphy mentioned Reagan's run-in with John Hinckley, the comedian scolded the guy, then one-upped him by poking fun at the Pope. "And they shot the Pope. I mean, who would shoot the Pope? What's your intention in shooting the Pope unless you're saying, 'Look, I want to go to hell and I don't want to stand on line?' I mean, whoever shot the Pope, they'll say to him, 'You shot the Pope?' Get in the express line, motherfucker.'"

In 1983, *Playboy* neatly summed up this non–rebel without a cause: "Eddie Murphy was no rebel: He was a comedian of the middle class, a young American for his *own* freedom."

The comic wanted people to laugh, not form picket lines. Murphy wasn't uninformed; he was indifferent. A $15 million film deal buys a lot of complacency. He recognized racism in America, but when you're living more than the American dream, the American fantasy of super wealth and fame, it's hard to feel persecuted. As his star continued to rise, others didn't share his complacency and criticized it loudly. Murphy recalled, "A very militant black woman said to me, 'How come no serious black actors get the same kind of deals you get or Richard Pryor gets? How come it's always a comedy?' I said, 'Because America is still a racist society.'"

But like many middle class blacks of his generation, Murphy never felt the sting of racism growing up. Richard Pryor grew up in his grandmother's brothel in Peoria. He dropped out of school at fourteen. Murphy slaved away at night and summer schools to graduate from high school on time.

A universe away, Will Smith, the star of two summer hits in a row, once explained why he didn't effect the angry-young-black-man pose which many of his equally successful contemporaries did. The rage in interviews with Denzel Washington and Spike Lee is almost palpable. In a conference room at NBC headquarters in Burbank, where his sitcom *The Fresh Prince of Bel Air* was then a Top-10 hit, Smith told me that his father was an industrialist and his mother a college professor. He grew up in a tony suburb of Philadelphia and turned down a scholarship to MIT to go into show biz. By the age of nineteen, Smith had made $2 million. "What," he asked me, "do I have to be angry about?"

Although Murphy didn't enjoy Smith's upscale upbringing, his formative years were comfortable, and so he felt comfortable about the issue of race. For public consumption, he might declare America a racist society for typecasting blacks as comedians, but at $1 million per comedy, Murphy might well echo Smith's question, "What do I have to be angry about?"

Murphy answered the question: "I'm not angry. I didn't learn this stuff hanging out with junkies on 158th Street. I have never been much of a fighter. If somebody white called me 'nigger' on the street, I just laughed."

In fact, Murphy never encountered a white racist until he was eighteen. Like most of his take on reality, his view of the white world during his formative years came exclusively from television. "I thought all white people were like *Father Knows Best* and *Leave It to Beaver*." By the time he went into the wide, white world with his self-image largely formed, out-

and-out racism was an amusing oddity rather than a resonat-
ing experience. Murphy's sangfroid was socioeconomic and
also generational, but not racial, according to one editorial
writer. Richard Grenier wrote, "The difference between
Richard Pryor and Murphy might be generational...When
Martin Luther King was assassinated, Pryor was 27, Murphy,
6. Murphy, Cosby and Michael Jackson might be the first
black superstars of post-racist America."

Others felt this view of racial harmony was discordant, if
not outright delusional, that Murphy was living in a fantasy
universe, insulated by the color-blind respect that money and
fame automatically provide. (This may explain Dennis Rod-
man's teflon immunity.) Some nonfans had the temerity to
confront Murphy about this in person, and not in the safe
pages of an intellectual periodical. At a Manhattan disco, a
Buppie in suit and tie approached Murphy's table and complained that he had played a convict in *48 HRS*. The angry
young black man wanted to know why Murphy didn't play a
doctor or lawyer. Murphy patiently explained to his inquisi-
tor, "I'm not a conservative-type black man. I wouldn't be
believable as a doctor or a lawyer. I'm an aggressive black
man." The interloper wasn't mollified by the explanation or
intimidated by Murphy's self-description of "aggressive." The
Buppie went on, "You're not setting a good example for black
people." As usual, Murphy had at least one bodyguard with
him, childhood pal Derrick Lawrence, who has a black belt in
Okinawan-Kenop karate. But Lawrence didn't rely on his
lethal hands. He always carried a briefcase which contained
something called a Cobra, a 10-inch steel pipe knobbed at one
end and a spring coiled at the other to give the weapon a snap
when used. To his credit, Murphy didn't call on the services of
his bodyguard or pet steel snake to get rid of the obnoxious
Buppie. Instead, he got up from the table and walked away.
The guilt-tripper screamed after him, "Cicely Tyson wouldn't
do that." If Eddie hadn't already disappeared, his reply might

have been, "Cicely Tyson doesn't get $1 million per film. In fact, she doesn't get much work at all."

Still, the criticism rankled. No one likes to be called an Uncle Tom, even if the cabin happens to be a palatial estate in New Jersey. When black comic Franklin Ajaye complained that the star lacked "social consciousness," Murphy defended himself articulately. "A lot of the old comics like Franklin are just frustrated and maybe jealous. I do Buckwheat because I think it's funny, and the character is too absurd, abstract, and ridiculous to be taken seriously. White people don't look at Buckwheat and say, 'Yes, that's the way blacks dress and act.' It's stuff like *The Jeffersons* that's a step back for blacks." He referred to the hit seventies sitcom that purported to show a wealthy black family that moves from Archie Bunker's Queens neighborhood to a deluxe co-op on Manhattan's Upper West Side. In fact, his rap on Buckwheat emphasized white people's strange misconception of black people's universe. In Murphy's view, Buckwheat made fun of whites, not blacks. A bit from his club act:

"Who thought up names for that show? Now, I'm from a predominantly black family, and I have yet to run into a relative named Buckwheat. Go to a cookout and say, 'Hey, how you doin'? My name's Ed.' 'Oh, I'm Buckwheat, man, nice to meet you. No, I ain't got no last name, man. I'm serious. Ain't that right, Farina? My little sister over there, her name's Shredded Wheat. My nephew, he's retarded. His name's Special K. My big sister's a prostitute. Her name's Trix, and my brother, the homosexual, Lucky Charms. He's over there with his friends, the Fruit Loops.'"

The introspective comedian knew the pitfalls of a black man doing blackface, and he felt nothing but contempt for colleagues who stepped and fetched for Nielsen ratings. "I do have a black point of view, obviously—and a real black isn't Jimmie Walker grinning like an idiot and going, 'I knooooow.' He was America's favorite little black boy—and

look where it got him. He's no place now," he said about the
star of another fantasy sitcom, *Good Times*, set in the projects
where it was clear the white writers had never set foot.

Sometimes, however, Murphy's self-assurance about
race faltered, and he worried about being a highly paid one-
man minstrel show for white America's entertainment. "I
don't want to butter my bread being America's favorite funny
little black boy," he said, shortly after signing a $25 million
deal with Paramount after *Beverly Hills Cops* grossed $235
million in the U.S. alone. But basically, racism was somebody
else's problem, not his. "I never got the real nigger treatment
in Hollywood. You hear a lot of artists talking about Hollywood is a plantation. I never sold out. Ain't no black person
that is going to take Eddie Murphy as a Tom. I don't disgrace
my people on screen." In fact, just the opposite. Roger Ebert
of the *Chicago Sun-Times* and syndicated television once
accused him of basing his career on making white people
look stupid. Or, as a kinder critic wrote, "His comedy comes
from outsmarting whites."

Friend and colleague Keenen Ivory Wayans believes
Murphy's opinion of racism has darkened considerably since
the early, heady days of instant movie stardom. Wayans told
me in the summer of 1997, "I think if you asked Eddie about
that quote today, he'd have a different take on the 'nigger
treatment,' as he put it. The nigger treatment is not confined
to Hollywood. Unfortunately, racism in America is institu-
tional. I think both of us have had that treatment. It's your
every day experience. I'm sure I could attribute a lot of things
to being black. On the other hand, it could have just been that
I didn't have the right sticker on my car when the cops pulled
me over. If you try to attribute every obstacle to [racism], you
just can't survive."

On stage, Murphy pooh-poohed the existence of racism.
Off stage, he displayed a more ambivalent attitude, because
he had felt its effects directly. "I ain't hooked up into all that

racism," he said in an HBO special. "My motto is be happy. Racism ain't so bad as it used to be anyway. They don't even call niggers niggers anymore....I went to Texas positively lookin' for racism. I come in at the airport and this white guy says to me [in meek little white voice], 'Is this your suitcase?' And I say [feigning rage], 'Yes, it's my suitcase. A black man doesn't have a right to a suitcase?'"

In real life, Murphy didn't tolerate racism by blacks or whites. He poked fun at all races and most minorities. But it was for the sake of a punch line, never a punch. A man who labeled himself apolitical could be surprisingly doctrinaire when racism manifested itself in all its ugly, unfunny forms. Outside his trailer on a movie set, he noticed a fan carrying a placard that said, "Get whitey." Murphy walked over and lectured him sternly on the stupidity of racism.

In his act, he could poke fun at the angry young black man mad at the world, but his few encounters with racism in real life didn't seem funny at all. Many black stars have confided in me their shock turns to fury when someone fails to recognize them and they're treated like a member of a persecuted minority. ABC's White House correspondent once interviewed the president, then stepped outside to hail a cab and no one stopped. Will Smith, who was amused, not angered, by his experience—perhaps because of its rarity— recalled a stewardess in first-class demanding to see his ticket not once, but twice, certain that he belonged in coach.

When Murphy managed to be incognito, he still got noticed, but the attention bore no resemblance to the kind the superstar had grown accustomed to. "I used to carry the bill of sale [for his Porsche] for when they'd pull me over and say, 'License and registration—I know you stole this, pal.' Bill of sale right there. 'Not only do I *own* it, it's more than you make in a fucking year.' Cops have been fucking with me ever since I started driving a nice car. They go, 'There's a nigger in a nice car, let's pull him over.' I say, 'I'm Eddie Murphy from

Saturday Night Live,' and it *all* changes. That fucking *burns* me. 'Can I have your autograph, pal?'"

Racism shocked him because he encountered none growing up in his homogeneous neighborhood. In fact, it wasn't until he was eighteen and down South that anyone directed a racial slur at him. Entering a grocery store in Ft. Lauderdale, where he was performing at a club, a white man cut in front of him. Murphy didn't get angry. He laughed at the man's New York–style pushiness in the languid subtropics of Florida. The man wanted to know why he laughed. "Florida is funny," Murphy said, still in a good mood. The redneck said, "No, it isn't. *Spades* are funny," and jabbed his finger into his chest, adding, "Aren't they?" Murphy was stunned rather than furious. He had heard about such people, but never met one until then.

Murphy didn't have to go all the way to Texas or Florida to find evidence of racism. It was alive and unwell in one of the richest, hippest enclaves in America. "I stayed at a house in Bel Air, in Los Angeles, and yet I couldn't go onto the golf course right behind it. I'm supposed to be an upper crust black person, and I'm still subject to racism," Murphy said.

New York was just as bad. Rushing with an interviewer to get out of the rain and into a Cadillac, he pointed to a nervous woman they passed at a trot. A running black still scares some people. "See that lady?" he asked the reporter. "She thought I was gonna mug her." When they entered the Caddy, Murphy made it clear that the car belonged to his manager. He refused to drive such a stereotypical vehicle.

Enormous wealth is better armor than a thick skin when it comes to deflecting racism. Murphy insulated himself with money as though it were a mylar police vest; racist insults just bounced off him. "Racism hurts when you don't have; when you're confused and not sure of what you want to do, and on top of that, somebody says you're this and that. But when you have your feet on the ground [and a $25 million deal at

Paramount], and some truck driver calls you a nigger, you can say, 'So what? *You* drive a truck, mutha.'"

His grotesque impression of Stevie Wonder's Tourette-like tics offended handicapped people of all colors. Murphy assumed his usual pugnaciousness when people complained. "Stevie says he listens to the show, and *he* loves it. So the critics can kiss my ass!" His sense of humor quickly replaced his anger, and he added that if Wonder did object, "I'll kick his ass."

After poking fun at a blind artist, Murphy had the nerve to complain that "people have a warped sense of humor now." Then he described his own comedy style as "mean. I'm a lovely person, but I like to see stuff like *Kung Fu Classroom—* kicking little girls through walls. But you can't beat up children on TV," he said, with apparent regret. "You *can* beat up old people. You can't beat up cripples. But if you beat up old people, like ninety-year-olds, people go into hysterics. I'm writing a sketch where Mr. T meets E.T." In the sketch, The *A-Team* star beats the hell out of the cuddly extra-terrestrial. The *L.A. Times* capsulized the Murphy mystique. "He takes pride in being a taboo buster extraordinaire, in imagining Mr. T as a growling gay, in smirking about Michael Jackson's sexuality and James Brown's enunciation."

Walter Hill, the director of his first film, gave another reason why Murphy could shock without offending. "This kid is so enormously talented he can get away with anything." Not with everyone, however, and not forever. By 1985 the backlash had begun. Murphy gave detractors a lot to object to. His obscenity-laced act started to pall on even such traditional sycophants as the trades. *Daily Variety* editorialized, "His laughs are caused by the obscenities he utters....Without them, he has no act." The *Chicago Tribune* disagreed and remained a member of the Eddie Murphy fan club: foul language, the paper said, didn't explain his success.

If blue material were all it took to create a star, "we'd be in the middle of a Buddy Hackett revival right now"—Hackett's nightclub act being fouler than Lenny Bruce's, without the redeeming brilliance.

By 1985, Murphy began to make some career and public relations missteps, which were ominous signs of bigger gaffes to come. He turned buddy Stevie Wonder down flat when asked to appear on the music video "We Are the World." Rebuffing a beloved blind man and a children's charity in one stroke didn't help a public image that was already beginning to show feet of clay. Murphy's reason was understandable. He feared that because of the critical lambasting his musical efforts had received, in the "We Are the World" video he'd be stuck in the back row with the likes of Sonny Bono and LaToya Jackson and told to sing "quietly."

In more serious areas, like career development, the star continued to be ill-advised by his managers and all those relatives who held executive titles at his production company. In 1985, he turned down the role that turned Bill Murray into a superstar, *Ghostbusters*. More than a decade later, the decision still rankled, and he admitted, "I regret not making *Ghostbusters*."

He never publicly admitted it, but an even bigger regret had to be his debut musical album, *How Could It Be*, released by Columbia Records in 1985. Its musical style could most kindly be described as "easy listening," a mix of upbeat dance tunes and sad-sack ballads. The record looked like a winner. The first single, "Party All the Time," released prior to the album in 1984, tested the waters and found them chillier than the North Atlantic. In a prerelease interview to hype the album, the *L.A. Times*'s R&B critic, Dennis Hunt, accurately predicted that it would "probably be trashed by the critics," including Hunt, who conceded, "Murphy's voice really is rather thin. There's nothing especially adventurous about his songs."

Murphy launched his musical career on a fluke. After buying a piano for his new home, he decided it should be more than an expensive, unused piece of furniture. "I spent a lot of time by myself sitting and tinkling with this piano. Then I started buying recording equipment. I was thinking maybe I could do something in music." Murphy was following a lamentable trend at the time, when superhot actors felt their success in one medium would automatically translate into another. Hey, if it worked for negligible talents like Ricky Nelson and Bobby Sherman in the fifties and sixties, why not for certifiable superstars? At least that's what Bruce Willis, who took the pseudonym of Bruno, and Don Johnson, who took the brunt of reviews that compared his vocal range to Minnie Mouse's, believed when they went into the recording studio and violated vinyl.

Columbia, which had already made a gold mine from Murphy's two gold comedy albums, took a deep breath and humored the wannabe pop star. The company must have hoped this was just a phase and soon he'd return to cracking jokes, not cutting tracks.

The transition from movie to pop star had seemed like a natural progression, but his debut's quick trip to the remainder bin showed that Murphy should stay away from sound studios and go back to the soundstage. His most recent film, *Beverly Hills Cop*, had remained No. 1 for a record-breaking eleven consecutive weeks. *How Could It Be*'s performance on the charts didn't break any records, although disappointed fans of his films felt like doing that with *How Could It Be*. After five weeks in release, the album had climbed to a cavernous fifty-first place on *Billboard*'s Top 200. For any other first-time artist, the showing would have been respectable, the *Times*'s Hunt said. But there were huge expectations for Murphy that his musical record would duplicate his film record.

Murphy urged fans to lower their sights. He certainly

had. "People expect so much from this album. They think it's
supposed to be as good as my comedy. They forget I'm new at
singing. I thought the album would be doing much better
now. I look at *Beverly Hills Cop*. About 60 million people saw
the movie. You'd think at least one million [platinum sales]
would go out and buy my record. Unfortunately, I see now
that it doesn't work that way."

By this time, Murphy didn't need money, so his album's
lackluster sales hurt his ego more than his bank account.
Much more painful were the complaints from fans. Seeing
yourself vilified in print was bad enough, but some fans had
the temerity to diss the star to his face. Murphy was not above
obsessing over such criticism. One fan of his films, but not
his music, told him, "Stick to comedy." Surrounded by yes
men whose job descriptions included saying things like, "You
great, Eddie," this kind of unvarnished put-down seemed all
the more shocking. "That would bother me all night," Murphy said. "Somebody could destroy my night saying the
wrong thing."

On a happier note, Murphy's surroundings continued to
improve as he traded up from one mansion to another, bigger
one. By 1983, he had moved out of his one-bedroom apartment in Hempstead, Long Island, near mom, and was living
in a thirteen-room spread in Freeport. The usually reverential *Ebony* magazine commented that the kitchen sink was
filled with dirty dishes, while the fridge was empty. Perhaps
by way of explanation, the magazine said he didn't employ a
maid. "I don't have maids and chauffeurs, and I clean my own
house," Murphy said. In 1985, he briefly lived in what one
magazine called a "relatively modest five-bedroom estate" in
Alpine, New Jersey, that cost $500,000 and nestled on two
acres. The house had been decorated by his mother, who
lined the walls with magazine covers of her bare-chested boy
and posters with giant close-ups of his face. Murphy explained all these pecs as icons with, "Chest sells." Maybe the

iconography was too much even for a man of Murphy's healthy self-estimation, because he left his Alpine aerie after living there for less than a year to take possession of a twenty-two-room, $3.5 million estate on 3.5 acres in suburban Englewood Cliffs, New Jersey. His new pad was christened "Bubble Hill," slang for party, which Murphy liked to do a lot of. Typically, the ratio of women to men "bubbling" chez Murphy was three to one. A frequent party-heartier at the Bub, Arsenio Hall, insisted that nothing sinister should be read into the disproportionate number of female guests. "We've had parties, but they're strictly what I'd call ego-fests—it's not sex. We never kicked it like that, man. It was never like, 'Let's go out and get some girls, come back and fuck 'em...'"

Dick Cavett, who liked to hang with Eddie in the mid-eighties, hinted that more than egos were getting a massage at these allegedly platonic orgies: "There's always a group of ladies who've been acquired somewhere, who sit quietly in the corner until needed." Not that Murphy needed a court jester, since he was supposed to be the one in his entourage cracking jokes, but Cavett seemed to enjoy playing the Learing Fool in the kingdom of Eddie. Cavett said, "He would dare me to do things. Eddie would say, 'Slap that bald man at the bar on the head!' So I did." At a Diana Ross concert, Murphy dared Cavett to squeeze Call Her Miss Ross's derriere. Cavett, who was once called the Noël Coward of talk show hosts for his epigrammatic flair, took the dare and groped the singer on stage. Murphy's Boswell again: "We ended up at Diana Ross's concert—I'm not proud of all this—and Diana came, in her regal way, into the audience. He said, 'Grab her ass, Cavett!' When she came by, I did. I grabbed the left cheek, as I recall. But she had her revenge—I cut my hands on the sequins on her dress." Miss Ross's reaction went unrecorded.

Murphy was a mercurial host at these egocentric extravaganzas. At one New Year's Eve party, he played the perfect host, personally fetching guests drinks and urging them to sample the buffet with the compulsiveness of an Italian mamma saying "*Mangia, mangia.*" On other occasions, the star turned into Howard Hughes, with better grooming habits, hiding in the bedroom upstairs while revelers downstairs boogied in a private disco the size of Studio One or Studio 54.

One visitor described the Colonial Revival mansion as "Tara-esque," complete with antebellum columns out front. Even more imposing were century-old oaks shrouded with ivy. A manicured lawn surrounded a driveway with four sports cars and a limo the day a reporter visited. The gardeners must have been frustrated that all their landscaping efforts were upstaged by a giant satellite dish that took up most of the front lawn. *Cosmopolitan,* which has been in most of the homes of the obscenely rich and exhibitionistically famous, gave Bubble Hill a four-star recommendation, saying "It could belong to the CEO of General Motors."

One neighbor didn't share *Cosmo's* bullishness. A woman who must have been spying on Murphy's secluded house with binoculars took objection to the number of cars parked outside Bubble Hill. She actually jumped the hedge and knocked on his door. "How many people live in this house?" she asked the lord of the manor; explaining and threatening at the same time, she added, "Because there are so many cars in the driveway and we have town ordinances, you know...." Another neighbor complained about the tennis court light. Murphy dismissed such pettiness without anger. "I mean, it's just a light on a guy's grass by the fence. It's all such silly stuff."

When *Beverly Hills Cop* producer Don Simpson—no slouch in the acquisition of realty himself—first saw Tara, uh, Bubble Hill, he exclaimed, "God, this looks like *The Great Gatsby!* Oh, Great Gatsby Murphy." The two-story brick structure sat on top of a steep hill. If that didn't provide enough security, there was also a brick wall and guardhouse at the bottom of the funicular driveway. *US* magazine called it a "secure compound." Another guest felt that the private police car on the front lawn with red lights on top and a uniformed, armed guard inside reinforced the feeling of a home—and possibly owner—under siege. Other visitors would say the fortifications and paramilitary personnel reflected a walled-off superstar and the beginning of Murphy's increasing reclusiveness.

The 9,000-square-foot home apparently wasn't big enough, because as soon as he moved there in 1985, Murphy began construction of a west wing. A few years later, he took Barbara Walters and her millions of viewers on a "You Are There" tour of the little place he liked to call home. A magnificent foyer with imported white marble flooring and a *Phantom of the Opera*–sized Lalique chandelier greeted visitors and seemed to proclaim that not only the guests but the host had "arrived" too. A plaque in the entrance hall said even more about the master of the house. A framed sign composed in elaborate calligraphy bore the title, "The Penalty of Leadership." The managers of Elvis Presley's estate, perhaps hearing that the King was Murphy's hero, had sent him the document unsolicited. It contained an essay by Theodore MacManus that said, "In every field of human endeavor, he that is first must perpetually live in the white light of publicity. When a man's work becomes the standard for the whole world, it also becomes a target for shafts of the envious few." The sentiment, with its focus on envy, hints at a term which would soon be applied to Murphy: paranoid. If the essay had been more prophetic, it might have added that when a man's work is no longer "the standard for the whole world" and his career goes into freefall, the "shafts of envy" turn into what the Germans call *Schadenfreude:* derision and delight in someone else's misfortune.

Just as Murphy loved to juggle a variety of characters on TV, and later in film, each room in Bubble Hill was decorated in a different style: country, Far Eastern, French Provincial, Victorian, modern. One room was done up entirely in black. His bedroom was stark white, surgical in its pristine decor. There were formal rooms as well as fun rooms. Murphy spent nine years renovating his home and installed a game room devoted solely to pinball. Other rooms accommodated a pool table and a racquetball court. The inevitable swimming pool was under glass for year-round use. The pool house, *GQ* gushed, was the size of San Simeon's and "looks like a small-scale model of a walled city." If guests overheated but didn't feel like a dip in the pool, the disco at Bubble Hill featured a rain-mist machine to cool off sweaty dancers. A tennis court, with basketball hoops bookending it, provided R&R for his underemployed entourage. A rec room looked out on the pool and tennis court. One observant visitor couldn't resist reporting that you could also see from the rec room a backyard littered with fried-chicken bones and boxes scattered by raccoons that had dined out in Murphy's garbage cans. The rec room contained a TV monitor that covered an entire wall, flanked by a bank of stereo gewgaws. The recreation area also housed a shrine to Eddie: a life-sized freestanding cardboard cutout of the star wearing his favorite material of the time, leather. Bubble Hill inevitably featured the staple furnishing of the ultrasuccessful in the arts: a screening room.

Murphy installed an underground recording studio reached by a tiny elevator that one guest said resembled the transporter room on *Star Trek*. In another part of the basement, which was so cavernous a guest asked, "Who's your architect? Piranesi?", Murphy practiced Vernon Lynch's boxing tips on a punching bag. An admiring female reporter mentioned that he boxed with his shirt off. Chest sells.

Rolling Stone disagreed with Don Simpson's Fitzgerald analogy. "Regal trappings, zealous security, sycophantic hangers-on—the role model is not Jay Gatsby, it's Elvis. Bubble Hill is glitzier than Graceland." And about ten thousand square feet bigger. Elvis might have been king; Murphy was emperor when it came to housing.

Elvis's presence dominated Murphy's bedroom. A seven-foot-tall oil portrait of his idol hung on the wall. A reporter from *Interview* magazine, Elvis Mitchell, failed to say if the painting had been done on velvet. The interviewer, however, did place a lot of significance on the presence of Murphy's idol dominating the room. "The bedroom [painting] offers the biggest clue to the heart of Eddie Murphy. Murphy admits having grown up worshiping Presley, but he worshiped at a distorted temple—Presley movies on TV. Presley's pristine self-containment is what seems to have caught Murphy's eye. Murphy, too, is tickled with his own presence." Although the Elvis analogies seemed forced, they enraged Murphy when the article came out in September 1987. He told another interviewer, "I was raped. The guy came to my house, and he was the nicest guy in the world, then he tore me up." Murphy felt so burned by this bedroom invasion, he refused interviews for a time, even keeping Barbara Walters and crew waiting outside his mansion gates for five hours. *GQ* wrote a venomous piece about Murphy at this time, when he refused to get out of bed for a scheduled interview. *Rolling Stone* had better luck, but it had to bend to the star's fear of the fourth estate when visiting him. The original reporter was allegedly rejected by Wachs for the sole reason that the reporter was a woman. Murphy's behavior with the *Stone's* male reporter suggests why. The superstar greeted his guest in underwear. Later, he asked another guest about a recent date. "Did you fuck her?" His entourage of bodyguards and other companions earned their salaries. *Rolling Stone* claimed they followed their boss around Bubble Hill saying, "You great, Eddie." Nice work if you can get it. Murphy wasn't embarrassed by this pond of toadies; they even became fodder for his stage act: "All my old friends work for me now. Just so's they get their paycheck, they'll say anything."

Dick Cavett claimed the bodyguards *et al.* weren't on staff to pump Murphy's ego but to protect his hide. "The gang," Cavett said, served as protection when Murphy went among the hoi polloi. They served as a physical buffer between the star and idolatrous mobs that occasionally turned into Bacchae, trying to tear apart the god they worshiped.

The employees had more labor-intensive tasks than burnishing their employer's self-esteem and stiff-arming autograph seekers. A reporter from *Playboy* mentioned that during their chat, Murphy spit chewing gum on the marble floor and said, "Don't worry. Someone will pick it up." Roseanne once said she and then-husband, Tom Arnold, were America's worst nightmare: white trash with money. You wonder if she and Eddie ever exchanged housekeeping tips—perhaps Martha Stewart's worst nightmare.

(*Right*) Eddie, age eight. Mom Lillian said, "He was such a lovable kid. He'd sit on your lap until you moved him. Eddie was always a good child." (Courtesy Academy of Motion Picture Arts and Sciences)

(*Below*) Eddie's third-grade class picture at P.S. 87 in Queens, 1969 (*second row from the top, at center*). The class clown was adored by classmates, who voted him most popular. (Courtesy Academy of Motion Picture Arts and Sciences)

(*Above*) All in the family. Stepdad Vernon Lynch (*far left*) serves as chairman of Panda Merchandising, which licenses Eddie Murphy products. Half-brother Vernon Jr. (*second from left*) cowrote the story for Murphy's 1995 film *Vampire in Brooklyn,* and runs his brother's record company. (Courtesy Academy of Motion Picture Arts and Sciences)

(*Left*) Ticket sales for Murphy's stand-up act at Radio City Music Hall in 1985 broke the previous record set by Diana Ross. (David McGough)

(*Opposite*) The superstar ranted and raved in *Eddie Murphy Raw,* the most successful concert film of all time. One critic wrote, "To review *Raw* was to leave the domain of criticism for psychiatry." (Bruce Talamon)

With friends Lisa Figueroa (*left*), Patricia Matthews (*opposite*), Gina Scurto (*below left*), and his latest, transvestite prostitute Atisone Seiuli (*below*). (David McGough)

When Jerry Lewis (*center*) hosted *Saturday Night Live* in 1983, the show's producer begged Lewis to take the troubled Murphy under his wing. Lewis declined. *Far right,* Joe Piscopo, Murphy's personal friend and professional rival. (David McGough)

In *Trading Places* Murphy plays a con man who pretends to be a legless vet. He says to one disgusted passerby, "What's the matter? Ain't you ever seen *Porgy & Bess?*" (Paramount)

As a tough Detroit police detective suffering culture shock in L.A.'s Platinum Triangle, *Beverly Hills Cop* transformed Murphy from star to superstar. Judge Reinhold and John Ashton play his witless partners against crime.

Another 48 HRS. was an unsatisfying sequel to Murphy's first film in which the neophyte actor played Nick Nolte's sidekick. In the sequel, Nolte played second banana to the superstar. (Bruce Talamon)

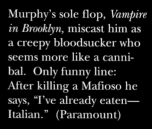

Murphy's sole flop, *Vampire in Brooklyn,* miscast him as a creepy bloodsucker who seems more like a cannibal. Only funny line: After killing a Mafioso he says, "I've already eaten— Italian." (Paramount)

Chapter 8

......

Golden Child, Tarnished Idol

In February 1985, when ShoWest conferred the fiscal equivalent of an Oscar on Murphy, the emcee at the Vegas gala said before introducing the star, "In just two years and three motion pictures, Eddie has become the No. 1 box office attraction in America." A few years later, ShoWest would name him star of the decade.

Murphy not only owned the screen, he also dominated the concert stage. The same month ShoWest honored him, ticket sales to his Radio City Music Hall appearance beat previous records set by Diana Ross and Barry Manilow. (This, however, was Murphy's stand-up, not musical, act.)

After *Beverly Hills Cop* grossed half a billion in *1985 dollars* worldwide, Murphy just about owned Paramount, the studio his film had so enriched, and the suits who seemed to run the studio in his name. Murphy described these executives' subservience toward their resident superstar. "I could say, 'Hey, guys! I got a great idea for my next film. I'm going to throw shit at the screen,' and they'd say, 'Great idea. Here's thirty million.'"

Arsenio Hall felt secure enough in their friendship to criticize Eddie's creative omnipotence. "There came a point in his life where if Eddie would say, 'I think I'm going to shit on the stage,' people would say, 'Yeah, that's funny, Eddie, shit

107

on the stage.' And these were people on his payroll. He realized that a lot of them wouldn't be honest with you anymore when you're Eddie Murphy." Surrounded by yes-men, Murphy needed someone to say no. It seems only Hall had the courage, but then Hall wasn't on his payroll and had a burgeoning career of his own as a talk-show host.

In the same frenzy, other execs would later throw $200 million at Kevin Costner for *Waterworld* and $110 million at Bruce Willis for *The Fifth Element*. Murphy automatically got the greenlight and carte blanche. At this point in his career, if the star had wanted to make an all-singing, all-dancing Busby Berkeley musical based on the Tibetan Book of the Dead, the green light would have been flashed quicker than you could say No. 1 at the box office eleven weeks in a row.

An unnamed movie producer summed up Murphy's Midas touch mid-decade: "You make a movie with Eddie Murphy and you are guaranteed a substantial hit, if that's not too much of an understatement. Eddie's gold."

For his next project, Murphy left the mean streets of Detroit and charmeuse-covered showrooms of Rodeo Drive for...Tibet. Fortunately for nervous execs at Paramount, the film wasn't based on that country's bible of death. In fact, *The Golden Child* wasn't risky, it was cautious and overtrodden Murphy terrain, thematically, if not geographically. The premise of the film, in fact, duplicated *Beverly Hills Cop*'s fish-out-of-water high-concept.

Unlike film executives, filmmakers had no trouble just saying no to Murphy. With his self-assurance even stronger, now that it was reinforced with three No. 1 hits, Murphy had the *chutzpah* to ask Francis Ford Coppola to direct *The Golden Child*. Today, that would be like Jim Carrey asking Antonioni to bring his sign-language interpreter to the set and direct *Dumb and Dumber*. Coppola demurred. With even more self-confidence, Murphy then told Paramount he wanted to direct the film. This was probably the only demand the studio had the *cojones* to reject. The executives were happy to throw increasing amounts of money at their biggest moneymaker to keep him happy and in-house, but turning over the reins of a $40 million movie with complicated special effects to a twenty-five-year-old neophyte scared the suits even more than saying no to their greatest living asset.

Like his three previous hits, *The Golden Child* was a hand-me-down, a Mel Gibson reject. ICM, which represented both stars, had developed the script for their white client and sold it to a producer who offered it to Paramount. Paramount never considered Murphy in the lead until Gibson bowed out. By now, Murphy showed that he could take other stars' dross, like *Cop*, and turn it into box office gold. *The Golden Child* was an ironic title for a film that just as easily could have been Murphy's nickname, although he had an even more appropriate one, "Money." (His personal file in a cabinet at Eddie Murphy Productions on the Paramount lot was also labeled, "Money." Arsenio Hall's was a drawer below under "Little Money.")

Paramount wasn't showing preferential treatment when it offered *The Golden Child* to Gibson first. Besides, Murphy had more heat behind him than Gibson, despite the latter's smoldering good looks. It was simply that the storyline didn't seem like an Eddie Murphy vehicle, except for the generic fish-out-of-water gimmick, which Murphy had made his specialty.

In the action-adventure comedy, the star plays a social worker called the Chosen One. Unwillingly, he has been chosen to rescue a Tibetan child living in L.A. who has been kidnapped by an evil sorcerer. The kid's a reincarnation of the Buddha, but the bad guy isn't religious. He wants the youngster because Buddha Jr. also possesses magical kinetic powers. But the stakes are higher than that. If the Golden Child isn't rescued by the Chosen One, the world will end. Thematically, the film was a promotion for Murphy. In previous films, he had cleaned up Beverly Hills and saved a young stockbroker's hide; here, Murphy was saving the world.

Like the underwritten *48 HRS.* and the custom-designed *Beverly Hills Cop,* much of *The Golden Child*'s dialogue wasn't on the page; it was in the febrile mind of the star. As his career evolved, Murphy and his advisers would show that they weren't porcine script analysts able to sniff out a truffle of a blockbuster by visualizing what the script would look like on screen. But Murphy was a brilliant ad-libber, as his stint on *Saturday Night Live* and his improvs on *48 HRS.* and *Beverly Hills Cop* had proved. Director Michael Ritchie, a respected veteran, encouraged Murphy to let loose with his stream-of-consciousness rap while the cameras rolled, knowing that the actor's riffs in previous projects had set them apart from all the other buddy-cop-caper comedies. Ritchie recalled Murphy's golden touch on the set of *The Golden Child.* "One of the funniest scenes in the picture was scripted with no dialogue. I suggested to Eddie that he pull off a joke about a scavenger hunt to explain why he was in the backyard of these people having a barbecue. Well, he had never *heard* of a scavenger hunt. So he made a few jokes; then he went and sat down in his chair for a second, and said, 'Okay, I think I've got something.' It's the funniest scene in the movie."

Murphy wasn't laughing when the production had to go on location in Tibet. Murphy was an unrepentant travelphobe. While others might be delighted at the prospect of an all-expense-paid trip to one of the most exotic places in the world, Murphy agreed with Oz's Dorothy that there's no place like a $3.5 million mansion, surrounded by a nurturing group of friends and family, all on the payroll. He loved New Jersey and tolerated L.A. when business demanded his presence there, but he loathed everywhere else. For *Beverly Hills Cop,* Detroit's bombed-out inner city was a nightmare and a shock after his tidy, all-black suburb of Roosevelt, Long Island. The upcoming sequel to *Beverly Hills Cop* had been set in London, until Murphy visited the place and discovered he was no anglophile. Tibet was a brackish backwater that gave Murphy mal de mer. Years later, one suspects he only agreed to remake the Victorian-era *Dr. Dolittle* because the story was now set in the present day and could be filmed without going any further than the Fox backlot in west Los Angeles. You can be sure he will never star in another remake of *Around the World in Eighty Days* unless the studio agrees to fake Mogul India and other far off locales on a soundstage in beautiful downtown Burbank.

In his trailer on the set of *The Golden Child*, Murphy played his disenchantment with the freezing location for laughs, but his anger was real, not feigned. Riding a yak in the middle of a blinding snowstorm, Murphy spoke directly to people in the theater watching the film's trailer. "If I'm the Chosen One, how come I'm freezing while you're sitting in a warm theater? Chosen One, my behind! Why couldn't someone choose me to go to the Bahamas?"

At least he had his leading lady to keep him warm. Charlotte Lewis, a striking black Eurasian model, played the social worker who propels Murphy on his quest for the holy kid. While their romance flowered offscreen, it was snipped out of the film. In a prerelease interview with *US*, the magazine noted that *The Golden Child* was not only the first Murphy film to contain special effects but also his first screen romance—with his off-camera inamorata. It didn't require a whole lot of acting on Lewis's part, since she was smitten by her leading man. "I was touched by his openness and sincerity. He's one of the nicest, sweetest people I've ever met." Murphy also made a great confidante, and Lewis really needed one. Her father, a police officer, had died recently, and his death, she told Murphy (and *US*) had traumatized her.

Fans who read the article in *US* must have spent the entire film anxiously looking for a hot make out scene, which never materialized. Murphy didn't complain at the time, but a few years later, he revealed a profound bitterness at this cinematic gelding of a black stud. "There's this big thing about blacks in Hollywood that they [studios] try to hide their sexuality. Lots of blacks feel the studios don't want them to be portrayed as sexual on film." An unnamed studio executive insisted the excisions were made because the love scene was "timid and ridiculous," which seemed to prove Murphy's point about the industry discomfort with overt black sexuality. When was the last time you saw a timid love scene with Madonna or Mel Gibson? Although over the years, Murphy's public comments—especially about press reportage on him—grew increasingly angry, his complaints about sex and blacks in the cinema were dead-on and even prophetic. A few years later, Kevin Costner's lovemaking with Whitney Houston in *The Bodyguard* would end up on the cutting room floor. Denzel Washington's affair with Julia Roberts in *The Pelican Brief* never even made it to the script stage, although the two characters in John Grisham's novel became lovers. White America feels uncomfortable with threatening black men, and the emotions run even deeper in regard to black men as sex symbols. The O.J. Simpson trial fascinated America for months in no small part because of its subliminal Othello-Desdemona psychodrama and all the issues of interracial sex that added titillation to the tragedy.

The polar weather of Tibet and his on-screen emasculation were all forgotten in the euphoria of *The Golden Child*'s commercial success—or almost forgotten. Murphy never forgot a reviewer's barb, and the reviews of this effort were particularly stinging. Michael Ventura, the kamikaze critic for the alternative newspaper, the *L.A. Weekly,* was fierce. "Hasn't he degenerated merely into Hollywood's favorite nigger, a pickaninny doll who laughs when we want him to laugh, at what we want him to laugh at?" When Murphy told *Interview* magazine that the critics were out to get him, it wasn't his paranoia talking. Even paranoid people, etc....

Until now, Murphy had been treated by the press like the new kid on the screen mostly praised, rarely reviled. But after five films, he was an established star and fair game for personal and artistic drubbing. Hemingway once said artists and gangsters have one thing in common: the public loves to build them up so it can tear them down.

The demolition of Eddie Murphy, which would go on for another decade, had begun in the press. *Newsweek* was barely kinder than *L.A. Weekly:* "What a wasteful comedy this is: it literally goes to hell to get a few off-the-cuff laughs." *People* magazine called *The Golden Child* a "golden turkey, Murphy operating at reduced levels of energy, sass, and humor." This was the same magazine that only one film earlier had praised Murphy's performance as "the funniest screen cop since the Keystones."

Murphy suffered short-term memory loss when it came to critical raves and condemnation. He forgot the encomiums for *Beverly Hills Cop* amid the opprobrium for *The Golden Child.* "So what do the critics know? It's the way audiences react that matters. I just don't have any use for critics....How can they fix their mouths to say some of the stuff they say about me? They don't know why I do what I do. So why do I need what they say about me?"

Many stars confess that they forget the glowing reviews and only remember the sulfurous ones. Murphy not only remembered, he obsessed. Four years after *The Golden Child* had received the critical reception of an abstract art exhibit during the Third Reich, the slings and arrows of the fourth estate continued to pummel and pierce his ego. "Things are still written about the fucking *Golden Child*, which made a hundred million dollars, saying it sucked. People still talk about *Best Defense*. It wasn't even my movie, but it always gets three or four lines in a story." By now, Murphy's incipient paranoia had grown to the point where he didn't realize just how paranoid the following statement would sound to everybody but him. "Most of the people who want to talk with me, I feel want to get me. But I understand it. That's the cycle. They can only write so many good articles about you before they're writing stuff they wrote before. A lot of my reluctance to speak is also rooted in the idea of 'What's to talk about?' For instance, after I do this interview, I won't do another one for five years. You never know who's gonna stick it to you." Murphy's fear, however, was surpassed by his work ethic. He worked just as hard marketing a film as he did actually making it. It was a love-hate affair with the press. His love of publicity for the product outweighed his loathing of journalists bent on "sticking it" to the star. The same year—1990— that he threatened a five-year boycott of press interviews, he was doing a press junket for the sequel to *48 HRS*. The same kid who worked exhausted in a shoe store by day to please his parents, while doing stand-up at night wasn't about to abdicate his promotional obligations, even if it meant getting in bed, psychologically, with really intrusive interviewers like David Rensin, whose article is quoted above.

Critical barbs sting. Imagine picking up the paper or a national magazine and finding your work and yourself vilified for the entertainment of a million readers. It's the Roman circus with witty put-downs instead of lions and Christians. But big box office is a potent balm. The analgesia of an $80 million domestic gross must take the sting out of being labeled a nigger and a pickaninny by a left-wing newspaper. Eventually, the realization that the press was right also made the attacks seem less mean and more justified. Or as Murphy said only four years after its release, "*The Golden Child* was a piece of shit."

The Golden Child represents an interesting point in the arc of a superstar's career. The old saying has it that you're only as good as your last picture. That is, of course, nonsense. How do you explain Michael J. Fox and Pamela Anderson's embarrassing reappearances on the big screen when the small screen seems too large a venue for their modest talents? Actually, you're only as good as your last four or five pictures, when studio chiefs finally see the writing on the theater wall. A corollary to this rule explains why superstars are allowed to fail upward. After the release of one blockbuster, the film immediately following it, no matter how dreckful, is almost guaranteed to do well at the box office. It's nothing more complicated than coasting on a past success, although the ride is a short one, rarely lasting more than two flops in a row. Murphy is only one of several superstars who embody this Peter Principle. Whatever they throw at the screen sticks. How else do you explain the $100 million-plus gross of Tom Cruise's *Mission Impenetrable?* Easy: a crackerjack popcorn film, *Interview With the Vampire*, preceded it. Jim Carrey similarly coasted with *Dumb and Dumber*, but the audience would only forgive him one laughless farce before boycotting *The Cable Guy*.

As far as the studios were concerned, it seemed as though the only papers executives read were *Variety*'s weekly box office report. No barbs there, just the bottom line, exactly where the moneymen liked to be. All this meant that Murphy was besieged with scripts, no matter how inappropriate the vehicle. He had become the Cadillac of stars, but that didn't stop desperate studios from offering him everything from Bentleys to Yugos.

A list of projects in development in development at Eddie Murphy Productions in the mid eighties makes interesting reading. It also underlines screenwriter William Goldman's famous estimation of Hollywood savvy: "Nobody knows anything."

If the following were projects Murphy was considering, imagine the stuff he rejected. A screenwriter who asked for anonymity—no point in alienating a possible future collaborator—described the avalanche of slush that descended on the Murphy dreamworks. "For a while there, anyone with a half-baked idea and a typewriter could get a meeting. I've heard everything from *The Three Faces of Eve* to *Mr. Smith Goes to Washington.*" The latter idea wasn't as far-fetched as it seems. In fact, the pitch was prescient. Six years later, Murphy would play *Mr. Smith* with an attitude in *The Distinguished Gentleman.*

In the euphoric afterglow of *Beverly Hills Cop,* its producer, Don Simpson, believed Murphy and gang were wise enough to separate the goo from the gold. Simpson was being too kind, considering later films from Murphy Inc. Simpson said, "They're getting a lot of crap thrown at them, and fortunately, they're smart enough to turn *most* of it down." "Most" was the most telling word in Simpson's evaluation. Maybe the producer had some of the following in mind when he included the caveat "most."

In the movie industry inferno, turnaround is the worst circle to end up in, but almost as close to the flames is development hell, where an unshootable script gets tweaked by committee until it goes one of two places: turnaround or the screen.

Of the scripts that languished on the shelf in Murphy's offices at Paramount, some seemed to be viable projects that just needed a little adjusting before they were camera-ready. Others sound like a parody from Robert Altman's *The Player,* where everyone in the film claimed to have a script that would be perfect for Julia Roberts, no matter how unsuitable the role or subject matter. You can imagine the adlines: "Julia Roberts as Madame Curie, whose passion for nuclear physics was only surpassed by her passion for her husband Pierre."

Some of the projects that passed by Murphy's desk or his handlers', sound even more inappropriate and fictitious, but they actually existed—at least in the mind of wannabe screenwriters and the producers attached to them.

Perhaps the most outré concept, announced in the trades as being in active development, was something called *Big*

Baby. The hero crash-lands on an island inhabited by adult-sized rulers who look like babies. A *Wild in the Streets* for preschoolers, the script's premise created a universe where adults are considered evil, so Murphy pretends to be a baby. *Screen International,* notorious for its sycophancy even for a trade paper, concluded the announcement of the project with, "Oh, brother!"

Speaking of concepts from hell, there was a script based on *Dante's Inferno,* called *Satan's Key,* written by Murphy himself. But even the superstar couldn't get this project off the ground, which says more about the quality of the script than his clout, which was still prodigious at that time.

Bumptious involved a black talent agent and the adorable twelve-year-old actress he represents. It would pay homage to another black man/white kid pairing, Shirley Temple and tapmaster Bill "Bojangles" Robinson. Although Drew Barrymore was attached to the project, Disney took one sniff at this stinker and threw it in the circular file. That was until Murphy showed interest. Suddenly, the studio that Mickey Mouse built was all ears, just waiting to hear Murphy say yes.

The actor loved Westerns, and there were several on his schedule. One was a remake of *The Magnificent Seven* with an all-black cast. The racial composition of these sagebrush mercenaries would be hard to explain in the Old West, but with Murphy on board, an all-black cast of *Othello* would have gotten a green light.

Another Western announced as a "go" sounds so formulaic you can almost hear the chairs of the committee members squeaking as they came up with the idea in an executive conference room. *Out West* transferred the generic black-and-white-buddy-cop-urban-fish-out-of-water-action-car-chase-partner-two-days-from-retirement-before-he's-killed-by-bad-guys to the Old West circa 1880. Murphy would play a cop from Philadelphia sent to a frontier town to transport a desperado wanted for crimes committed back East. None other than Tom Cruise was set to play the local sheriff, a yokel who clashes with Murphy's wisebutt urban cop. Someone called this concept by committee Cuisinart art. Throw in successful ingredients from previous blockbusters and pray the resulting puree does similar business. Typically, you end up with mush instead of a moneymaker. In the case of *Out West,* the project never got to the mush stage, where film critics would be forced to sit through it before warning readers to stay away. Even with Walter Hill of *48 HRS.* attached, *Out West* went south.

In 1985, Murphy said, " I want to direct and write and score and produce—like Chaplin used to do. Nobody does that anymore." *The Butterscotch Kid* would give Murphy the chance to pay homage to his role model by remaking the director's biggest hit, 1921's *The Kid.* Chaplin's widow, Oona O'Neill, was not a fan, however, and she refused to surrender the rights. The star later dismissed the notion as an "experiment in self-indulgence."

Murphy was also stymied in his attempts to get a biopic on Little Richard off the ground. Maybe the rock 'n' roller had seen Murphy's wicked impression of an effeminate Little Richard Simmons on *Saturday Night Live.* For whatever reason, the singer refused to grant the rights to his life story unless he got script approval. That was out of the question, since Murphy loved to improvise scenes, especially with a target as lampoonable as the sexually ambiguous composer of "Tutti Frutti." Still, the trades remained optimistic: "With Murphy starring, pic's sure to be a box office winner even if the screenplay's written by Crusader Rabbit." Rabbit seemed to be the only one not on Murphy's factory-sized payroll.

An even scarier biopic was one on Malcolm X, with Murphy starring in and directing the life of the radical Muslim activist. Another biopic, however, fit Murphy like a boxing glove. He optioned the rights to Sugar Ray Robinson's life story. All those years sparring with Vernon Lynch and punching a bag in Bubble Hill's home gym would pay off. They wouldn't even need to hire a trainer, since Murphy already knew all the moves.

Unlike the risible casting of Eddie in *The Three Faces of Eve (Steve?)*, another remake was actively considered by the Murphy camp. *The Sob Sisters* would update *Some Like It Hot*, but instead of musicians on the lam from the St. Valentine's Day Massacre, the contemporary reworking would star Murphy and another actor as newspaper reporters who go undercover to investigate political corruption in Chicago. The journalists, as in the original movie, would spend most of the film in drag. Paramount loved the idea and planned to make the film with or without its biggest star. (Why Murphy refused to do drag himself but later put best bud Arsenio Hall in a dress in *Coming to America* may be explained by the star's May Day misadventure in 1997.)

Batman was the No. 1 film of 1989, and Murphy its No. 1 fan. Word got out that Murphy had always wanted to play a superhero. Paramount offered to add him to the cast of the next *Star Trek* feature. Universal offered something a bit fresher, *The Green Hornet. Hornet* fans may have been disappointed the film never got the greenlight, but Trekkies rejoiced when Murphy failed to invade the bridge of the *U.S.S. Enterprise.* Murphy held a top-secret meeting with director Leonard Nimoy to discuss the actor's participation in *Star Trek IV.* David Kirkpatrick, Paramount's executive vice president in charge of production, didn't want to offend the studio's golden child, but his comment on the casting sounded less than enthusiastic. Kirkpatrick said, "There is a character that could be right for Eddie in the next movie." Off the record, other executives were horrified at what an injection of Murphy's street sass would do to the stately series. The negative synergy would be worse than Richard Pryor's contribution to *Superman III*, in which he upstaged the title star and turned the tongue-in-cheek flavor of its predecessors into a slapstick mess. As for *Star Trek IV*, it's hard to imagine what role Kirkpatrick had in mind for Murphy. The fourth installment was the "Save the Whales" episode. No character in the film even vaguely resembles Murphy's screen persona. Proprietary Trekkies and studio execs both breathed a sigh of relief after the film came out. It remained faithful to the spirit of the first three, and, more importantly for studio bean counters, IV became the biggest moneymaker in the series (until the latest, *Star Trek: First Contact*, took that honor).

A few years later, when I interviewed William Shatner for the *Chicago Tribune* on the occasion of his directorial debut, *Star Trek V*, Captain Kirk explained the real reason Murphy never went where no black man had gone before. "Paramount's two biggest franchises are *Star Trek* and Eddie Murphy. The studio didn't want to dilute both these powerhouses by putting them in the same film when they could gross the studio millions starring in separate blockbusters." Sometimes the bottom line is good for the cinema. At least that's what Trek purists must have felt when IV came out Murphy-free.

As time passed, manager Bob Wachs was no longer content simply to get his client $25-million deals. He also wanted to be part of Murphy's creative team and came up with a story called *Fountain of Youth*, about two old con men who find the title's watering hole and become young again. *Trading Places* on testosterone replacement therapy. Best friend Joe Piscopo, whose career post-*SNL* was floundering after several film flops, would get a big boost and play the other senior citizen. The project never got further than the outline stage, although Wachs insisted, "It's a project we all like."

Wachs fared better as Murphy's aesthetic tribune, vetoing surreal projects before they disturbed his client's consciousness: among the high concepts were *Cyrano de Boogie*, *The Black Musketeer*, *A Black Yankee at the Court of Queen Liz*, and *Count Cool and the Knights of the Round Table.*

Murphy also passed on a comedy about death called *Critical Condition*, which Richard Pryor, in a major downturn, gratefully accepted. It was the sad comedian's turn to take sloppy seconds after having given Murphy so many of his hand-me-downs. But unlike Murphy, who took his idol's rejects and turned them into hits, Pryor bombed in *Critical Condition*, adding another paragraph to his career obituary.

It's impossible to overstate how hot Murphy was in the eighties. He was the No. 1 box office attraction of the decade, inheriting Burt Reynolds's crown from the seventies. How hot was Eddie? Neil Simon, the most commercially successful playwright of all time, whose works have been seen by more people than Shakespeare's, wrote a script on spec for the superstar. Simon didn't even get a reply, according to one press account. Another had the two men meeting at Simon's home in Los Angeles to discuss the playwright's vehicle for Murphy, titled *Mr. Bad News*. For the first time in a career that was eventually honored with a Pulitzer, Simon stooped to creating a high-concept movie. Murphy would play a luckless fellow born under a curse that condemned everyone he met to bad luck. Fortunately, Simon only wasted fifty-four pages on the project, because although in 1985 the *L.A. Times* proclaimed it an "odds-on favorite" to become Murphy's next film after *Beverly Hills Cop*, *Mr. Bad News* ironically lived up to its title and died in development.

Murphy seemed to be open to all comers. In 1985, during an interview with the *L.A. Times* at his home, a neighbor knocked on Murphy's door and gave the star a script. Murphy politely accepted it and was glad he did. Although the neighbor had never sold a screenplay before, Murphy liked the idea so much he put it on his to-do list, which by now was encyclopedic. Hopefully, the neighbor didn't move to Hollywood to begin his new career, because the script was added to a pile of two hundred other contenders and ended up like most of them: unproduced.

The scripts were purchased, not optioned—a less expensive, well, option. In a manic reaction to *Beverly Hills Cop*'s performance and the Paramount deal, Eddie Murphy Productions went on a shopping spree. What shoes were to Imelda, scripts were to Eddie, only much more expensive than Manolos. As far as screenwriters—both novices and Pulitzer Prize winners—were concerned, it was a seller's market. "Eddie Murphy is every writer's favorite lottery ticket in this town," said a twenty-something screenwriter who sold two projects to the star. Neither got made. Producer Don Simpson disagreed with the lottery ticket analogy. "Eddie's not the ticket, he *is* the lottery!"

Not all the projects represented impulse-buying. But even the class acts never made it to the screen. The Broadway classic, *Fences*, about a former Negro Leagues baseball player and his family, won August Wilson a Pulitzer in 1987. A year later, Eddie Murphy Productions bought the rights. Actually, Paramount paid the cash and *gave* the play to Eddie. One of Hollywood's most respected black directors, John Singleton (*Boyz 'N the Hood*), was attached to the project and spent hours discussing it with Murphy. Set in the fifties, *Fences* explored the complicated relationship between a retired ballplayer and his son, Murphy's role. One hesitates to call *Fences* Murphy's dream picture, like Tom Cruise's *Born on the Fourth of July* or Kevin Costner's *Dances With Wolves*. Those films proved that their stars could stretch into serious roles outside their usual genre, popcorn entertainments.

Fences could have been a sure bet for an Oscar nomination and the respect due a star who takes a risk and succeeds beyond Hollywood cynics' greatest expectations. As the years went by and the film went unproduced, Murphy's dream project seemed more like an albatross, a Moby-Dick of a picture that would obsess the actor and drag him down. The failure of *Fences* to get off the ground seemed to prove the critical consensus: Eddie Murphy was not a risk-taker. He would continue to play it safe in uninspired action comedies that proved only one thing: Murphy could open a picture. This is not a label that is followed by "for your Oscar consideration."

For years, Murphy had been hobbled by handlers who mismanaged his career and personal life. *Time* magazine said, "He surrounded himself with a coterie of yes-men, buddies and family members who rarely try to persuade him to do something he isn't immediately enthusiastic about." On those rare occasions when a yes-man (or woman) said no to Murphy, the star still went with his own instincts. Witness *Best Defense* and *The Golden Child*. For once, an adviser gave him good advice, and Murphy ignored it.

Linda Morris, executive vice president of development for Eddie Murphy Productions, knew exactly what was wrong with his filmography and told him so. "We're now looking for more mature roles for Eddie because he's reached a point in his career where it's time to take the next step." Murphy never did. Instead, Manager Wachs gave this let-them-eat-cake reply when queried about the fate of *Fences*. "Eddie thinks that *Fences* is so good, it's irrelevant when we make it."

The actor tried to put a racial spin on his refusal to take the plunge in dramatic waters. He pointed out that dramatic black actors didn't get $25 million paydays from major studios. Black clowns and cops did. "America is still a racist society," he said, after earlier claiming that race was a nonissue in his career and personal life.

Wachs explained Murphy's aesthetic cautiousness as a matter of taking care of fans. As much as Murphy might want to stretch, moviegoers wanted a predictable product. At least that was Wachs's operating philosophy, no matter how hurtful it would be to his client's prestige. Wachs said, "Eddie

Murphy is interested in one thing and one thing only—quality. Eddie is a perfectionist, and he doesn't want to get into something where his fans would be disappointed."

In a 1985 article titled "The Eddie Murphy Script Derby: Winner Takes All," the *L.A. Times* listed twenty projects in the Murphy hamper. Everything from Murphy as an angel to Murphy as a faith healer, a kid-show host, a Pinkerton security guard, and a washed-up gumshoe. Some were just talk, and Murphy wasn't doing the talking. The origin of a black Robinson Crusoe movie consisted solely of comedian Alan King approaching Wachs at the Russian Tea Room and saying the title of Daniel Defoe's novel. "That's the last I heard of it," Wachs said. And yet the trades and the *Times* dutifully reported the nonproject on Murphy's roster.

Although the list of projects under consideration had Murphy playing everything from an African prince to a zany Klingon, one obvious role was missing—romantic leading man. Paramount was ready to let Murphy put the White Pages on film, but the studio got nervous about the actor in bed with a woman. A screenwriter working on yet another Murphy vehicle revealed the studio's reluctance to yank the action star out of his cop car and onto a bedroom set. "That's the thinking at the studio," the unidentified writer said. "They don't tell you explicitly, but that's it. The real question is, when is Eddie Murphy going to be allowed to fall in love?" Wachs rejected this hypothesis and insisted his client's screen neutering had nothing to do with racism. Murphy agreed with the studio that he was too young to play Mr. Right, even though teen and twenty-something romances continue to target the prime demographic of moviegoers. And love on screen wasn't ruled out for Murphy. In fact, his manager mentioned that *Mr. Bad News* provided the star with a love interest. The picture, of course, never got made, even with a brand name like Neil Simon on the label.

Ominously, at the end of the *Times*'s list was a script

called *King for a Day* that would come back to haunt the star and drag him into court. Tellingly, of the twenty scripts under consideration, only one got made, and it was a no-brainer decision that suggests just how cautious—artistically—the star and his advisers had become. A sequel to *Beverly Hills Cop* screamed to be made, and Murphy Inc. listened attentively.

But first, the star decided to make what would turn out to be the most successful concert film of all time. And yet despite the commercial success, it was a decision the comedian would come to regret.

Chapter 9

......

Not Well Done

"**S**OMETIMES I WONDER if the audience is going to get mad at me, but they never do," the actor said in 1983, after he invited a a woman in the audience to fellate him.

That same year, however, a segment of ex-fans did get very mad. Murphy starred in his first filmed concert, an HBO special called *Delirious*. A rare bit of cross-merchandising for the time, the special also came out on video and as an album that went gold.

The concert was filmed at Constitution Hall in the nation's capital, the same venue the Daughters of the American Revolution banned black opera star Marian Anderson from performing at in the fifties. (Eleanor Roosevelt, one of the Daughters, noisily tore up her membership card and invited Anderson to sing in front of the Lincoln Memorial, which didn't have a color code; one hundred thousand people showed up for the show.) Murphy reveled in the fact that thirty years later, a black man held court on a stage that had been denied to a black woman. The context he placed his appearance in, however, was more profane than historical. "So here we are. It's not even fifty years later, and a black man is on stage, getting paid to hold his dick. God bless America."

While Murphy was breaking the color barrier with his concert, he was slamming into another minority's sensibilities. A sketch in *Delirious* called "Faggots Revisited" so offended homosexuals that they took out an ad in the trades calling for funds to treat the disease of Eddie Murphy Syndrome. Gays also formed the Eddie Murphy's Disease Foundation, renaming homophobia after him as its most famous victim. The group distributed bumper stickers which said "Eddie Murphy Disease Can Be Cured." In *Playgirl*, which has long been rumored to have a larger gay male than straight female subscriber base, the foundation took out another ad which included a P.O. box address to get more information. The tone of the ad campaign was tongue-in-cheek, but it concealed anger, which a spokesman for the group expressed by calling *Delirious* "exceedingly harsh," especially his AIDS jokes that were "nothing short of inflammatory."

In the aftermath of *Delirious*'s homophobia, Murphy expressed mixed emotions, alternating with defiance, contrition, and terror of what furious gays might do to him. "I'm afraid of gay people," he said in 1984. "Petrified. I have nightmares about gay people. I have this nightmare I go to Hollywood and find out that Mr. T is a faggot." In London—a city he loathed—to promote *Trading Places*, his tone turned exculpatory. "I kid homosexuals 'cause they're homosexuals. 'Any faggots in the audience? No? Good. Let's talk about them.'"

Almost immediately, the comedian abandoned his apologetic tone and denied that gays frightened him. "I think homosexuals didn't get offended by this," Murphy said, somewhere in another world, on the banks of a river called Denial. "Faggots who have nothing to fucking do but sit around with tight asses and feel like people are pointing fingers at them. People who are insecure got offended. The way I feel about it is, what they did helped my album, because the majority of the country is heterosexual and they read that the homosexuals don't like Eddie Murphy, and they think [imitating redneck accent], 'Hey, all right!' They're wasting their money.

They blew it all out of proportion, and if they want to, I don't give a fuck. Do all the ads you want to. Kiss my ass." Here, perhaps, Murphy was following in the footsteps of his idol, Richard Pryor, who, coked out of his mind, went on stage at an AIDS fund-raiser and told the audience, "You can kiss my rich black ass." Not missing a beat, gay-friendly Bette Midler shouted at Pryor, "You can kiss my rich white ass."

Soon, Murphy was backtracking. This time, he claimed, his gay jokes were just a tool for poking fun at a straight guy. "This is what I have to say about homosexuals. I am not the first comic to do homosexual jokes. When I said I was afraid of homosexuals, all it was was a setup for my Mr. T joke." No one ever thought to ask Mr. T what he thought about Murphy's routine. Maybe timid reporters were afraid to tell the *A-Team* star that Murphy joked that Mr. T asked to be sodomized and got his wish.

Murphy continued to backtrack. "I don't have anything against homosexuals. I'm not afraid of them. I know homosexuals. It was a joke. I make fun of everybody. I poke fun at anything that I think is funny. It's comedy. It's not real."

In January 1985, *Saturday Night Live* invited its most successful alumnus to return as guest host. Murphy used the gig to engage in more fag-bashing. During his opening monologue, he held up a Ken doll, Barbie's boyfriend, whom Murphy implied was Barbie's beard, not her boy toy. He said, "Remember Ken? Check out Ken's pink shirt. Check out the way he combs his hair. And look at his posture. Moms and dads, unless you want your sons to live in the Village [Greenwich Village, New York's gay ghetto] and skip to work, keep them as far away from Ken as possible, all right? I tell you, before I finish I must stress once again, keep your children away from the Ken doll! OK? Because if your little boys play with the Ken doll, they may turn out like this guy." Implying that homosexuals were converted, not born, Murphy had invaded Jerry Falwell territory.

The star soon made what sounds like an apology mixed with the excuse that it was all the folly of youth. A more mature Murphy, allowed to grow up outside the limelight, would have been a kinder, gentler comedian. "My attitude was 'Fuck everybody. This is me, this is the way I express myself on stage.' Then, after the special came out, I was scared. People got offended. Now I'm thinking, whatever I'm doing, I have to be doing it right. It doesn't mean I don't feel guilty about anything I've done, it's just that I know I'm growing into something else. It's fucked up that I have to grow up comedically in public. If I could change one thing in my career, it would be to put off success until I was thirty years old." (Ironically, Murphy would get the reverse of his wish: at age 28, his career went into free fall. But that's a few chapters down the line.)

Four years after *Delirious* ticked off gays, the comedian managed to infuriate more than just the homosexual population. And instead of tongue-in-cheek ads, there were boycotts, pickets, and denunciations on op-ed pages, as well as more mocking ads in the trades.

Today, *Eddie Murphy Raw*, a filmed version of his stand-up act, is more curio than controversy. The 1987 release managed to offend a huge portion of the audience, but *Raw* didn't keep others from patronizing it to the tune of $50 million, putting the production in the record books as the No. 1 concert film of all time.

As he had on *Saturday Night Live* with his impressions of hairdressers and pimps, *Raw* offended a kaleidoscope of colors and ethnicities, only much more crudely than anything NBC ever let him get away with at 11:30 on Saturday nights.

Raw's apt title was about anger in all its raw manifestations, Murphy's personal fury and the Furies that tormented him. Even fans found themselves squirming during ninety minutes of what seemed like psychotherapy rather than comedy. The film critic for the defunct *L.A. Herald-Examiner* said that everything was on stage except the couch: "To review *Raw* was to leave the domain of criticism for psychiatry." The comic as analysand. The *New York Times* wrote, "*Raw* exposes rather more of him than he may suspect." A psychotherapist provided a technical explanation. "He was obviously in pain, and *Raw* was his way of acting out."

A personal manager said the film "was like watching a public death, a private life fragmenting on stage and film. It's painful to watch." In happier times, *Newsweek* summed up the actor's abrasive charm. "He's not bad; just naughty." *TV Guide* said, "Some feel anger in his characters, but no real rage in him, no carryover frustration from a deprived childhood, no hatreds."

Not after *Raw*. The same magazine that had called him naughty now labeled him a "walled off, paranoid movie star." He was more than naughty, he seemed downright nasty. What fueled Murphy's fury? Lisa Figueroa for one: The filming of *Raw* coincided with the end of their three-year romance. Who dumped whom changed, depending on the interview and the interviewee's mood.

The comedian attributed *Raw*'s rage to the breakup, which didn't explain why he also performed a rainbow demolition of minorities. Murphy insisted, "I was real bitter when I did *Raw*. I had just gone through a breakup. That's why a lot of the material was about relationships—'Never get married, they'll get half your money' sort of material." Misogyny might be a logical reaction to the messy end of an affair, projecting one woman's rejection onto the entire opposite sex. But what had homosexuals or Italians or Asians or blacks for that matter ever done to Eddie Murphy?

Whoever ended the relationship, Murphy's bitterness also spewed out of an even unlikelier venue, his home answering machine. When the comedian vented, he didn't care who telephoned him. According to attorney Pierce O'Donnell, author of *Fatal Subtraction*, an account of a lawsuit O'Donnell litigated against the star, "Murphy once put his ex-girlfriend's sobbing pleas on his answering machine's outgoing message, so that anyone calling could hear her say, 'Eddie! Take me back! Please, Eddie. Please, I love you, Eddie. Take me back.'"

This is the same Murphy who said, "I'm basically a sensitive person."

Murphy's misogyny came wrapped in an obsession with money and his fear that cash was all women wanted him for. In the mid-eighties he said, "Women were using me and hurting me." On stage, his paranoia served as a punch line. "I'm a target. If I get married I have to go off to the woods of Africa and find me some crazy nekkid zebra bitch. She gotta be buck-naked on a zebra and know nothin' about money." He imagined the headline on the cover of *Jet* magazine: "Murphy Marries Bush Bitch."

At the time Murphy filmed *Raw*, Johnny Carson was making headlines after paying his ex-wife half of his $300 million fortune in a divorce settlement. Murphy's monologue on Carson's payout lasts ten minutes—forever in a stand-up act —this time with no punch line, just unvarnished venom. Again, even paranoid people have enemies, and Murphy's fears of being divested of half his fortune were justified, since he had such a large one. In 1987, *Forbes* magazine proclaimed him the fifth richest entertainer in America, earning $27 million that year alone. Murphy justifiably suffered separation anxiety since he had a lot to be separated from.

For sheer hatred of women, *Raw's* stridency is shocking, but, less forgivably, it's just not funny. The video is embarrassing to watch. A DSM buff would have a field day analyzing Murphy's mix of gynecology and money metaphors. He refers to "pussy-control, pussy-on-lease, pussy-on-layaway." The stage becomes a bully pulpit for the importance of prenuptial agreements. Or, as the *New York Times* said, "In *Raw*, Mr. Murphy... seems to be searching for the name of a perfect tax lawyer" to write the premarriage contract. If a Freudian had caught the show, he might have used the term "castration complex." Murphy imagines a woman responding to his infidelity. "I'd wait 'til you were asleep, then I'd cut off your dick."

The film pays homage to Freud—or at least psycho-dynamics—in its opening sketch, written by the star and Keenen Ivory Wayans. Set in 1968 Brooklyn, a seven-year-old Murphy shows the origin of all the scatology and hypersex-uality in his act. After doing a tap dance, the child tells a joke that involves the bodily functions of jungle animals. It's Thanksgiving, and most of the family members are horrified. Two relatives, however, think he's hilarious, a prediction of the comedian's appeal and distastefulness in adult life.

Four years after *Delirious* sold half a million albums, *Raw* continued his history of homophobia, but he realized from the uproar over *Delirious* that gays were one pressure group he couldn't offend—at least not at length. A relatively brief joke about a screaming queen providing the siren on a San Francisco cop car represents his only incursion into dangerous territory. This time there'd be no jokes about AIDS and its origins in a romance between green monkeys and gays.

In retrospect, perhaps the most horrific segment occurs during a swipe at Bill Cosby. Murphy does a dead-on impres-sion of the Cos and the phone call he made to Murphy telling him to clean up his act. Murphy literally says "fuck you" to Cosby during this routine. But its another Cosby that gives the viewer goose bumps today. A fictional account by Cosby's son Ennis on all the new dirty words he learned after a Murphy concert has a creepy resonance in the wake of the young man's murder.

While Murphy pokes fun at Japanese tourists and other foreigners, who he claims stop him on the street and repeat phrases from his act, thinking they're complimenting him

("Suck my dick, Eddie!"), another target is potentially far more dangerous. He portrays Italian-Americans as strutting racists pumped up after *Rocky* movies who try to beat up "moolies," a supposedly Italian term for blacks which I, as a third-generation Italian-American, had never heard before. Still, he sees a fraternity of sorts between the two antagonistic groups. "Italians act like niggers. They hold their dick more than we do."

As the preceding snippets suggest, *Raw* is a cesspool of profanity. Extending the metaphor, one critic said of his toilet humor, "Murphy's Oedipal ravings about doing it to your mother represent a fetid stream of consciousness in dire need of a sewage filter."

Not that the comedian didn't have his defenders—although his backers weren't exactly disinterested parties. Comedian Robert Townsend came to his friend's defense. "Eddie is out for Eddie, but he is loved because of his arrogance, his guts, and his balls. There are not a lot of African-Americans who speak their minds, and Eddie dared not to be liked. And he is the only one to break away, the only one whose movies break a hundred million, the only one whose audience is almost everybody." Well, not everybody, but enough unoffended viewers to earn *Raw* $50 million. Townsend's boosterism isn't surprising, since he directed the concert film.

It wasn't just the critics and minorities who objected to Murphy's triple-X-rated monologue. Murphy claimed that studio executives would have been happy for him to relieve himself on screen and give it a two-thousand-screen release, but after Paramount saw *Raw* in rough cut, the studio found it way too rough. Nervous lawyers from Paramount descended on Bubble Hill with a dirty laundry list of one hundred "watch fors" to avoid an X rating—box office death—since Murphy's demographic included teenagers. It's testament to the star's clout that the studio called all these problem areas "watch fors" rather than a more forceful "cut it out." The laundry list was more like a wish list. The lawyers wanted references to orgasms, Eddie's pelvic thrusts, masturbation jokes about Michael Jackson's song "Beat It," and gags about TV's *Webster*'s pint-sized genitalia excised. As anyone who has seen *Raw* knows, the lawyers didn't get their wish. But somehow *Raw*, which included descriptions of sex that alternated between gynecological and proctological, managed to snatch an R-rating.

As sole writer credited for the concert portion of the film, Murphy ignored his own epiphany a few years earlier that four-letter words were passé. In 1983, he seemed to renounce raunch after *Delirious* raised so many hackles. "A few years ago, all you had to do to get a laugh was say, 'Let's have sex.' But the country's not in a wild and crazy mood anymore. I don't know what it is, maybe the economy, but people seem frustrated and uncomfortable. A lot of their laughter is nervous laughter. Comedy's getting more disgusting and the movies more dangerous. Audiences like to see that somebody besides them is screwed up." *Raw*'s personal psychodrama proved the last point.

The comedian's obsession with poop is so proctological it even caught the attention of a scholar who specialized in the stuff. Professor Tim Jay, a psychology professor at North Adams State College in Massachusetts, attempted to deconstruct Murphy's comedy in a magazine article that could been subtitled, "The Psychopathology of Everyday Smut." In the cable TV guide article, which ran when *Raw* hit pay-TV, the fastidious Dr. Jay counted 151 four-letter terms "for the act of reproduction, eighty-one synonyms for a digestive by-product, and sixty-seven 12-letter nouns implying a too-intimate relationship with one's mother." The shrink wasn't writing tongue-in-cheek. He explained perhaps why *Raw* had grossed $50 million and managed to become the top concert film of all time. "A joke is funnier if it contains four-letter words because dirty words cause distress. We laugh not only at things that are funny, but at things which make us nervous." If you listen to *Raw*'s soundtrack, however, the most noticeable thing is how thin the laughter is. Lots of applause, but the giggles seem smothered by something else, maybe choking.

Dr. Jay divided humor into two phases: a "boost phase" in which anxiety is aroused, followed by a punch line, which eases tension. While Murphy avoided describing AIDS in a gay context, he expressed his own fear of contracting the disease. Dr. Jay understood the urge. "AIDS is a matter of life and death. When you have this kind of anxiety, you have subject matter for humor." Gallows humor and chemotherapy comedy.

Even Murphy's use of the f-word every three seconds comes in an historical context, courtesy of Dr. Jay. "'Fuck' has been used since 1400 A.D.," happily just missing Chaucer's era. "There are reasons why these expressions have persisted for so long. Swear words not only amuse and titillate us, but help intensify and dramatize the emotional content of what we're saying." Stealing a page from Freud's totemic work, Jay noted that breaking a taboo is just plain funny. And more acceptable. In the Middle Ages, a court jester could diss the king without a trip to the block for lese majeste, the professor said. Critics in the late 1980s were less royal about pardoning Murphy's language.

Murphy's material was part of the evolution of humor. Dr. Jay again: "Most of humor in contemporary America is sexually aggressive. Since World War II, the taboos have progressed from religious to sexual." One joke the psychologists quoted from *Raw* neatly combines Murphy's profanity, misogyny, and obsession with money. "I've had my share of pussy. But even if the pussy was great and sparks shot out of the pussy, no pussy is worth $150 million." Mrs. Carson's haul still haunted him.

Finally, Jay makes a suggestion that would get the U.S.

Surgeon General fired. Parent and kids should watch *Raw* together and then discuss the differences between men and women, blacks and whites, the poor and the middle class. Dr. Jay wrote, "*Raw* is not nearly so bad as kids hearing their parents use four letter words in an argument."

The same year that *Raw* hit cable in all its antiblack and white glory, the NAACP gave Murphy its Image Award as Entertainer of the Year. One wonders if they showed clips from the film at the awards banquet.

Raw's ills screamed for a spin doctor, and Murphy showed he had an M.D. in spin. Less than a year after *Raw* came out, he was making his mea culpas. "I did *Raw* at a really bitter stage in my life. I look at it now and cringe. It's not so much that I think *Raw* wasn't funny, but I can't believe what I was feeling then. I was on tour and I had broken up with Lisa. I was feeling sorry for myself. It was that old cliché, 'Who's gonna love me for me?'" which happened to be the lyrics to a song he wrote.

Some gay activists were not mollified by the apology. One said Murphy seemed to be making amends with the mixed emotions of John Wayne Bobbitt doing a public service announcement for spaying and neutering pets. Plus Murphy's later travels and travails on Santa Monica Boulevard suggest what gays have long considered a truism: noisy homophobia in public often conceals the quiet self-loathing of a closeted homosexual.

Within a few years, Murphy's mea culpa would turn into an unrecovered memory. Psychologists call it repression. Asked why he had harangued gays, women, Bill Cosby, Michael Jackson, and Mr. T, Murphy dismissed everything as growing pains, although it was the audience, not the comic, who felt the sting. "I was a child," he said. "What you saw was an artist growing up; a kid going through stages. Did you believe all that? People say they saw *Raw*. *Raw!* I can't even remember it. I would probably like it even less than the *chicks* who were offended by it." *Plus ça change, plus ça meme.*

Lisa Figueroa wasn't the only woman who fueled Murphy's misogyny and fear of gold diggers. *People* magazine speculated that his tantrums in *Raw* were also caused by a paternity suit filed in Los Angeles Superior Court April 22, 1987, by Nicolle Rader, claiming her daughter Ashlee had been fathered by the comedian and demanding child support. Details in Rader's petition kept the tabloids busy, as she alleged that instead of child support, Murphy had offered her $50,000 to have an abortion.

The actor categorically denied paternity. "That was bullshit," he said. "It wasn't my kid." If little Ashlee Murphy had been his, he added, "I'd have taken care of the kid. But I'd have no responsibility to that woman. When the child got old enough to understand the relationship that I had with his mother, then I would start seeing him. [sic] But I wouldn't be forced into a relationship with a woman just because I had a child with her."

Despite his fear of contracting venereal diseases, which he joked about in *Raw* by imagining a patient seeing a doctor because fire was literally shooting out of his genitals, Murphy obviously wasn't practicing safe sex at this time. He also got around, because less than two years later Paulette McNeely gave birth to Murphy's son. McNeely, unlike Rader, didn't have to seek redress in the courts. Murphy not only acknowledged paternity, he gave the kid his last *and* first name. Now there was an Eddie Murphy Jr., who would be ready to be a Not-Ready-For-Prime-Time-Player in the year 2008, if he duplicated dad's early success at age nineteen.

One can only hope that Junior turns out as macho as Senior; if not, little Eddie is in store for Vernon Lynch–like discipline in the basement boxing ring. Although David Bowie is a personal friend and frequent guest at Bubble Hill, and Murphy admires Prince's music, he loathes their penchant for women's clothes. "Elvis sang and acted like a guy. If I had a son and he was watching some guy making music on TV and he came downstairs with makeup and his mother's shoes and said, 'I want to be like so-and-so,' I'd beat the shit out of him. 'Take that shit off!' I want my boys to wear men's clothes and my daughters to wear women's." Psychotherapists make mortgage payments on second homes from such stuff as this. If you beat your kid for *any* reason, he may need a shrink.

A therapist might disagree that Murphy seemed paranoid about gold-diggers and parasites. An unwed mother wasn't the only person who wanted a piece of Eddie at this time. In April 1987, the comedian was hauled into a Mineola, New York, court by a man who claimed he was Murphy's long lost manager. Murphy must have wished King Broder would stay lost, but Broder, a fringe agent/manager of magicians and housewife strippers, found a contract from seven years earlier. At the age of nineteen, Murphy had indeed signed an agreement with Broder to represent him for life. It was the kind of uninformed deal a beginner without representation would be delighted to sign—even with a minor player like Broder, who booked comics and magic acts into mountain resorts from his Long Island office. The press characterized Broder as a real-life Danny Rose, Woody Allen's talent agent of last resort for the hopelessly untalented.

In Broder's mind, he was the creator of the one-man industry called Eddie Murphy Inc. "I taught him how to dress, how to behave," Broder testified in court. An observer at the trial suggested otherwise. Murphy showed up in banker's pinstripes. Broder wore an obvious toupee and tinted aviator glasses with a plastic crown glued to the lens. Murphy's career-making break on *Saturday Night Live* was also his doing, Broder claimed, even though Bob Wachs and Richie Tienken brokered that deal through their personal contacts with *SNL* producer Jean Doumanian, a muckety-muck who wouldn't have even returned Broder's phone calls. Murphy denied Broder's claim, but conceded he had signed a contract with him. However, the star insisted he had canceled the deal only five months later by phone.

More accurately, Broder said that from day one his client's profanity drew complaints from the clubs he booked him into.

After an eight-day trial, the star's notorious short attention span and the impending startup of *Beverly Hills Cop II* led to a settlement with Broder. Murphy got off cheap. Broder had demanded twenty-five percent of the star's income for the past seven years, which he estimated at $120 million. Under cross-examination, Murphy was forced to do something he hated, disclose his income. Murphy's estimate was considerably less than Broder's, a mere $58 million since 1980. Broder settled for a fraction of Murphy's wealth, a piddling $700,000, riches for the manager, chump change for America's richest entertainer. Unlike his monetary battles of the heart with women, Murphy didn't seem to resent paying Broder to go away. "I always liked King," he told reporters outside court. The comedian in him, however, couldn't resist one last swipe at his opponent's déclassé appearance. He grabbed a reporter's notebook and wrote, "Murphy then became outraged and snatched off everyone's hairpiece."

The same year that *Raw* left such an unpleasant taste in people's mouths, Murphy found the perfect mouthwash: A non-controversial film that would become the biggest money-maker of 1987. While *Raw* made many whites and blacks see red, the color of money proved to be a more powerful hue.

Chapter 10

......

The Art of Roman Numerals

THERE WAS AN HISTORICAL inevitability to *Beverly Hills Cop II*. Like Talleyrand's description of Napoleon: If the sequel hadn't existed it would have had to be invented. Axel Foley's first trip to the Platinum Triangle grossed nearly half a billion worldwide; no. 2 was a categorical imperative.

An early draft ignored the title and planned to send Murphy's Detroit cop to London to team with Scotland Yard. The fish-out-of-water gimmick would be even more dramatic in stiff-upper-lip Britain than in merely stuck-up Beverly Hills. The studio, however, wasn't merely anglophiliac; it envisioned turning the *Beverly Hills Cop* franchise into a series like James Bond, spawning sequels into the millennium. Murphy, however, first wanted to test the waters of this new angle, and he found the temperature too bracing. He loathed London, and the limey *Beverly Hills Cop* script wound up in Paramount's dumpster, which was already overflowing with stuff like *Cyrano de Boogie* and *A Black Yankee in King Arthur's Court*. Another draft put Murphy in the City of Light, but a quick trip by the Accidental Tourist to the banks of the Seine also axed this locale. Desperate for a change of scenery, the studio wrote in Hawaii, but even this paradise on earth seemed hellish to the confirmed travelphobe.

Director Martin Brest, a class act who would later work with Robert De Niro and help Al Pacino win his only Oscar, couldn't be wooed back for the sequel, no matter how much money or how many gross points the studio threw at him. Paramount must have been even more delighted with his replacement, Britain's Tony Scott, white hot after the previous year's box office champ, *Top Gun*. Scott had already proved himself adept at handling delicate superstar egos, and his finesse would come in handy for the handful that Murphy had become. In retrospect, the moody, image-conscious Tom Cruise would seem like Oprah after Scott's collaboration with Murphy.

The star, however, wasn't impressed with the director's pedigree. He only agreed to work with the graduate of the Royal College of Art after the two men played pool together at Bubble Hill. Scott's bank shot rather than his track record made Murphy amenable to the collaboration.

The final draft of *Beverly Hills Cop II* trod the same territory, not only geographically, but thematically. Murphy chasing drug dealers with explosions and car chases coming every five minutes, whether or not the storyline justified them. The script, though, did have one original plot point. The bad guy was actually a bad girl, Danish amazon Brigitte Nielsen, Mrs. Sylvester Stallone. While the film made a rich Murphy even richer, it impoverished an intimate relationship, his friendship with Nielsen's husband. Murphy regretted the loss. He felt close enough to Sylvester Stallone to discuss their common battles with clinical depression. When Murphy wondered, "Why the fuck am I depressed?" he'd console himself with the recollection that both Stallone and Michael Jackson had told him they asked themselves the same question.

Stallone must have been even more depressed when the groundless rumor began circulating that Murphy and Nielsen were more than professional colleagues. When Murphy heard the allegation, he immediately called his friend on the phone. Murphy recalled their last conversation. They didn't talk again. "He thought I fucked his wife. He heard the rumor and believed it. He came after me and said, 'YOU FUCKED MY WIFE!' I said, 'Down, brother, I didn't fuck your wife!' We talked about it, but I guess somewhere in the back of his head, he'll never really know the truth. Sly and I liked each other, too, but after the weirdness with Brigitte, it was ruined. I didn't fuck her. Did I ever want to fuck Gitte? No, she's not my type. She was married. And married to somebody who was my friend. I'm not that kind of guy."

Stallone didn't believe Murphy's protestations of innocence. The strain on their relationship became so great that Stallone couldn't even stand to be in the same room with the man he was sure had betrayed him. Murphy did more than phone his friend to mend the relationship; he showed up at Stallone's house. "We were real cool for a hot minute; I'd go up to his house; we'd talk on the phone a lot. And suddenly, it stopped." Murphy recalled going to a party and being told Stallone had fled the place as soon as Murphy entered the room.

His off-screen woes were beginning to show on camera. Whether it was depression or boredom with exploring the same old movie territory again, only his psychotherapist would know. By now, the actor was just going through the motions and some felt his face expressed motion sickness. One critic wrote, "His eyes go dead in *Beverly Hills Cop II*, a soporific movie that also happened to be the No. 1 box-office hit of 1987." Eddie was bored with Axel Foley. The public wasn't.

His disenchantment with the project expressed itself in expensive petulance. During a publicity shoot for the film, Murphy refused to pose unless the studio bought him a Ferrari identical to the one he drives in the movie. Paramount happily coughed up a piddling $200 grand—gas money compared to the potential half billion the film might generate.

He could also be a scary dinner guest: the man who came to dinner—with an entourage. After the New York premiere of *Beverly Hills Cop II,* director Scott and manager Wachs cohosted an intimate soiree at 21. It was instantly unintimate as soon as Murphy arrived. While everyone else brought one guest, Murphy showed up with fifty-six. Six of his companions never left his side. Fortunately, dinner was a buffet, so there was no mad rush for an additional fifty-plus place settings.

Murphy's entourage may have provided him with a sense of protection and insulation from fans who might literally want to tear him apart in Beatlemania mode. Others felt the gang was reminiscent of Elvis's sycophantic hangers-on. The human buffer was more isolating than insulating. At this time, the press began to compare him to Elvis, and the comparisons weren't flattering, they were cautionary. Bob Wachs, wrote a reporter who was invited to interview the star then got stiffed at the door, said the manager was turning into Elvis's eminence grise, Colonel Parker. A colleague said, "Eddie doesn't need all those bodyguards. Somehow it must play into his own fantasy."

A visitor at this time described life chez Bubble. "At twenty-six, he lives a strange existence not unlike the one his hero Elvis lived twenty-three years later in his life—sequestered from reality by his fame, fawned over by courtiers, loved by millions, and ultimately alone."

Murphy denied he was reclusive. He wasn't avoiding the public, just the press, which he felt had burned him one too many times. "Rape" was what he called his interactions with interviewers. An article by a black journalist, Elvis Mitchell, still rankled a year after their meeting. Particularly galling was Murphy's feeling that he had been done in by one of his own people, who should be rooting for, not raging at, the most successful black entertainer in the history of the biz. "They talked me into it, then they raped me bad.... You have to get hurt when somebody says something bad about you, especially if there's a little bit of truth in it. You're human, you know. I don't think I'll ever get to the point when I don't care what someone says about me."

I found the ten-year-old Mitchell piece in the archives of the Academy library in Beverly Hills. It's hard to understand what made Murphy feel like a rape victim. The journalist is as reverential as a reporter for *Access Hollywood;* he even praises Eddie's singing voice! Perhaps Murphy resented Mitchell's faithful transcription of the taped interview, which included calling pals Prince and Stevie Wonder egomaniacs and gays "faggots." He also mocked David Bowie's effeminacy even though the singer was on his way over to help Eddie with his new record. During my quarter century as an entertainment journalist, I have often been shocked by what celebrities revealed while my tape recorder whirred beside them. Murphy wasn't press-savvy enough to realize the reporter you're confiding in will repeat what you say to millions of readers.

Avoid the press at your own peril, as Michael Jackson and other stars playing Garbo have found. If you don't let journalists have access to your side of the story, they devote all their ink to the other side. Plus, miffed that they have been stiffed, reporters typically will fill the space where the star's comments would have run with nasty innuendoes and hypotheses about what the star has to hide. Two extremely influential magazines, *Vanity Fair* and *Esquire,* showed up for scheduled interviews only to be told that Murphy was napping and didn't like to be awakened. The journalists got their revenge in a series of nasty pieces.

At a press conference for *Cop II* the press-shy star said he was more like Garbo than Elvis. He didn't "vant to be alone." He vanted to be *left* alone. He wasn't reclusive; he was fourth-estate phobic. "If I want to go outside, if I want to go to a store, I go to the store. I refuse to be a prisoner of my fame."

It wasn't just the press, however, that he kept at arm's length. His own manager, Bob Wachs, more responsible than any other person for Murphy's stunning rise, had to play hide and seek with his mercurial client. Wachs once spent three days trying to get to Murphy. Finally, he stowed away on Murphy's tour bus. For all his efforts, he was only allowed to ask his client one question. And unlike the press, Murphy wasn't even mad at the man who had made his fortune.

He did get mad, however, when his best friends diminished his success. By 1987, Murphy was so famous some of the glitter rubbed off on his buddies. Enough to warrant a cover story in *Vanity Fair* on the "Black Pack," Murphy's recreation of Sinatra's star-studded entourage of the '50s but with a different palette—if you don't count Sammy. To his credit, Murphy didn't hang out with nonentities to make his star burn brightly. Members of the pack were notables in their own right and included stand-up comic Paul Mooney, super-hot director Keenen Ivory Wayans, *Raw*'s director Robert Townsend, and of course his Boswell, Arsenio Hall.

Ironically, the Black Pack was the fanciful creation of a white journalist desperate for an angle, according to one of its purported members, Wayans. "It's funny, but the Black Pack never existed," Wayans told me. "It was something Eddie said in jest. It just sounded good, but it was never like an organized pack. We just happened to be friends. Eddie made a play on words, on Rat Pack, in the same way those guys were friends. Everybody in our group went on to make their own place, which is great."

Whatever you call it, the friendship was sometimes troubled by the jealousy of less successful packers. Hall recalled an angry outburst by Murphy during a pack attack at the staid L'Ermitage Hotel in Beverly Hills. An unnamed friend claimed that any of the other guys in the gang would have enjoyed the same success given Murphy's launching platform on *Saturday Night Live*. Murphy, per Hall, exploded. "You know I hate that attitude. You motherfuckers think I'm not talented and anybody can do this. Does *good* have anything to do with this? That pisses me off. That was my shot, and I did with it what a lot of people couldn't do." Perhaps overly sensitive, Murphy was nevertheless dead-on. Other black comedians like Garrett Morris and the brilliant Chris Rock failed to prosper post-*SNL*.

Chapter 11

······

Coming to Blows

ALTHOUGH THIS ISSUE would later involve a precedent-setting lawsuit, Murphy originated the idea for his next film, *Coming to America,* in 1987. It was the tale of Prince Akeem of the mythical African kingdom of Zamunda. Murphy played a poor little rich boy who finds the local girls lacking and comes to America to find a sophisticated bride. The plot point was the exact opposite of Murphy's threat in *Raw* to visit the continent of his forbears in search of a non-mercenary "black nekkid zebra bitch."

The pitch meeting for *Coming to America* spoke volumes about the star's clout. The pitch to Paramount executives was a formality. The fecal aesthetic was in full force, and Murphy could shovel anything he wanted on screen. Maybe as a courtesy, Murphy deigned to tell Paramount's President, Ned Tanen, the concept for the film the studio would be spending $45 million on. That this was a courtesy, not a supplication, was underlined by the fact that Tanen, one of the most powerful men in Hollywood, came to Murphy's office on the backlot. Or as *Vanity Fair* punned, "The Paramountain came to Mohammed."

The meeting was more pep rally than solicitation. In the middle of his description of *Coming to America,* an executive had the temerity to interrupt the star, who didn't mind because he liked what he heard, which was, "Stop, stop. This is *great*. You guys go write it."

"That was it,'" recalled Arsenio Hall, a participant at the pitch and costar of the film. This hands-off-the-fatted calf policy worked on this occasion, but the studio's laissez-faire attitude would barbecue its bottom line on the next Murphy project.

Coming to America represented a career shift and some image repair. After the venom of *Raw*, Murphy wanted a vehicle that would show what a sweet-natured guy he really was. "I needed to be something different. A character who talks loud and goes wherever he wants to go—I had to get away from that. This movie isn't as raunchy as anything I've done before," he said. The press noticed a desire to change off screen as well. Garbo had turned into Bob Hope, press-friendly to a fault. The *Boston Globe* said, "In 1988, he's conciliatory, charming. A few years ago, he would have done an 'I'm bad' act."

The comedy would also offer his first on-screen romance, after critics' complaints that Hollywood was afraid to portray a sexual black man. Cons and clowns, Okay. Casanova, no. Murphy agreed with the complaints, and he made sure he finally got a little sugar in the movie. "There's this big thing about blacks in Hollywood that they try to hide their sexuality. Lots of blacks feel the studios don't want them to be portrayed as sexual on film."

The film would also be the first—but far from the last—to let Murphy play multiple roles on the big screen. He had had plenty of practice on *Saturday Night Live*, but this time the stakes were much higher. Murphy played an ancient black barber, a Jewish customer at the barbershop, and a Rick James impersonator.

The big budget, of course, raised the stakes, but even more important was the need to continue Murphy's flop-free track record. As Burt Reynolds and Ted Danson have learned, to their peril, one big expensive turkey can stall a superstar's momentum and lead back to TV.

The supporting cast of *Coming to America* would also allow Murphy to answer the complaints of black activists that his previous films were lily-white except for the star. *Coming to America* boasted a nearly all-black cast.

Despite his overwhelming clout, Murphy found he had to beg the brass for one big concession. He wanted John Landis, his brilliant collaborator on *Trading Places*, back in the director's chair. While Paramount was willing to let Murphy photograph paint drying, it balked at rehiring Landis, who had fallen on hard times with torpid caper films like *Into the Night* and *Spies Like Us*, not to mention the ultimate career-spoiler, *Twilight Zone—The Movie*.

Murphy has said that the only time he had fun making a movie was with Landis on *Trading Places*. The star wanted to have some more fun, and he really went to bat for the player he wanted. Murphy said that the studio "had reservations." Murphy persisted: "I'm gonna use Landis." The director, by ignoring his recent track record and demanding a ridiculous fee, almost screwed up Murphy's campaign to get him the job. The studio might be willing, reluctantly, to overlook Landis's recent failures, since it had the insurance of Murphy's services, but the bean counters refused to be mugged by a down-and-out filmmaker with a delusional concept of his worth and clout. Murphy said, "He came in demanding lots of money. Paramount was saying, 'Hey, come on, Eddie, we're getting fucked here.'" Murphy told the executives to lie back and enjoy it. "I made them pay his money. They bent over backward."

Landis didn't appreciate Murphy's advocacy. "After he got the job, he brought along an attitude. He came in with this 'I'm a director' shit. I was thinking, Wait a second, I fucking hired you, and now you're running around, going, 'You have to remember: I'm the boss, I'm the director.'"

Murphy would come to regret this act of kindness, lending a helping hand to a colleague, a gesture that would literally turn into a stranglehold.

The star was a different person and a phenomenon by 1988, the most successful box office star of the decade, black or white. When he first worked with Landis on *Trading Places* in 1983, the twenty-two-year-old was a TV star still feeling his way in the bigger league of the movies. Landis was his mentor; Murphy the novice, respectful and grateful for the guidance. His first film, *48 HRS.*, hadn't hit theaters when *Trading Places* began filming, so Murphy had no track record to demand coequal treatment with the more established auteur of *Animal House* and *Kentucky Fried Movie*.

By 1988, Eddie Murphy had become EDDIE MURPHY, an 800-pound gorilla with a King Kong-size box office and a permanent fifty-man staff paid for by a grateful studio. Like a successful version of Willie Loman, Eddie agreed with Mrs. Loman and felt attention must be paid.

Landis wasn't paying attention. He seemed to be the only person unaware of his protégé's metamorphosis from David to Goliath. "John approached the project like I was still the twenty-two-year-old who he'd worked with on *Trading Places*, and he was still this hotshot director, you know, rather than this guy who just went through this big trial and had, like, four flop movies in a row," Murphy said.

To his horror, after pressuring Paramount to hire the director, Murphy discovered Landis held a five-year-old grudge against the star. Murphy had failed to attend Landis's trial for child endangerment and manslaughter on the *Twilight Zone* set. Two child actors and the star, Vic Morrow, died when a helicopter crashed into them. Landis was ultimately acquitted, but Murphy stayed away from the courtroom. "I considered John a friend, but I didn't go. It was like, you know, 'You were directing the movie.' I would never say that to him. But that's what my feelings were. So I was like, 'Hey, if you get acquitted, I'm happy for you. But I'm not coming and sitting down, you know, because some kids died.' That was the way I felt." The outspoken director didn't worry about making his feelings known to his star.

When Murphy contacted Landis about directing *Coming to America*, instead of gratitude, he got lip about Murphy's no-show at his show trial. "He said, 'Where were you at? They almost sent me to jail!'" Murphy's lack of court support obsessed the director.

No one would call Landis starstruck; he was star-tough. The director irritated Murphy by frequent allusions to his tough love treatment of another superstar. "One of his favorite things was to tell me, 'When I worked with Michael Jackson, everyone was afraid of Michael, but I'm the only one who would tell Michael, "Fuck you." And I'm not afraid to tell *you*, "Fuck you."' And sure enough, he was always telling me, 'Fuck you, Eddie. Everybody at Paramount is afraid of you.'"

The relationship went downhill from there. It didn't help that crew members were whispering outrageous allegations in Murphy's ear. One claimed Landis had called the film's choreographer, Paula Abdul, a nigger. Another said the director's wife, Deborah Nadoolman, the film's costume designer, had made the same racial slur against the star when he kept her waiting for more than an hour. Murphy's reaction sounds like a mix of paranoia and well-grounded suspicion. When Landis and Murphy posed for a picture with Mike Tyson, who was visiting the set, Murphy claimed the director had an "I-have-to-stand-by-this-nigger?" look on his face. The star never explained exactly what an "I-have-to-stand-by-this-nigger" look looked like. But Murphy's alienation was justified by mistreatment that was unequivocal. Landis feared Murphy was making the move on costars Shari Headley and Allison Dean, and played Cupid with a poisoned quiver. According to

Murphy, Landis warned the women, "Don't go out with him. He's going to fuck you if you go out with him, and it will fuck the movie up. Stay away from him."

On another occasion, Landis told several production assistants not to be afraid to boss Murphy around. Murphy decided to prove the director wrong. Coming up from behind, Murphy put a full Nelson on the director and asked his companions, "What happens to a guy who is not afraid of me?" A toady supplied the correct answer: "They get fucked up."

It got even more physical behind closed trailer doors. Landis escalated the fight in his Winnebago by grabbing Murphy in an unexpected place. "John reached down and tried to grab my private parts," Murphy said in a deposition for an unrelated court case. Landis's temerity and Murphy's restraint are both amazing. A well-trained boxer, Murphy could have creamed the director with a single blow. Showing rare restraint, Murphy put his hands around Landis's neck and squeezed. "I cut his wind off. And he realized I was serious. He started crying and said, 'Eddie!' and ran out of the room." Another account had the director almost passing out before Murphy released his chokehold.

Murphy was kinder and gentler with another crew member. As his huge year-round payroll suggests, Murphy is a generous, supportive employer. His personal valet on the set expressed an interest in getting into the movie business on a level higher than washing his boss's socks. When Landis offered the man a job as his personal assistant, Murphy let the valet go with his blessings. In fact, Murphy went without the services of a personal assistant on the film. One report mentioned that he folded his own underwear.

If only the same bonhomie had existed at the top of this food chain. With monumental understatement, Murphy summed up the relationship, "John is a talented director, but we had personal differences. I don't like him anymore, and he doesn't like me." Murphy later claimed the two men never came to blows, but the set of *Coming to America* was not a happy place. "We didn't get along that cool. It was personal. I never hit him, like some stories said. We had some disagreements. A bunch of personal stuff. He's a good director, but no, I won't do another movie with him." Or, as he tastelessly said on Arsenio Hall's talk show, "Landis has a better chance of working again with Vic Morrow than he does with me."

That was a threat Murphy didn't keep. A few years later, as the careers of both floundered, they would embrace like two drowning men holding on to one life preserver on *Beverly Hills Cop III.*

Perhaps the kindest thing Murphy said about his ex-mentor was to label him a "control freak."

Despite his on-the-set behavior, Murphy decided to tone down his image, if not his actions. One reporter contrasted his outfit for *Beverly Hills Cop II* interviews and his formal attire at a press conference for the following film, *Coming to America.* For the *Cop* junket, he seemed to have stepped off the stage of *Raw,* wearing a leather suit and no shirt. To meet the press for *Coming to America,* he looked like a studio executive, not its biggest star, in a conservative pinstriped gray suit, black loafers, camera-friendly blue shirt with white collar, and a navy blue tie. Instead of gold jewelry on a shirtless chest, the only ornament he wore was a gold tie pin. His clothing was inspired by Brooks Brothers, not Ace Hardware.

The antagonism between star and director off-camera didn't show up on-screen. *Coming to America* was a feel-good movie. It certainly made the audience, not to mention Paramount's suits and stockholders, feel terrific. The film grossed $300 million worldwide and reinforced Murphy's position as the box office star of the decade.

The critics again played party pooper. The *L.A. Times* called the film "a hollow and wearying fairy tale." The *New*

York Post: "There's the danger that this abrupt change of character could backfire, leaving fans of his raunchy stuff disappointed, and those previously put off by him unwilling to give him a second chance."

Murphy must have really felt damned if you do, etc...when black activists also found fault with the film. To answer such critics, Murphy made a point of making a movie with a largely black cast in contrast to his previous, paler forays into Beverly Hills and Tibet. But black pressure groups complained that the film presented a fantasy of black culture, a pastel universe unconnected to an America divided between black and white.

Professionally, Murphy was at the top, but typically, his personal life remained in the dumps. His love life suggested a naive romantic, a man who wears his heart on his sleeve and keeps an engagement ring in his pocket as an impulse item. In November 1988, however, romance seemed to be on fast-forward when his engagement to a recording artist was announced. Murphy asked Brit Lorraine Pearson, a twenty-one-year-old member of the brother-sister pop duo, Five Star, to marry him only five days after they met.

Murphy fell in love with a photograph of Pearson she had sent him. Intrigued, he phoned her and they were soon spending three or four hours a night talking transatlantically. Murphy was surprised by his own behavior because he hates chatting on the phone and his calls usually last about five minutes.

A day after he gave her a $50,000 heart-shaped diamond ring, the marriage was off. Pearson read in the tabloids that he was also dating a Swedish cocktail waitress, Maria Bayer. In fact, the same night he popped the question to Pearson, he had gone out earlier with Bayer.

The cause of the split differed when Murphy described it. His suspicion that women were only after his money and

One big happy family at the Los Angeles premiere of *The Nutty Professor* in 1996. *From left:* Shayne, wife Nicole, Miles, Eddie, and Bria.

Fans felt Murphy deserved an Oscar for the multiple roles he played in *The Nutty Professor.* Eddie as his flatulent father (*above left*), loving mom (*above right*), foul-mouthed grandma (*below*). . .

... sleazy brother (*above left*), a Richard Simmons–like fitness guru (*above right*), and the lovelorn title character, with makeup magician Rick Baker (*below*). (Bruce McBroom)

According to former adult-film star/director Geoff Gann (*left*) a.k.a. Karen Dior (*below*), he and Murphy spent quality time in a limo in 1990. "He had beautiful manners," the lovely transvestite told the author.

fame wasn't all based on paranoia. Pearson's father, not Murphy's roving eye, had poisoned the relationship, according to the actor. Dad insisted that when the couple went out, a security contingent accompany them. "Her father fucked up the whole relationship before it could get started. She couldn't go out unless security people came along. Even to the store. I said, 'I know y'all are Five Star, but even I go to the store'" without an entourage. In retrospect, Murphy felt Pearson's ardor was career- not heart-oriented. Five Star's new album had just come out and promptly fallen into the remainder bin. Or, as Murphy lyrically described the group's predicament, "Their new album was going into the shit house. So the father probably said, 'Let's get something in the paper' and invited me out to the house. They probably sold another 20,000 records from that alone. Which weirded me out. I got used."

Fueling Murphy's fears about gold diggers, Pearson dumped the guy and kept the ring. "I thought about sending it back," his 24-hour fiancée said, "but he wants me to keep it." Murphy insisted the expensive bauble was a friendship ring. "There was a crush, but never an engagement," he said.

There was also a crash at this time, literally. During some R&R in the Bahamas, Murphy's yacht was rammed by the boat of a crazed fan. After his near-death experience with the mob at the record-store signing, is it any wonder that Murphy became more and more isolated and surrounded by a human buffer? You can't, however, put muscle in the water, and the collision almost killed the star. A blood clot lodged in his jaw muscle. A little further north, and Murphy would have gone out like his idol, Elvis, prematurely. Murphy wasn't litigious. He had been to court twice before fighting the alleged mother of his child and an alleged manager, and he didn't feel like being in the dock again. "Lawsuit? No. I'm happy to be alive. Maybe it was an omen. I was down in the Bahamas recording some songs for an album. When the boat cracked up, maybe it was somebody saying, 'Shut up!' I'm about seventy-five percent recovered, but I can't sing now. A lot of people say, 'You couldn't sing before.'"

Murphy avoided a lawsuit this time, but the same year he would find himself hauled into court and accused of the worst charge that can be hurled at a writer—plagiarism. He could buy his way out of fatherhood and an unwanted manager, but his good name couldn't be preserved with a financial fix. A judge would do that, but first the reclusive Murphy was forced once again to reveal more of himself in public than he did even in a therapy session called *Raw*.

Chapter 12

......

Coming to Court

In 1985, THE *L.A. TIMES*'S LIST of twenty films in development for Murphy ominously included a project called *King for a Day*, which the paper said was based on an idea by humorist Art Buchwald, the grand old man of syndicated newspaper columns. The *Times* also mentioned what seemed like a throwaway line about a project that was on its way to the dumpster. Paramount executives hated Buchwald's idea, and the newspaper predicted it would share *Cyrano de Boogie's* fate.

Whether or not *King for a Day* landed in the circular file, the issue would be debated in a messy, multi-million-dollar lawsuit, pitting a movie studio and its biggest star against one of the most beloved wits in America.

On November 21, 1988, Buchwald filed suit against Paramount (but not Murphy) in Los Angeles Superior Court for breach of contract. In 1983, Paramount had optioned a treatment (script outline) by Buchwald about an African prince who comes to America in search of a bride. For his efforts, the studio paid Buchwald $65,000 up front and promised him 1.5 percent of the net profits. Buchwald was truly a naïf in Hollywood, where the joke goes you can always tell who your real friends are; they're the ones who stab you in the *front*. Whoever negotiated Buchwald's contract for the treatment should have been sued for malpractice. In the

157

movie industry, net profits are derisively called "chump points." Superstars and directors like Steven Spielberg always sign on for "gross," not net. Gross participation means the lucky recipient begins earning a percentage of the movie's revenues from the first ticket sold. Net profits are another animal, a chimera. After the studio deducts the costs of the star's gross, which increases as the movie makes more and more money, plus marketing (TV ads around the clock, full-page newspaper ads), the theater owners' cut (30 to 50 percent), and bottom-line expenses like prints of the film ($3,000 per print multiplied by 3,000 theaters for a wide opening), even hit films sometimes allegedly run in the red. The studios behind *Forrest Gump, Batman,* and *Alien* had the chutzpah to claim those blockbusters failed to turn a profit when the writers demanded their cut of the net. It's a time-honored accounting trick called double-entry bookkeeping. Some critics of the industry call it legalized fraud.

After *Coming to America* grossed nearly $300 million worldwide, Buchwald wanted his 1.5 percent of the net. Paramount told him the film hadn't earned back its costs. The studio seemed to stop just short of offering him a deal on prime real estate in Florida's wetlands.

Although Murphy hadn't been listed as a party to the suit, he would become a star witness in more than one sense of the word. Also, his reputation and ethics were being tried in the court of public opinion, which opined that Murphy was a plagiarist. *Coming to America*'s credits said "story by Eddie Murphy," which meant the star had originated the idea.

That was news to Buchwald—and fighting words. The venerable columnist wasn't a litigious crank. Before filing suit, he and his attorney, Pierce O'Donnell, who would write a bestseller about the lawsuit, tried to settle pretrial for $5 million, not an overweening demand for a concept that had generated $300 million. Paramount said, we'll see you in court. The studio would come to regret its hubris.

Murphy's manager, Bob Wachs, tried to minimize his client's involvement, but no amount of damage control or spin medication could obscure the star's prominent place on the sidelines. Wachs said, "This is between Mr. Buchwald and Paramount. Eddie has nothing to do with it." Not quite. Wachs added, "I know that Eddie Murphy wrote that story."

Buchwald and his lawyer made a tactical decision not to sue for plagiarism but for simple breach of contract. Unless the plagiarist practically Xeroxes your script, such suits are nearly impossible to win. The humorist put a whimsical spin on what was pure legal strategy. "I want to sue Paramount, a big conglomerate that eats up little people like me," said the writer, whose column runs in over 500 papers and earns him millions annually. "I have nothing against Eddie Murphy."

Except for a minor matter of who was the real originator of *King For a Day/Coming to America*. Buchwald's eight-page outline was far from a photostat of *Coming to America*'s final draft. Written in 1982, when Murphy was a rising movie star wooed by everybody in L.A. who owned a typewriter or word-processor, Buchwald's synopsis revolved around the arrogant ruler of an oil-rich African kingdom. The king visits Washington, where he gets the royal treatment, until a rival foments a rebellion back home, and the monarch suddenly finds himself without a country. Soon the red carpet is rolled up, and his Washington embassy throws him out on the street. A genuine *Out of Towner*, the king gets mugged by teenagers who steal his clothes and leave him in boxers and socks. A ghetto resident befriends the king and gets him a job as a waiter. Meanwhile, the CIA plots against the dethroned king because it prefers the right-wing politics of his successor.

Paramount's legal muscle jumped on the dissimilarities between *King* and *Coming*. The film version took place in New York, not D.C. Buchwald's heroine is an Ivy League grad. In the movie, she works at her father's McDonald's franchise.

Buchwald's attorney, O'Donnell, dismissed the discrepancies. All he had to prove, he argued, was that his client provided the creative "spark" that ignited the firestorm at the box office. In a letter to the studio, O'Donnell said, "Writers like Mr. Buchwald sell their unpublished story ideas to a studio fully expecting them to be substantially modified during the creative process.... Writers also expect that they will be compensated in accordance with their contracts."

Buchwald was lucky to have O'Donnell's services. Every other entertainment attorney in the incestuous fraternity of Hollywood had turned him down, not wanting to offend its biggest star and hottest studio. O'Donnell, it turned out, had created a niche practice devoted to studio-bashing. The attorney predicted the trial would set precedent. It certainly would attract international headlines, because a supporting player was an international star. The same day he filed suit, Buchwald spoke to the *Wall Street Journal*. He described his angst, while holding on to the sense of humor that made his twice-weekly column a must-read for millions of Americans. Buchwald recounted his frustration the previous summer as *Coming to America* broke box-office records its opening weekend, enriching the studio and the star, but not the creator. The columnist at first avoided seeing the film, but curiosity overcame his irritation. "It did not show off Eddie Murphy at his best," Buchwald said, echoing most reviews. The writer added, "For legal purposes, I thought it was the greatest movie ever made." He had three hundred million reasons to back him up.

One magazine hyped the tort as the "case of the decade." *Forbes* called O'Donnell the new Perry Mason, on a par with TV's talking heads Alan Dershowitz, F. Lee Bailey, and Melvin Belli. O'Donnell modestly called himself the Red Adair of the movies, extinguishing studio greed instead of burning oil wells.

Murphy wasn't the only player in the supporting cast.

John Landis, Disney chairman Jeffrey Katzenberg, and Paramount's chief Frank Mancuso all made cameos and kept gossip columnists busy penciling in "BOLD" above the names dropped.

For those who missed the daily blow-by-blow account, O'Donnell cowrote *Fatal Subtraction: How Hollywood Really Does Business*, a pinstriped version of *You'll Never Eat Lunch in This Town Again*. O'Donnell's experiences explained why Buchwald had had so much trouble finding legal representation in the first place. When the attorney subpoenaed Katzenberg, former head of Paramount during *Coming to America*'s inception and even bigger in 1988 as Disney's No. 2, an attorney for Disney urged O'Donnell to rescind the subpoena—or else. "In the years ahead, in your cases, you're going to need expert witnesses, friends around this town. Don't count on getting them," the Disney lawyer warned him.

The pretrial depositions, by law available to the public, made dishier reading than anything Jackie Collins ever mythologized about the movie industry. The choking and genital torture that occurred between Murphy and director Landis only came to light during the deposition. Ditto Murphy's answering machine message with his girlfriend's lament.

Details of the deposition were an embarrassment of riches for journalists and plain old embarrassment for major industry players. Very few of them came out untarnished after O'Donnell chewed them up during the deposition process. Landis and his wife's alleged use of the "N" word surfaced. Murphy noted that Landis had suffered "four flops in a row" before the star took pity on him and turned his career around with *Coming to America*. Jeffrey Katzenberg looked like a fool or a liar when he claimed Murphy had not been a star in 1983 when Buchwald wrote *King For a Day* as a vehicle for him. This was the same year *Trading Places* and *48 HRS.* ranked No. 4 and 5 at the box office.

Other tidbits from the depositions revealed a studio desperate to keep its goose happily laying golden eggs. No request was too big or too petty to be denied. O'Donnell gleefully interrogated Paramount execs who admitted that the studio paid the year-round salaries of fifty people solely devoted to the care and feeding of Murphy's ego. Employees of his TV and film production companies also got their paychecks from Paramount. When a Murphy film went into production, $600,000 was spent for even more retainers, half a dozen relatives, cronies, a personal valet and trainer, twenty-four-hour limo service, and a Teamster for his out-sized motor home. No item was too small for the plaintiff, including Murphy's $235.33 tab at McDonald's. The star must have needed his motor home to transport over $200 worth of Big Macs and fries, but can a Winnebago squeeze past the drive-in window?

It also came out that the studio had installed a king-sized bed in his office on the lot. A personal note: In 1988, I interviewed Arsenio Hall in the Eddie Murphy building at Paramount. The genial Hall suggested we do the interview in Eddie's office. Sure enough, most of the floor space was taken up by the bed. There was only one chair, and Hall and I ended up sitting on the bed while we talked.

The reclusive Murphy claimed having his personal quirks and perks logged into the public record didn't distress him, but the racial spin he put on the intrusion suggested irritation, if not outrage. "I think they wanted to open my whole life anyway. I was this odd nigger they didn't know anything about, so let's open up the nigger's books and see what he makes. I know that's what it was, so I didn't trip on it."

An unnamed executive at Paramount told O'Donnell that Murphy would be "great" during his deposition. The entertainer lived up to his billing, appearing in O'Donnell's conference room with an unbuttoned shirt that exposed chest hair and gold jewelry. Murphy's first words for the stenographer were, "Dah-*DAH!*"

His sartorial tastes and body hair weren't the only things exposed in O'Donnell's Century City law office. The superstar came across as a disengaged dilettante with the attention span of a puppy. Former Paramount VP David Kirkpatrick, whose job title detractors said was "executive in charge of Eddie Murphy," described story meetings with the star as "M.E.G.O." for "my eyes glaze over." Kirkpatrick, now at squeaky clean Disney, which had no use for the foul-mouthed star of *Raw*, came clean. Murphy never read scripts, made artistic decisions, or even paid attention during business meetings. Wachs, per Fitzpatrick, who was there, called all the shots. Fitzpatrick didn't care if he burned his bridge to Hollywood's blue chip commodity. He testified that during a screening of *Coming to America*, then-Paramount President Jeffrey Katzenberg whispered, "I can't believe this? Who are they kidding? That's *King for a Day!*"

Paramount felt compelled to defend its in-house prince, since his name was on the story credit. To settle Buchwald's suit would also be to call their biggest star a plagiarist. The studio claimed Murphy had never even heard of the country's most famous humorist.

In his deposition, Wachs valiantly tried to earn his ten percent. (Actually, when the two men split, in 1991, it would be revealed that his cut was 50 percent of Murphy's income!) The manager kvelled that his client knew the lyrics of every TV show theme. Murphy could also recite dialogue from his favorite Saturday morning cartoons ad infinitum. More to the point, Wachs said both he and his client hated *King For a Day* —this after Murphy said he had never even seen Buchwald's treatment. Wachs said he advised against the project because Buchwald's king was no prince. "I didn't feel it was advantageous to Eddie's career to play a spoiled-rotten despot who treats his subjects badly."

After three years of testimony the *National Enquirer*
would have spiked as too unbelievable, Judge Harvey
Schneider found for the plaintiff. For Buchwald, the victory
was Pyrrhic but the process fun. Judge Schneider called
Paramount's Alice in Wonderland bookkeeping "unconscion-
able," but awarded its victim only $150,000 of the $5 million
he had sought. Since legal costs had soared to $2.5 million,
no one, as usual, made money except the lawyers. Buchwald
remained unremunerated for an idea that enriched everyone
else. The columnist was still in the red—the same color as the
faces of the suits exposed during the deposition and the trial.
On the plus side, Buchwald got fodder for the maw of his
syndicated column. His attorney got a best-seller that earned
him millions and comparisons to Alan Dershowitz. At last
report, O'Donnell was writing a novel á la John Grisham,
based on his practice. The deal he negotiates with the studio
for movie rights might make another novel in itself. Buchwald probably won't write the treatment.

Chapter 13

......

"For Your Oscar Obliteration..."

In 1983, Eddie Murphy made his first appearance at the Oscars. During his presentation speech, he gently chided Academy voters and urged them to become more color-conscious. "My dream is still the same. I want African-Americans to be able to win Oscars, to do films about our people when we want to, to get films made and to do what we want as artists. All we want is to be accepted as equals," he said. Overflowing with limousine liberals, the audience cheered.

Five years later—a year after *Raw* enraged minority groups—Murphy was back on stage, acting out again. But instead of the mere millions angered by the concert film, Murphy managed to discomfit an audience of one billion at the 60th Academy Awards.

Before he presented the Oscar for best picture on April 11, 1988, Murphy ignored the TelePrompter and did a little editorializing. Maybe it was Spike Lee calling him an Uncle Tom or the *L.A. Weekly* labeling him Hollywood's favorite nigger. But Murphy decided to condemn the academy for honoring only three blacks with Oscars during the organization's sixty-year existence. Murphy added that he almost stiffed the ceremony because he was so angry about the underrepresenation of blacks at Oscar time. "They haven't recognized black people in motion pictures because only three have won Oscars in over sixty years. At that rate, we ain't due 'til 2004." His crystal ball turned out to be clouded, or maybe he managed to tweak the white liberal guilt of academy voters. Only a year after his diatribe, Denzel Washington would take home a best-supporting-actor statuette for *Glory,* and the following year, Whoopi Goldberg would win for her supporting role in *Ghost,* the first black female honoree since 1939!

Backstage, the event's organizers were ready to barbecue the comedian. The show's producer, Samuel Goldwyn Jr., one of the friendliest honchos in Hollywood, turned apoplectic, screaming at Murphy, "How dare you use my show to voice your personal grievances!" Murphy told him not to worry; he'd never show up at the Oscars again. Goldwyn's complaint was disingenuous. Everyone from Brando's cigar-store Indian Vegas showgirl Sacheen Littlefeather, to the Palestine Liberation Organization's publicist, Vanessa Redgrave, has used Oscar's McDonald's-sized audience to air their angry laundry. Plus, Murphy's criticism was hardly a personal pet peeve.

Editorialists lined up behind Goldwyn. *Vanity Fair* called Murphy's outburst "graceless and rambling." Even white liberals said the Oscar show was the wrong place to tackle 300 years of discrimination.

The incident even entered urban legend—or whatever it is the tabloids create. The *National Enquirer* reported that Cher had also joined the cheerless leaders backstage. "I'm outraged. You put a damper on the whole night." Cher was not outraged, but she was horrified when she read of her alleged outburst, which she felt made her sound racist. "What Eddie said is not an idea that I think bad," she said while announcing a $15 million lawsuit against the tab she referred to as the "toilet paper magazine." The story—surprise!—was a fabrication. Amid the distractions of the gala, Cher said she hadn't even heard Murphy's speech. Murphy took Cher's word over the *Enquirer*'s. There were obviously no hard feelings because later that year, he took the actress's white-elephant mansion in Beverly Hills's Benedict Canyon off her hands for $6.5 million.

The aftermath of the incident, however, proved that Murphy wasn't simply experiencing a manic episode with one billion people serving as therapist. While his speech enraged Goldwyn, it seemed to have guilt-tripped and galvanized studio greenlighters. One week after the Oscar blowup, the *New York Times* reported that the film industry was suddenly awash with new projects on the '60s Civil Rights movement, including *Mississippi Burning, The Stick Wife,* and *The Heart of Dixie.* Industry guilt turned out to be short-lived. Only *Mississippi Burning* made it to the screen.

The year 1988 was not one for the Murphy scrapbook. Encouraged by Buchwald's success, two loonies came out of the woodwork and sued the star. One claimed to be a Nigerian prince. His Highness Johnny Osseni-Bello alleged Murphy had stolen his life story, even though Nigeria is a dictatorship, not a monarchy. Shelby M. Gregory, who claimed he had written Osseni-Bello's biography, also filed suit for $10 million. Neither case came anywhere near a courtroom.

To add to the public embarrassment of the Buchwald suit, Murphy's private life was not prospering. The impulsive romantic once again announced his engagement to yet another coed, Musanna Overra, an eighteen-year-old beauty, who attended Howard University. A wedding band never joined the engagement ring on her hand. Overra may have been scared off by seeing photos of her "fiancé" squiring Whitney Houston and *A Different World*'s Jasmine Guy at concerts and clubs.

Chapter 14

......

Dog Days, Harlem Nights

IF 1988 WAS DIFFICULT FOR MURPHY, 1989 would be a night-mare as he fought a far more serious allegation in court and suffered his first box-office disappointment.

Way back in 1983, when he was at the top of his game, he had premonitions of his mortality in terms of box office viability. His position as king of the till was ephemeral; a fall could be fatal. "I'm hot right now, but nobody stays hot, because generations keep changing," said the star of the No. 4 and 5 films that year. Also in 1983, a cheeky British journalist asked Murphy how he would cope with a flop. A former attorney, Wachs interrupted with a lawyerly answer: "If one considers it inevitable to do a bad movie, then it's our job to push back the inevitable as far as possible." Wachs and company accomplished this Sisyphean task for most of the decade.

The "inevitable" turned out to be *Harlem Nights*, which was released in 1989. To call the period comedy a vanity production doesn't begin to encompass Murphy's octopus-like involvement, with a tentacle in every pie. Murphy not only starred as a Harlem nightclub owner during the Depression, he also wrote the original story and screenplay, execu-tive-produced and, most ominously, directed. His screen credits totaled six. During the opening crawl, his name flashed so frequently on screen, the audience at the press preview I attended giggled. Murphy wore so many hats that crew members started calling him Hedda Hopper—behind his back, of course. A critic said he did everything but cater the food.

Murphy insisted it was logistics, not vanity, that had him in front of and behind the camera and everywhere else on the set. "I'm stuck in this weird position. Directors have big egos, and really big directors have huge egos," Murphy said, failing to mention movie stars' Winnebago-sized sense of entitlement. "Most directors, when they become stars, don't want to work with big, big actors. They work with no-name actors or character actors so they can be in control. Also, when it's time to put a project together and I want to get a big director and get moving fast, these directors aren't available for three years. Only *schleppers* are available. Rather than get a half-assed job, I figured I might as well do it myself."

Later, Murphy would admit that maybe a little ego had contributed to his decision. That and peer pressure, although he really had no equals at the box office before *Harlem Nights* spoiled a perfect track record. "All my peers were directing. Keenen [Ivory Wayans], Robert Townsend, Spike Lee. I was like, 'Shit, I'm the big cat on the block; let me see what it's like to direct.' So I just did it. I didn't dig it."

In 1989, Murphy's position at Paramount was, well, paramount. The *Ladies' Home Journal* said, "He could release home movies of his trips to the dry cleaner's and people would probably line up to see them." Jerry Bruckheimer, coproducer of both *Beverly Hills Cop* films, called the star a cynosure. "He's such a wanna-see guy—you wanna see what the hell he does next. If he was available, there'd be a wild melee of people trying to get to his trailer, their pockets full of money." Instead, Paramount would play solo bagman. There were many celebrity members of the Eddie Murphy fan club. *Raw* had turbocharged director Robert Townsend's career, and he was suitably grateful. "Comedy is, after all, timing. And with his career, Eddie's timing has been solid gold."

In less than a decade, his films had earned the studio $1 billion, Spielberg territory. Studio executives didn't object to Murphy's directing; nor did they have a problem with his desire to cast a bunch of marquee-challenged comics like Redd Foxx and Richard Pryor in supporting roles, not to mention nonprofessionals, like singer Della Reese. His title of executive producer was just a name on a contract. But the suits blanched when they read Eddie's first stab at screenwriting.

Showing rare courage, then-Paramount Chairman Frank Mancuso begged Murphy not to make *Harlem Nights*. This proved to be a big mistake. When word got out that Mancuso had angered Murphy and the superstar was thinking of decamping to a friendlier backlot, Mancuso got the ax. The rest of the Paramount board members and nervous stockholders knew that chairmen were a dime a dozen; throw a dart into the dining area of Morton's and you're sure to hit one. A guaranteed blockbuster manufacturer like Murphy, on the other hand, came down the assembly line only once every decade or two.

A movie star with clout can be a scary thing. After an actor enjoys just one huge hit, the white-hot star supernovas and become bankable. That means the actor can get just about any project off the ground. Hey, Julia, you want to do a musical based on the erotic lesbian diaries of Anaïs Nin? Hey, go for it, kid. Love ya, and see you at Le Mondrian. Oh, Mel, you want to hide that gorgeous mug under ten layers of latex scar tissue...*and* direct the thing? Here's a blank check. Oh, and the subplot deals with pedophilia? No sweat. Not surprisingly, these star-generated vehicles often crash and burn. A good actor is not necessarily a good script reader; that's what development executives get paid for. One wonders how deeply the D-boys at Columbia gulped when Schwarzenegger showed them the script for *Last Action Hero* with its homages to *The Seventh Seal* and Olivier's *Hamlet*.

When a star whose only talent is acting decides he is a filmmaker, it's more often than not a recipe for disaster. The list of stars who think their box office performance has earned them the mantle of auteur is long and full of embarrassments. Bruce Willis came up with a storyline based on his experience with a wind called the Hudson Hawk that whips through Manhattan's concrete canyons. The film has become a touchstone for comedians when they want a quick reference for the quintessential flop, replacing *Howard the Duck* or *Heaven's Gate*. Goldie Hawn imperiously recut *Swing Shift* and changed it from a feminist buddy film to a romance flick emphasizing the role of her new boyfriend, Kurt Russell. Instead of Thelma and Louise fighting World War II on the home front, *Swing Shift* turned into a wan imitation of *The Way We Were* without the great theme song.

To be fair, stars who suddenly think they're Scorsese after doing blockbuster box office don't always create disasters. Mel Gibson's *Man Without a Face* didn't do *Lethal Weapon* business, but his directorial debut received respectable notices. And his follow-up about a 13th century Scot in a skirt cleaned up at the Oscars. Similarly, prerelease, *Dances With Wolves* was widely rumored to be self-indulgent hokum with Orion going along with Kevin Costner in the hope that his next film for the studio might be a sequel like *Robin Hood: Another Part of the Forest*. Clint Eastwood had been considered a journeyman director and fading box office draw until *Unforgiven* put him in the same pantheon as Anthony Mann and Howard Hawks. And even Whoopi Goldberg earned the respect of Disney executives after *Sister Act* became a hit. During filming, however, the commandants at Mauschwitz gave her so much grief when she demanded script changes that the actress showed up on the set wearing a T-shirt that read "Nigger-teer."

None of these stars could match Murphy's record of seven monster hits in a row, not to mention a billion-dollar

balance sheet. In 1989 Murphy was box office emperor;
Mancuso, a mere courtier who had been dismissed by impe-
rial fiat—and a nervous board of directors.

After Mancuso left Paramount, Brandon Tartikoff,
schmoozer to the stars, was hired for the sole purpose, it was
rumored, to patch things up with Murphy, using their mutual
involvement on *Saturday Night Live* as a fond memory to
counteract the present ill will. Tartikoff had his work cut out
for him.

Murphy practically owned Paramount, and he treated
the studio bosses like employees. The star and his hired
friends would race around the backlot in golf carts, using the
studio as a frathouse. His companions always let him win, as
they did with chess. While he wasn't rude to the execs, he
displayed a playful casualness that no one else would have
dared to exhibit in front of such powerful men. Pulling up in
a customized golf cart with a faux Rolls Royce hood, Murphy
shouted at Mancuso and *his* entourage, "Hello, suits!" A
reporter said the executives "chuckled. They have to. By 1989,
Eddie has made the snowcapped mountain top that is Paramount $1 billion. One billion buys a lot of chuckles." It can
even buy off their reluctance to hire a B-list director for an
A-list star's film (Landis). Or hire an A-list star whose directorial ranking doesn't even make the alphabet.

As an actor, Murphy could be as temperamental as an
opera diva. As director, he intuitively realized that part of his
job description included nurturing the talent. During on-the-
set interviews for *Harlem Nights*, TV cameras recorded a soft-
spoken father figure, not the usual tough-talking superstar.
The cast thrived under Murphy's touchy-feely direction—
except for one who sued him, but that's a story for later.

Redd Foxx, delighted to be employed again, said, "He's
on top of the world, and he's doing a hell of a job. He sure
knows how to handle people with sensitivity. He'll come over

to your side and give private direction—he never embarrasses anyone."

Another career rescuee, Richard Pryor, loved working on the production, which was more like group therapy. "It's turning out to be more pleasant than I expected. He's wise enough to listen to people. I see him be very patient with his actors. It's not a lark to him. He's really serious." Murphy didn't use John Landis as his role model for interpersonal relationships. Lucky for the actors Murphy was so nurturing; some of them needed a lot of nurture. Two were seriously ill. Shooting slowed while the director played doctor for infirm stars. Redd Foxx suffered from heart disease, which would eventually kill the hard-living-drinking-smoking comedian. Pryor's multiple sclerosis diminished his usual hypertensive screen presence.

Pryor appreciated his director's compassion and commended him for repeating the hiring practices of *Coming to America,* using an all-black cast. "You walk around here and look at the people—have you ever in your life seen this many black people on a movie set? I haven't."

Some people didn't like what they saw on screen, and it wasn't a nervous studio chief worrying about how an all-black movie would play in all-white suburbs. Forty black actors in New York signed a petition condemning Murphy for shooting *Harlem Nights* on a soundstage in Hollywood instead of on location in Harlem; the actors' real beef was that because of the location, they didn't get hired. Their complaints were unrealistic. And Murphy wasn't ignoring his roots—not that he had any in Harlem—by choosing the safety and convenience of the studio on Melrose Avenue in Hollywood. Shooting in the ghetto would have been a nightmare of crowd control and security, plus, present-day Harlem doesn't look like the Depression era 'hood.

In late 1989, *Harlem Nights* enjoyed a huge first weekend,

proving that Eddie Murphy could still open a movie. But cranky reviews and worse word of mouth saw the second week's audience fall off by half, a disastrous statistic for a movie with blockbuster aspirations, since the only way a movie can top $100 million is by teenagers returning to theaters over and over again.

The *L.A. Times* said, "Like many superstars, Eddie Murphy may have gotten so tangled up in the myths and myopia of high-power movie making that he can't get back to the gritty, pungent, kick in the throat awareness earlier audiences loved." By now, *Raw* seemed cutting-edge rather than off-putting. *Newsweek* headlined its review, "Eddie Murphy's Sorry Night." *Time,* which a year later would refer to him in the past tense as though he were dead, called the film "self-destructively primitive, offering a depressing answer to the question, 'Will success spoil Eddie Murphy?'" *GQ* joked that *Harlem Nights* was "conceived, written, directed, and catered by Murphy." Referring to all his hats, the magazine added, "The director failed to direct his actors, the writer fed them idiotic lines, and the star got away with murder."

The worst "review" came from industry analyst Mark Manson, who said that a Murphy movie "may be a guarantee of revenue, but it is not a guarantee of profit." *Harlem Nights* earned only $33 million in rentals. Since it cost $50 million, you don't need to be a CPA to calculate the loss to the studio, although Paramount's accountants were probably having coronaries as the trades trumpeted the film's failure every week until it fell off the box office list. In retrospect, Mancuso seemed sane rather than insubordinate to rein in Paramount's billion dollar man.

To his credit, Murphy took the blame, especially for donning the writer's hat. "The reaction to *Harlem Nights* was like having a mortar shell go off in your front yard. I had never had a flop picture before. And all of a sudden there was a flop. It was, like, 'Oh, shit.' The script was shitty. I wrote it in two weeks. And it shows. But I had to direct to see if I was going to dig directing." The failure of *Harlem Nights* was expensive for Paramount, but instructive for the star, who never sat in the director's chair again.

Once again, the crazies came out of the woodwork and into court. Art Buchwald's success inspired others. In 1990, Hafiz Farid of Newark, New Jersey, filed a $100 million suit claiming Murphy had plagiarized his idea, as did Micheale Greene of Hempstead, Louisiana, who wanted $35 million. The litigation disproved conventional wisdom that success has a thousand fathers while failure is an orphan.

Amid the lawsuits and grim signs of professional death, Murphy fell in love—again. He was clearly smitten with a twenty-one-year-old model, Jacqueline Davis, whom he picked up at her hotel six nights in a row. Davis had been a switchboard operator at the St. Moritz in Beverly Hills, but by the time she and Murphy hooked up, she had been promoted to resident of the expensive hotel. Murphy's nightly courtship miffed other hotel guests, since he showed up with flowers and entourage. Louisa Moritz, the hotel's owner, said, "Yes, there are people in the lobby late at night. We got a couple of complaints about noise." White people freaking out over a large contingent of blacks in a posh hotel sounds like a routine in Murphy's act.

The year 1989 was not Eddie Murphy's favorite. Plaintiffs crying plagiarism weren't the only people hauling Murphy into court. Friends had nicknamed the star "Money." His busy attorneys must have fondly called him "Billable Hours." On May 8 of Eddie's least favorite year, actress Michael Michele sued the star for $75 million in New York Federal Court, alleging sexual harassment and "lascivious interference with an actress's contract." Michele also sued Paramount for breach of contract. In her petition, Michele said that his "attempt to attain a personal, sexual relationship" led to her ouster from the cast of *Harlem Nights*. "When it became clear to the defendant that plaintiff would not accede to his sexual demands, Murphy had plaintiff discharged from *Harlem Nights* and her services terminated immediately. Murphy has defamed, slandered, and deprecated plaintiff in an effort to rationalize his unwarranted termination of her services in favor of another actress," Michele's petition said. She also claimed Murphy had prevented her participation in a TV pilot based on *Coming to America*.

The gorgeous twenty-two-year-old first caught Murphy's eye during auditions for *Coming to America*, and he cast her as his jilted African bride. Their relationship must have been cordial, since she was promoted to leading lady in *Harlem Nights*.

The first day on the set, Michele said Murphy treated her like a princess. A day later, he was a tyrant. "I was sitting reading my script," Michele said. "Eddie taps me on my shoulder and says, 'Bravo. You deserve an award for not looking at me, Michele. Good. Real good.' I wasn't being unfriendly. I admired him.

"But then during rehearsal, he yells, 'Speak up! Speak up! I can't hear you!' angrily." At the next rehearsal, Murphy "asked me out." When he then tried to "fondle and caress" her, "I said no. He stormed off." Michele later heard from co-workers that Murphy was boasting on the set that he had fired her. According to *People* magazine, Paramount confirmed Murphy's braggadocio.

Murphy insisted that nothing untoward had taken place. His explanation, however, suggested that, like Talleyrand's description of treason, sexual harassment is merely a matter of dates. A reporter had the temerity to ask the superstar if he had "ever come on to this woman at all?" Murphy said, "No. If I were trying to fuck her, I would do it *before* I gave her a job. As for her claim that I was touching her—realistically speaking, if you're gonna be a sleaze and try to fuck somebody, you try to fuck 'em before you give 'em the part. And second, I don't have to give a woman a part in a movie to fuck her. I mean, she painted a picture like my name was Murray and I was five foot three with a big bald spot and cigar, going, 'You want the part? Then open your legs!'"

Michele's accusation that Murphy got touchy-feely with her particularly grated. "The only thing that bothered me is that in her lawsuit, she says I tried to touch her, like I was a *pervert*. I *never* tried to touch this woman. We had, like, four conversations, each time with up to sixty people around us on a soundstage."

Michele's allegations, Murphy added, were "absurd and totally false. My integrity and professional behavior are being attacked." Murphy considered it a frivolous lawsuit, just another parasite trying to make some money off of "Money." "It's just a typical somebody-taking-a-shot-at-me kind of thing. I get sued a lot by people who just take shots," the actor said with understatement. He estimated that this feeding frenzy of litigation had cost him millions.

Manager Wachs responded to Michele's charges with the threat of a countersuit. "Women throw themselves at him. Why would he need to do this? Eddie felt her attitude was antagonistic. She did not fit into this movie's healthy environment."

Michele had an unusual defender in O. J. Simpson, who had starred with her on his cable sitcom, *1st & Ten*. O. J. expressed surprise that anyone would find the amiable actress antagonistic. He said, "She was a very pleasant young lady. A nice girl."

Murphy's firing of Michele had nothing to do with the anger of a jilted suitor. He simply wanted a bigger name on the marquee, so he fired the actress and hired *A Different World*'s Jasmine Guy. His explanation raised eyebrows among people who know how the industry works. Firing Michele after shooting began was an expensive decision; all her scenes would have to be reshot with Guy. As for Michele's name lacking marquee value, he had to have known this before he hired her. A more common euphemism for "get out of my face and off the set" is "creative differences," a time-honored way to paper over a sheaf of troubles between two principals on a movie set.

A native of the heartland, Indiana, and daughter of a furniture tycoon, Michele didn't fear being blacklisted as a troublemaker. "Everyone thinks I should allow this to happen because it's Eddie Murphy. But if keeping a job means lowering yourself to the casting couch, then we're in a bad place. And if having integrity, ethics, and morals means never being able to work in the entertainment industry, then maybe I did choose the wrong profession." Sadly, Michael was prophetic about her career prospects, although it's more likely that her disappearance from the scene had more to do with endemic unemployment among black actresses than any infamy about suing Eddie Murphy.

With his notorious short attention span, Murphy loathed depositions which were more like police interrogations. And he got antsy sitting around a courtroom. When you're worth $80 million or $200 million (Murphy and *Forbes*'s figures, respectively), you don't have to be bored. By 1992, Murphy's blue-chip attorneys had settled all the lawsuits without troubling their client with pesky grilling by plaintiffs' counsel.

Another casualty of *Harlem Nights*, besides ending Murphy's perfect track record of blockbusters, was his friendship with Richard Pryor. The two men had been so close in 1983 they appeared together on the cover of *People* magazine and did a joint interview inside, something stars of Murphy's magnitude rarely do. Asked about rumors that his idol had dumped his disciple, Murphy refused to explain why but substantiated the break. "Trust me, the brother doesn't like me. It's weird to find out that your idol hates you." Their estrangement deeply hurt Murphy, who not only considered the older man his idol but mentor as well. Cosby gave him grief; Pryor provided inspiration. No use crying over spilled milk, but Murphy decided that the glass was half full, not half empty. "If I dropped dead tomorrow, at least I'd know I finished what I set out to do. He's [Pryor] the reason I'm Eddie Murphy."

Pryor remained mum on why the platonic love affair had ended, but the failure of *Harlem Nights* had to have hurt the waning star, who must have felt appearing in a surefire thing like an Eddie Murphy movie would have resuscitated his career.

Harlem Nights had been an artistic departure for Murphy. His patented street punk had been traded in for a suave, romantic leading man. Instead of baseball cap and Mumford Phys Ed. T-shirts, he became a fashion plate in vintage double-breasted suits and silk ties. The public hated this new but unimproved persona. The audience's rejection must have rattled Murphy. He had stretched, and the box office had contracted. His next project would take him out of the boudoir and return to the friendlier milieu of mean streets. Carnivorous fans and critics would stop chewing up the man and stampede back to theaters, if only Murphy fed them what they wanted.

Or would they?

Chapter 15

......

Retreading Water

To CALL *ANOTHER 48 HRS.* paint-by-numbers filmmaking is to denigrate the art form. The sequel to Murphy's film debut had everything that made the original a sleeper hit—car crashes, verbal and knuckle sparring between buddy cops, a smart-alecky Murphy beating up white people, psychopaths galore—everything but *48 HRS.*'s wit and coherent storyline.

In Monday-morning-quarterback mode, Murphy conceded that caution, not creativity, had been the motivating force behind returning to over-fished waters.

"*Another 48 HRS.* was reactive. I got fucked up on *Harlem Nights*, so it was, like, 'Okay, let's do something that's a sure hit. Is *Cop III* ready?'" It wasn't. "*Coming to America Again?* The idea [for *Another 48 HRS.*] was contrived and we threw it together, and they wrote these big checks out and we did it."

A reporter who interviewed the star after he had endured four flops in a row had the chutzpah to ask why he made movies that were "obviously bad."

Ego, not the devil, made him do it, said the star, who was feeling introspective rather than persecuted by the press—for the moment. "My popularity after *Beverly Hills Cop*—all that 'He's-so-hot' shit—everything was going out of control. Everything came too easy....And when the laughs came too easy, you start doing things like walking through movies. You

180

get too comfortable. You start getting out of control. You start star tripping. You argue. You get the big head. You wear leather suits and a glove with a ring on the outside." And you make a concert film that irritates every other minority group in the country.

For once, Murphy was being too hard on himself. Although the critics reviled both *Harlem Nights* and *Another 48 HRS.*, his failure was one of perception. Because the reviews treated Murphy as though he had sold West Point to the Iraqis, the movies somehow became linked in the public perception with commercial failure. The stats showed that while Murphy got no respect from reviewers, his grosses were still respectable, if not in the same stratosphere as previous films'. The bottom line remained fine. And it was the only feedback that Paramount cared about.

His alleged slide was illusory. *Harlem Nights* grossed $60 million in the U.S. *Another 48 HRS.*, because of its tedious rehashing of vintage Murphy, was perceived as a bigger flop than *Harlem Nights*, but in fact earned a whopping $141 million worldwide. *Time* magazine said, "Even when his or her ticket sales are robust, a star can be perceived to be in a slump. Eddie Murphy's 'disappointing' *Another 48 HRS.* did better than *Harlem Nights*. But both films were badmouthed because they were costly pictures that had a hard time breaking even."

Murphy might have consoled himself with the fact that he received $12 million for *Another 48 HRS.*, the high end of the superstar pay scale in the early nineties. But his eye wasn't on the bottom line; it was on the screen and on sulfurous editorials proclaiming that the king was dead. In 1990, *Time* magazine made a creepy crack that sounded like a genuine obituary. "A moment's silence, please, for the late, great Eddie Murphy." The usually benign columnist Liz Smith didn't hesitate to kick a superstar when he was down: "Eddie began to mistake a billion dollar gross for a billion dollars worth of brilliance and rode a billion dollar ego into critical oblivion."

Murphy began to suffer from self-image problems that had nothing to do with bad press or perceived box office death. A self-described health freak who didn't touch alcohol or drugs, except for an occasional toke of marijuana, Murphy began to self-medicate with a different kind of drug, food. He became a compulsive overeater. And a rarity, since only one percent of victims of eating disorders are men. A friend said, "Eddie loves to eat. He is a maniac for really good food."

Murphy's description of his behavior sounds like out-takes from a French film, *La Grande Bouffe*, about men who gather in a mansion and decide to stuff themselves to death. Murphy didn't die, but he wanted to when he saw the blimp he had become magnified by the giant movie screen.

"After *Harlem Nights* I was so depressed that the movie was a flop I used to sit around and eat. I was 185 pounds at one time. I'm 5 foot 10 and weigh 170 pounds now. I used to just wake up, go, and eat lunch, come back home and sit down and watch videos and eat dinner, go out, go to dinner. All we did was eat every day, all day. By the time I got to *Another 48 HRS.*, I was a piece of shit.

"I had made *Another 48 HRS.*, and I was depressed at how I looked in that film. I let myself get fat. There's nothing like going into a movie theater and looking up on a screen and you're a fat guy in a bad movie. And then an article I read in *Time* magazine said I was on the fast lane to ex-stardom. That really went to the bone more than being fat."

Only five years before *Time* published his obituary, a poll conducted by several movie studios said that Murphy was the most popular performer in the country, citing his tremendous "crossover appeal," a euphemism that meant white folks patronized his movies. A similar poll in 1990 attributed the relative failures of *Harlem Nights* and *Another 48 HRS.* to the fact that whites had jumped off the Murphy juggernaut. The *L.A. Times* said flat out white people no longer liked Murphy.

Often his own worst critic, Murphy didn't play the race card. The failure of his films, he felt, had nothing to do with the color of his skin. He dismissed studio polls that said otherwise.

The actor handicapped his downturn: "What happened was a lot of the studio heads got wrapped up with charts and graphs and demographics and who is responding to what. And on *Harlem Nights* and *Another 48 HRS.*, the test results came back that white people didn't turn out like they had before, which is bull, because nobody goes to see an Eddie Murphy like, 'Oh, Eddie Murphy, let's go see him, he's a funny black man.' No, you go see Eddie Murphy because he's funny. Race has nothing to do with it. The reasons those movies didn't do well was they weren't as good, plain and simple."

Studio execs ignored their own polls. Word got out that Eddie wasn't happy at Paramount. Once again, money was obsessing "Money." While his $12 million paycheck for *Another 48 HRS.* put him near the top of the superstar pay scale, the summit was occupied by others like Schwarzenegger and Stallone, although neither had topped Murphy's box office record. Stallone's more muscular payday must have particularly irked Murphy, since the *Rocky* star had had a rocky career with many more misses than hits. The *Wall Street Journal* described the star as "mighty steamed at reports that Stallone and Schwarzenegger are commanding up to $20 million. And he is upset that many of what he considers Hollywood's best acting roles and hottest scripts aren't being offered to him or developed for him by Paramount." The *Journal* also said that Murphy's discontent at his home base had Disney and other studios "circling like buzzards" around a piece of very live meat. "Regardless of reviews, virtually every other studio in Hollywood would like to sign Mr. Murphy up," the paper said. In fact, the Magic

Kingdom seemed to be living in fantasy land. Disney had ten scripts in active development for Murphy, even though the star had an exclusive contract with Paramount at the time— wish fulfillment on a corporate scale.

Murphy would make one more film for Paramount before being railroaded into Duckau. Neither studio managed to find the right vehicle for him at this time however.

The lackluster reception of *Harlem Nights* showed that fans didn't want their Eddie debonair; reaction to *Another 48 HRS.* was even scarier. Moviegoers rejected his tried-and-blue persona as a street-wise operator. He seemed damned when he stretched and damned when he played it straight. Murphy was so nonplussed by both films' blah box office that he stayed away from the screen for two years, but he kept busy doing other things, like wielding the ax.

What does a rudderless superstar do when his ships keep sinking? Trying a new screen character obviously wasn't the solution. It was time for a drastic makeover, and major house-cleaning, a painful task considering Murphy's retinue of handlers and hangers-on, relatives and buddies from high school on the payroll.

The fish stinks from the head, as the aphorism goes, and Murphy in March 1991 decided to fix things by going straight to the top. He fired Bob Wachs, his comanager since 1980. (Richie Tienken, his other manager and co-owner with Wachs of The Comic Strip—Murphy's first big venue—had been dismissed in 1987. Interestingly, although Tienken had played good cop to the irascible Wachs's bad cop, it was the good cop who got dumped first.)

After eleven long years of suffocating devotion, Wachs's dismissal was most notable for its terseness. In a press release, Murphy expressed "appreciation" and thanked his manager "for years of work and effort" on his behalf, but decided "it is time to move forward in a different direction."

There were two obvious reasons Wachs got the boot—

Harlem and *HRS*. But other factors remained unknown outside Murphy Inc., until their split revealed some mighty dirty dry cleaning. The two film embarrassments were only the part of the iceberg visible above submerged resentments.

Wachs had rubbed people the wrong way for years. Eventually, he rubbed his only client the same way. The *New York Times* called him "contentious." Paramount executives felt he was an obstructionist buffer between them and the pit called "Money." Wachs rejected scripts without informing his client, and most of the time that was a blessing when oddities like *Big Baby Boogie* crossed Wachs's desk without making it to Murphy's. The buck stopped at Wachs's desk, but occasionally it should have been passed on to his employer. Such high-handedness inevitably led to rejecting the gold mixed in with the dross. Murphy was incensed when he learned Paramount had offered *Ghost* to the star only to have it intercepted and deep-sixed by Wachs. *The Golden Child* was another project Murphy had to find himself; neither Wachs nor the studio thought of casting him in the $80 million hit.

Rolling Stone said Wachs had turned into Colonel Parker, Elvis's meddling manager. The analogy was more apt than the magazine realized. In 1993, the *Wall Street Journal* provided a shocking glimpse of how badly Murphy had been used by his management team—ripped off would be a more accurate term. Just like Colonel Parker, who owned fifty percent of Elvis for life, Wachs and Tienken owned fifty percent of Eddie Murphy Productions, split evenly between them. Adding insult to injury, each of them also collected a five-percent management fee. Eddie's managers earned ten percent more than Eddie, according to the *Journal*! Murphy had once claimed he never got the "plantation nigger treatment" in Hollywood, but his managers' cut sounded like indentured servitude.

Other indignities were less costly but irritating. Wachs fancied himself a development executive and screenwriter. In

1989, he and Murphy's new comanager, Mark Lipsky, were actively developing their idea about two old con men who find the fountain of youth and re-experience life as young men. As the Buchwald deposition showed, Murphy hated reading scripts, but he must have forced himself to read *Fountain of Youth* because Wachs's big baby never made it to the screen.

The manager tried to sweeten the relationship with little gifts which couldn't make up for the fact that Murphy was on the wrong end of a 40/60 split. In 1986, Wachs endowed the Eddie Murphy Scholarship at the College of William and Mary in Williamsburg, Virginia, his alma mater, but he would have had to endow an entire university to make up for his and Tienken's sixty percent cut of Murphy's $200 million fortune.

Despite the irritant of *Fountain of Youth*, Murphy kept Lipsky on until 1996. That manager's profit participation was never revealed, but you can bet Murphy was no longer doing the fiscal equivalent of minstrel showtunes.

There was another shakeup at Team Murphy in 1991, although in this case the star didn't do the sacking. In a move I have never heard of during my twenty-five years as an entertainment journalist, Murphy's longtime publicist, Terrie Williams, *resigned* as the press rep for one of the most powerful men in Hollywood. The competition for celebrity clients is so fierce among personal publicists, who charge their clients up to $1,000 a week, press agents never voluntarily jump off these gravy trains. Williams, in a press release, mysteriously attributed the break to "irreconcilable differences." Typically, when a star suffers a spate of bad publicity, even if it's his own fault, the flack catches the flak and gets fired. When false rumors about her heroin addiction plagued Julia Roberts, she fired the most powerful publicist in the entertainment industry, Pat Kingsley, because Kingsley was powerless to stop the slander. It was unheard of for a publicist to fire a client, but that's exactly what Williams did. Murphy is now repped by one of the more accommodating press agents in the biz, Arnold Robinson of Rogers and Cowan, a firm known for working with the press rather than against it.

Chapter 16

......

Makeover Mavens

DURING HIS TWO YEARS in the wilderness after *Another 48 HRS.*, Murphy had plenty of time to read scripts, no matter how much he disliked the task. The reluctant reader got blue-chip assistance from his biggest fan in a suit, Brandon Tartikoff, Paramount's new chairman, hired to keep the studio's biggest franchise big—and happy. Murphy's two years of inactivity made Tartikoff's life miserable. He remembered their glory days when as programming chief he was making NBC No. 1, and Eddie was doing the same thing for *Saturday Night Live*. Maybe they could make magic again, only the stakes were infinitely higher now. A disappointing episode of *SNL* would disappear into the ether, whereas a $60 million film would show up on the balance sheet at the annual stockholders' meeting.

Tartikoff literally sighed when he remarked that the billion-dollar man was "on the sidelines because Paramount hadn't developed a movie for him. Well, Eddie Murphy should have been then, and will be now, priority number one at Paramount."

Tartikoff died last summer after a third bout with Hodgkin's disease. The brilliant television programmer had a less stellar fifteen-month tenure as a film executive, but he came to the job with high hopes for Paramount in general and its biggest, if flickering, star in particular. In 1992, the genial studio chief considered himself a savvy analyst of movie-star maintenance. He knew why Murphy's star had lost wattage. "As a performer, he's not been challenged. There's an adult audience waiting for a grown up Eddie."

The studio's top cheerleader for Team Eddie, Tartikoff did everything but break out the pom-poms. Because Murphy had been unhappy that other superstars made more money than he did, one of Tartikoff's first acts was to revamp Murphy's contract, making him at least temporarily the highest paid actor in film. Tartikoff felt it was money well spent. Both men had the same vision, and it was focused on the bottom line. Tartikoff said, "I don't have the feeling he wants to play Othello. Eddie wants what we want—to make movies that make $100 million." The new deal called for Murphy to earn $12 million for each of four pictures. The real sweetener, however, was that, unlike previous pacts at Paramount, Murphy was free to moonlight at other studios while Paramount continued to pay the salaries of his retainers. *Time* magazine, not content with writing his obituary, harumphed, "Eddie Murphy signs a multimillion dollar deal with Paramount Pictures. Have they seen *Harlem Nights?*" Of course, but Tartikoff had also seen both *Beverly Hills Cop* movies and felt the gamble was well worth it.

The production head could have found work as a lay analyst. He intuited that Murphy's discontent wasn't really about money, but the respect it reflects. Tartikoff hinted at what had made the deal fly. "I don't think there are too many deals today or in the past that can match the lucrative and *respectful* nature of the deal we've made with Eddie Murphy."

It was a mutual adoration society. Murphy sent his "boss" this billet-doux via a magazine interview: "All the people I had had trouble with at Paramount were leaving, so it was like getting a whole new studio, and I knew that Brandon wouldn't bullshit me."

Before Tartikoff came on board, Paramount had resisted

Murphy's desire to make a romantic comedy. Actually, what scared the studio was the project's largely black cast. The second thing Tartikoff did after making Murphy even richer was to greenlight the star's pet project, which would be a dramatic makeover of the Murphy image that had fallen on hard reviews.

With the romantic comedy *Boomerang*, Tartikoff intended to make his "number one priority" the black Cary Grant. "Whatever negative view that people came away from *Raw* with will be erased by *Boomerang*. It's a true leading-man role. A comedy with a classic form. The kind of movie Cary Grant would have made," Tartikoff said.

Boomerang's producer, Warrington Hudlin, jumped on the Cary Grant analogy. "After this movie, people are going to see Eddie Murphy as Cary Grant." Tartikoff earned his money as Murphy's protector; the affable production chief always seemed to be running interference against people trying to tackle Eddie's evolving gameplan. Hudlin, who was black, and Paramount executive David Kirkpatrick pressured Murphy to have the standard white sidekick in *Boomerang*. Tartikoff sided with Murphy, as did the director, Reginald Hudlin, the producer's brother. Director Hudlin said, "Eddie and I agreed that there should not be a thought given to having any white buddies in this. It's frustrating to have to reinvent the wheel, to prove time and again that an all-black cast does not marginalize a film." That was true only some of the time. *Coming to America* proved Hudlin's point; *Harlem Nights* demolished it. Murphy so enjoyed jettisoning the white buddy staple, he replaced it with not one but four black pals, who served as a Greek chorus commenting on the protagonist's lovelife.

Another "white" feature of the film discomfited the star. Murphy rejected comparisons to a dead white man with a Cockney accent—in other words, he refused to do Cary Grant in blackface. "Cary Grant did the Cary Grant thing already," he said. "I'm new shit. Don't color me Cary." A more mature Murphy diplomatically added, "Not to piss on Cary, but this is a new *shade* of Eddie," not Cary.

Boomerang was a romantic comedy with a twist and 180 degrees away from anything he had played before. In *Harlem Nights* he wore beautiful suits, but he was still gangsterish, if not a card-carrying member of the mob. In *Boomerang*, he was pure buppie, a black urban professional in Armani togs and Bruno Magli footwear. Gucci was his god, the gym his temple. *Harlem Nights* had revealed his binge eating on a huge screen, and the bloated image shocked him. For *Boomerang*, he dieted and pumped chrome. Murphy's makeover went all the way down to the follicle. The hairdresser on the movie said, "He has a new hair texture...revised hair. People at Paramount said he had a common street look. Now he looks more of a gentleman. Now he has a well-groomed look."

The creative director for an all-black ad agency, Murphy begins the movie not as Cary Grant but as Warren Beatty, an ultra-smooth operator who loves women and leaves them. He can sauté a salmon with rosemary and break a date's heart, all in one evening. The movie's unusual twist has Murphy meeting his match—in fact, Robin Givens, who plays his gorgeous boss, one-ups him in the sexist pig department. She's a female chauvinist, who uses Eddie as a plaything, then tires of the game. The smitten stud becomes a whimpering puppy dog, complaining when Givens doesn't return his phone calls or fails to show up for a date. Sounding like one of his previous rejects, Murphy whines, "Were you so busy you couldn't pick up the phone?" Givens's rejection is instructive for Murphy, who becomes a sensitive, caring man—and falls in love with another kind soul, the delectable Halle Berry.

As frothy as a thirties screwball comedy, *Boomerang* nevertheless had surprising depth. Its racial politics were largely implicit rather than preachy. The casting alone made a political comment, according to Murphy. "*Boomerang* is a very political film, because it is black, and yet it's about nothing to do with being black, and it cost $40 million. So if it's successful, then it will prove that you can do mainstream movies about blacks that are not just set in the 'hood.'" Actually, *Coming to America* had already proved that, but Hollywood had to keep learning the lesson over and over.

Boomerang dramatized the persistence of racism, even among the movie's gilded class of buppies in BMWs. In one scene, out of the blue, Halle Berry lapses into a foreign language. She explains to her date, "It's Korean for 'I'm so sorry I shot you, but I thought you were robbing my store.'"

Even more outré is a scene where Murphy and his beautifully dressed black pack try on suits in a Brooks Brothers–type store. A cranky white salesclerk tries to shoo them out of the store, saying they don't sell suits on layaway and returns aren't allowed. Comic Martin Lawrence, the group's Spike Lee, wants to punch the odious salesman out. Murphy, displaying his real life laissez-faire attitude toward racism, is amused by the dimwitted clerk and tells Lawrence to "chill."

The casting of *Boomerang* also shows a kinder, gentler Murphy. As he did with *Harlem Nights,* he gave employment to over-the-hill black comics and actors—Slappy White, Eartha Kitt, and Melvin Van Peebles came out of involuntary retirement for the film. Even more touching was Murphy's insistence on casting Robin Givens over Paramount's objections. The studio feared that Givens's torturous split with Mike Tyson would turn moviegoers off. Murphy, Givens's one-time lover, showed that at least some of the time he remained friends with former girlfriends. In fact, on the set, Givens came to Murphy's defense for not being more political about black issues. From her secure background among the haute black bourgeoisie, Givens felt it unfair that every successful black was expected to get up on a soapbox, preferably in the ghetto. "People look at Eddie and say, 'He's not doing anything.' but he's doing so much." Givens said, "This is a man who can relate to everybody. And everybody can relate to [him]. It's not necessarily the struggle to get out of the 'hood for all of us. There are other types of people in America, too." Givens's father was an industrialist; her mother a prominent business executive who founded her own computer company. "Eddie's a brother, too. But it's good for black people in America and around the world to see that there are different types of blacks and different types of experiences," the actress said.

Boomerang gave Murphy a dramatic opportunity to show that his consciousness didn't need any raising. The allegedly disengaged superstar personally strong-armed Paramount into hiring ten black interns to work on the film. Besides experience and a nice addition to their resumes, their participation also gave them the most coveted possession of a film tyro—automatic admission to the DGA, the director's union. And as a delicious extra, Murphy's good deed allowed him once and for all to stifle Spike Lee's repeated complaints about the actor's indifference to blacks. In 1988, Lee said, "Eddie needs to flex his muscles that can help black people get into this industry. Clout isn't just getting the best table at Spago." He also demanded the star use his clout to get Paramount to hire more blacks. Lee enjoyed playing the angry young man so much, he apparently failed to notice that the year before he went public with his criticism, Murphy had packed the screen with black faces in *Coming to America*. During a promotional interview for *Boomerang*, a reporter repeated Lee's three-year-old criticism. Murphy was the perfect gentleman, although his interviewer suggested it was fear rather than courtesy that elicited this measured response. "I had to take the show business position—[Lee is] new in the business, he doesn't know any better, they probably made him say it." Murphy was being too generous. By this time, Lee had been a major film director since 1986. He was hardly "new in the business." Murphy was polite in the press, but more confrontational with the director. "I would see Spike and say, 'Why'd you say that?', and he'd say, 'I didn't say that—they changed my words around.' And because it's show business ...where you smile when you're low and all that bullshit, you got to forget about it and let it slide under the bridge."

In 1992, Murphy had become a role model for up-and-coming black filmmakers, and one defended him. Matty Rich, who directed *Straight Out of Brooklyn.* said, "It was a silly statement Spike made—he should be ashamed. What is Spike doing? Is he giving a percentage to the community? Is a percentage of *Mo' Better Blues* going to the inner city? Come on—black men, white women, all that, that's garbage. If you really want to do something, start in the community." That last barb must have really stung Lee, who was criticized for opening his movie memorabilia shop not in the black ghetto of South Central Los Angeles, but on the West Side's trendy Melrose Avenue.

Other cast and crew members were not as sanguine as Murphy's champions, Givens and *Straight Out of Brooklyn's* Rich. *Daily Variety's* mole on the set reported that Murphy's tardiness and occasional no-shows "drove the crew crazy and helped push the film over budget." En route to a location in the nation's capital, Murphy decided to go for a walk and showed up so late the director decided to shoot another scene that didn't require his presence. When the star finally appeared and learned the crew wasn't ready for him, he walked off in a huff. Murphy developed wanderlust during another stroll to the set and decided to take in a movie on a Monday morning. Crew members twiddled their thumbs—and collected their hefty hourly wages—while Murphy sat through a two-hour-plus showing of *Cape Fear.* Murphy's apologists said the star didn't show up for the exterior shoot because it was raining. When the sky cleared, Murphy appeared. When Murphy did another disappearing act in Atlanta, it was attributed to his fear of the ongoing Rodney King riots. The star's late arrivals were matched by early exits before the day's filming had wrapped.

Variety also revealed the perks and power of what it called an "800-pound gorilla," who nevertheless could be as passive-aggressive as any powerless subordinate. When his personal assistant ordered ten compact discs for the stereo in Murphy's trailer, Paramount was penny wise and superstar foolish, refusing to reimburse the assistant. (Tartikoff must have been on vacation without a cell phone.) Instead of throwing a fit, Murphy ordered thirty steak dinners from a pricey restaurant for his entourage, and Paramount was told to pay up or else. The studio didn't have the temerity to call his bluff and discover what "or else" meant. The steaks and CDs were charged to the incredible inflatable budget.

Murphy alienated the crew by ignoring them. The rough-edged, blue-collar types who predominate behind the camera can't abide a stuck-up star, even a billion-dollar grossing one. No matter how big a star you are, it's not a good tactical move to tick off these "below-the-line" folks, because they can sabotage your scenes and allow stunts to turn into "accidents." When a temperamental actress antagonized the crew on another movie, they surreptitiously urinated in a pond before she shot a bathing scene in it.

A Murphy spokeswoman didn't deign to explain the star's aloofness, but she did address *Variety*'s claim that the star was often a no-show. Eddie wasn't being "difficult," he was being a perfectionist, according to his press rep. When a scene wasn't working, he would leave the set and return, refreshed, the next day.

Murphy must have felt a lot of scenes weren't working. His late arrivals, according to *Variety*, totaled 100 hours. The

average cost of shooting on a backlot soundstage runs into
the six figures an hour—even more if you're on location and a
swath of the motorcade-riddled capital has to be shut down.
Murphy didn't feel that punctuality is the courtesy of kings—
or even richer superstars. His tardiness cost the production
an extra $1 million, *Variety* reported.

While his spokespeople made excuses, Murphy didn't
seem contrite about his unprofessional behavior. "Every time
they write I'm late, they should also write that my movies
have made $2 billion." Murphy's biggest apologist was the
film's white producer, Brian Grazer, a Tartikoff-league
schmoozer to the stars. "Eddie might show up two hours late,
but he contributes to rewriting the script and does brilliant
things." The film's black producer, Warrington Hudlin, didn't
object to the star's budget-busting tactics either. "We'd rather
have a comic genius like Eddie late than another actor on
time." Interestingly, although both producers adored Eddie,
the star had a major falling-out with Hudlin but kept Grazer
close. In a later monster hit, *The Nutty Professor,* the movie
villains were named after Hudlin and his director brother,
while Brian Grazer had the honor—and gross points—of
producing the blockbuster.

Other defenders attributed Murphy's tardiness to professional rather than imperious reasons. They claimed that
Murphy's handlers had overbooked the workaholic star.
While shooting *Boomerang,* he was also recording an album
and holding production meetings for his next film. These
exhausting commitments accounted for Murphy's apparent
lack of professionalism on the set of *Boomerang.* His work
ethic, not the devil, made him do it.

All complaints evaporated when the opening weekend
figures rolled in. Murphy's gamble with a black cast and a
remodeled romantic image had paid off. *Boomerang* took in a
whopping (for 1992) $14 million its opening weekend. Despite
mixed-to-malicious reviews, Murphy proved he could still

open a picture and that he could keep it opened on screens nationwide. *Boomerang* went on to earn $70 million in the U.S., respectable business, if not a *Beverly Hills Cop* bonanza, for a film that cost $40 million. Triple the domestic take to account for foreign sales and the video release, and you can see why the Murphy-Tartikoff love affair was a match made at the bank and why the producers were happy to be kept waiting by the "late, great Eddie Murphy."

One powerful voice declined to make the romance a menage á trois. The *L.A. Times*'s usually kind-hearted film critic, Kenneth Turan, took the filmmakers to task for the scarcity of white faces in the black farce. *Boomerang*, Turan wrote, "takes pains to create a reverse universe where white people are invisible, except when comic relief is called for." Only seven white people appeared in the film, Turan complained. The critic said that setting *Boomerang* among black professionals was "silly and arbitrary and not dramatically motivated."

Murphy and director Reginald Hudlin were so irritated by the charge of reverse racism that each man (or more likely, their press agents) penned a rebuttal for the *Times*'s op ed page. Hudlin made the most telling point when he noted that *Boomerang*'s seven white folks were greater than the number of blacks who had appeared in all of Woody Allen's films, despite the fact that blacks and Latinos outnumber whites in Allen's beloved Manhattan.

To other critics' objections that *Boomerang* had created a fantasy world, Murphy suggested that the scenes depicting white racism were more documentary than fantasy. The episode in the clothing store, where the white clerk suspects Murphy and his buddies are shoplifters, was based on the real-life experiences of Oprah Winfrey and Oscar-choreographer Debbie Allen, whom he said had both been turned away from stores. The black producer of *Boomerang*, Murphy added, has found it hard to get a cab in New York City, a problem that seems endemic among blacks. As for the film's other alleged fantasy, a world of co-opped and coutured black people, Murphy quoted a trade magazine for buppies that said the top five black-owned companies on *Black Enterprise* magazine's annual Top 100 list raked in more than $2 billion the previous year. Murphy's million-dollar co-op and Givens's designer duds weren't fantasy; they were just a glimpse of a socio-economic group usually ignored by white filmmakers who focused on the underclass of pimps and junkies. *Boomerang*, in fact, reflected a less opulent version of Murphy's reality, where salmon comes with rosemary, and crack addiction is something you read about in the Metro section of the *New York Times*.

Although *Boomerang* had grossed a handsome $130 million worldwide, that wasn't *Cop* or *Coming to America* business. Murphy seemed to have accepted the misperception of critics that his career was on the downturn. At the time, he said sadly, "I was the best five years ago," when *Raw* and *Beverly Hills Cop II* made him No. 1 at the box office, if not in the hearts of certain minorities.

Murphy felt the banner year of 1987 had not been duplicated since. Being on top, however, didn't make him happy either. There was nowhere to go but down, and the perfectionist thought that was where he was heading in 1987. "Now I just want to be good and stay good. I just want to do stuff. And if I can't do stuff, I'll just chill. Because being the best is a fucking drag."

In 1992, he didn't chill, but spent a feverish year making back-to-back movies. After the critical drubbing of *Boomerang*, Murphy made a partial retreat from romantic comedy back to his trademark persona, a smart guy who outwits dumb white people in a political comedy, *The Distinguished Gentleman*. Romance was still in the picture, but it was a subplot to the main story about a Florida con man who uses the tricks of his trade to get elected to Congress, where he hopes to get his larcenous hands on PAC money and all the other perks and payola of elected office. His love of a beautiful, bleeding-heart attorney, who looks more like a fashion model than a member of the bar, reforms his larcenous heart, and he uses his power to reform Congress. Someone called the film, "Mr. Smith Goes to Washington and Gets Religion." Because of the return of his smart-aleck persona, another observer said it was *Beverly Hills Cop* with a better wardrobe.

The comedy allowed him to showcase his Streep-ish facility with accents, including Yiddish, Chinese, cracker, and a brilliant impression of a Boston Brahmin who makes William F. Buckley sound like a truck driver.

When *The Distinguished Gentleman* premiered in December 1992, Murphy proved yet again that he could open a picture. Despite heavy competition from *Home Alone 2*, *Aladdin* and *The Bodyguard*, *The Distinguished Gentleman* made $11 million during its first three days which put the film at No. 2. Only Macaulay Culkin's suburban comic nightmare revisited could best Eddie, and the winner had the benefit of being a sequel with a built-in wanna-see edge. However, the opening weekend was not a happy omen of business to come, since *Boomerang* ($13 million) and even the execrated *Harlem Nights* ($16 million) had made better debuts. The omen turned out to be an accurate prediction. *The Distinguished Gentleman*—or worse, Murphy—couldn't hold on to his audience, and the movie petered out at $47 million in American theaters. An executive at another studio said, "He can get it up, but he can't keep it up." A less Freudian box office analyst said, "A lot of pictures open to $20 million their first week, and the studio is having a party. But Eddie is not where Harrison Ford and Tom Cruise are. He ain't there anymore."

Some felt the premise of *The Distinguished Gentleman* was all wrong and played against its star's greatest strength,

sticking it to the Man. Fans didn't want their antiestablish-
ment icon turned into an idealist for the love of a beautiful
woman.

At this point, the wisdom of Brandon Tartikoff's new
deal with Murphy manifested itself. The pact had not only
soothed the superstar's hurt feelings, it allowed him to work
for other studios. Disney's Jeffrey Katzenberg, called the
Golden Retriever for his ability to sniff out hits and stars, had
lured Murphy over the hill to make *The Distinguished Gentleman*. Katzenberg had predicted Eddie would do for Washington what his Detroit cop had done for Beverly Hills. The
Golden Retriever lost his sense of smell this time. Disney's
Hollywood Pictures would have to absorb *The Distinguished
Gentleman's* losses, not Tartikoff's Paramount.

Within a few months, the box office disappointment
would be forgotten amid the euphoria of a major development in Murphy's personal life. While his career remained up
in the air, the troubled romantic would settle down with Ms.
Right. Like Gloria, little Eddie was happy at last.

Chapter 17

......

Wedding Bell Bliss

MURPHY HAD MET FASHION MODEL Nicole Mitchell in 1988 at a banquet for the NAACP Image Awards in Los Angeles. Five years and two children later, they were married on March 18, 1993. Unlike all his other ecstatic liaisons, their relationship evolved rather than burning intensely and then flickering out. "We got to know each other slowly," he said.

Mitchell, then twenty-one, met Murphy, twenty-seven, at a high point in his career, but at a low point in his personal life. *Coming to America* had been one of the biggest hits of the year, but the previous year's *Raw* and his unrequited infatuation with Lisa Figueroa had poisoned him on future romance. Murphy's misogyny had reached a high point; his self-esteem had gone in the opposite direction. Press reports at this time described him as heartbroken, "perhaps paranoid." Feeling sorry for himself, he hung out at clubs when he wasn't bingeing in front of the fridge.

Their initial meeting didn't augur well. The first thing he said to Mitchell was "Life's a drag."

Murphy may have been despondent, but he wasn't blind. The fashion model's transcendent loveliness registered with the jaded superstar. "The first thing I did when I saw Nicole, I turned to my accountant and said, '*Her* I would marry tomorrow—without a prenuptial.' That's what I *said*. I'll *always* have a prenuptial." It's telling that the first glimpse of

Mitchell made him think of money, not love or even good, old-fashioned lust.

There was a lot to lust over. Mitchell had been a fashion model since she was 10; magazine covers and runways had enjoyed her magnetic presence. By the age of twenty, she was earning $100,000 a year. She was the first self-supporting woman Murphy had ever fallen for. There would be no worries that she would spend his money on furs and jewelry á la Figueroa. Mitchell could well-afford to pay for her own trinkets and dead animal skins. Family friend Kathryn Smith said that the perks of stardom didn't dazzle Mitchell because she had already enjoyed them herself. She was accustomed to flying first class from her home in Sacramento to exotic fashion shoots; the back seat of a limo, according to Smith, was a second home. "She had already adjusted to the fuss. She helped him to grow more comfortable with himself and with his fame, too," Smith said. Mitchell centered Murphy and helped him settle down. Instead of barhopping with his entourage, Murphy cuddled with Nicole in front of the TV; their favored fare: Elvis concerts and reruns of *Amos and Andy*.

A year after they met, Mitchell, who was only twenty-two, gave birth to the first of three children, a girl named Bria. In 1989, Murphy was ready to be a doting dad but not a husband. He felt secure that Mitchell wasn't a gold digger but was not sure that she was Ms. Right and he definitely wasn't sure sure he was ready for monogamy. That same year, Paulette McNeely gave birth to Eddie Murphy, Jr. Eddie Sr., continued to live in the baronial opulence of Bubble Hill in New Jersey. Nicole and Bria lived at the other end of the continent in Sacramento, with Nicole's mother, who is a white Englishwoman, divorced from a black Air Force pilot she met while he was stationed on a military base in Britain.

Mitchell was different from the other women who had caught his fancy. "She was the first woman I had met on that whole romantic level," Murphy said. "Most of the girls I've gone out with are really nice *girls*. Nicole is a woman. You can talk to her. She's honest. She's straightforward. She's got a sense of humor," Murphy said. But her attractive personality didn't blind him to the bottom line attraction. "And on top of that, she's f-i-i-i-ne." *GQ* was ready to put Mitchell on the list of women it loved. Or as a writer for the magazine said breathing heavily, "Nicole's beauty is so extreme it doesn't really register."

Murphy had been slapped with a paternity suit in 1987 by Nicolle Rader, which he vigorously fought because he insisted the kid wasn't his. He embraced his paternity of Bria when Nicole told him they were expecting. Murphy felt he had gotten his Christmas present early. "I got a kid coming, and I'll have my first Christmas with my baby in December. I wanted to have a kid with Nicole because I was in love with her." At long distance. During his daughter's first year of life, Murphy was terrified of commitment and kept the mother of his daughter three thousand miles away. Murphy would fly to Sacramento sporadically; Bria spent one week a month in New Jersey with dad but without mom. Gradually Nicole began to visit Bubble Hill more often. *People* magazine said he acted more like an uncle than dad to his daughter.

At least he was a very generous uncle. Murphy put Nicole and Bria up in a lavish lakefront home he bought for them. For years, Nicole had lived modestly in her mother's home. Now her mother would live in Nicole's $1 million mansion. When Murphy made an appearance in this all-female household, he was more disciplinarian than doting dad. Where Nicole was a classic permissive parent, Murphy imitated his stepdad—without the boxing gloves in the basement. Murphy said, "With Nicole, it's, 'Oh, come on Bria, please have something to eat.' I don't negotiate with her. It's yes or no. Once she turns eighteen, she can do what she wants to. For now, I'm the parent, and she's the child."

Murphy claimed age, not fear of commitment, made him keep his distance. "I associated the whole family thing with being a middle-aged person. I was holding on to my youth. I could feel it pulling me in, but I was like, 'I'm still Ed. Still single. I'm a bachelor.'" Also, cohabiting would have really intruded on this bachelor life. Besides the odd paternity suit and other birth mothers, at this time the tabloids loved to show Murphy out on the town with gorgeous models (not Nicole) and actresses.

In the face of this documented unfaithfulness, Nicole displayed the forbearance of a Kennedy wife. Her own parents had separated when she was young, and she knew the ropes of single parenting. "Her mom never made single parenting look tough. Nicole learned by example," said family friend Kathryn Smith. She was an independent spirit who didn't need Eddie for a meal ticket. If the father of her child went the way of most flesh, there were always the odd runway job and magazine layouts to pay the bills.

Nicole never nagged about the girlfriends or pushed for marriage. "Nicole sits on the side and observes. Her strength is her reserve," said Smith. Once his fear of gold diggers was finally laid to rest, Murphy basked in this selfless love. Even so, it took him two years after Bria's birth to come to the epiphany that home life was better than night life. "After a while, going to a disco all the time ain't that much fun. Sitting in a room and shaking people's hands all night—it's not like you're having a great time," he said.

By 1992, the tabloids stopped running photos of Eddie and various arm ornaments out on the town. There was a simple reason for his absence from discos and double-truck spreads in the tabs: Eddie had gotten into cocooning. This newly minted homebody was horrified when Magic Johnson listed himself, Arsenio, and Eddie as "bachelors almost every woman in L.A. wanted to be with." The tragic consequences of Johnson's desirability soon became known. Murphy didn't want any part of this unholy trinity. "I haven't fucked any more women than anyone else," he said nervously. Johnson and Murphy had only met twice and *never* hung out together, according to the third corner of this alleged partners-in-crime triangle, Arsenio Hall.

As for the sybaritic lifestyle at Bubble Hill which was rumored to make Tiberius' vacation home on Capri look like Bible camp, the alleged orgies were strictly G-rated, says Hall.

Murphy's dating habits also deserved a G-rating. "I'm real prudish and real straight," Eddie said. "I could never go to a disco and meet a chick and take her home and fuck her. If you're going to go home with me and fuck me tonight, I know you've done this before. And if it's just a question of getting off, hey, I got someone I can get off with that I care about." Although she would never say, one wonders what Nicole must have felt when she read of her function as "someone" the father of her children could "get off with."

Murphy asked rhetorically, "Why go fuck some strumpet in a disco? I'm not saying I haven't had times when I wasn't tempted. But I can't recall the last time I met a chick in a disco. I got to go back ten years. Hey, man, I have a beautiful woman. Things are changing, and love is all right," Murphy added, quoting the philosophy of his third record. "The last thing I need to do is fuck some bimbo. I've been with Nicole for about three years now. Do I have a monogamous relationship? Yeah. Nicole is expecting in November. Little Edward is on the way." The name of the coming heir had to be changed to avoid confusion. Murphy had already sired an Eddie Jr. by Paulette McNeely.

The Moral Majority might criticize Murphy for fathering two children by different mothers in the same year. Psychologists might recommend a Sexual Compulsives Anonymous meeting. But conservative critics, not to mention the rest of us mere mortals, can't comprehend the sexual Mt. Olympus demigods like Murphy inhabit. How many of us could resist the temptations that Murphy and other stars encounter every time they step out of the house? A friend of mine who waited tables at a tony Italian restaurant in Beverly Hills recounted a telling incident a few years ago. Murphy walked in arm in arm with two women. "They were the most gorgeous creatures I had ever seen" my friend told me, "and Eddie had the full, uh, attention of both of them." If Helen of Troy or Lola Montez threw themselves at us, could we resist a come-on from a beauty whose "face launched a thousand ships and burned the topless towers of Ilium" or bankrupted the Kingdom of Bavaria? And why should we judge him, when Nicole or McNeely obviously didn't? McNeely never took Eddie to court or her story to the tabloids for big bucks. And Nicole eventually accepted his marriage proposal.

On Christmas Eve 1991, Murphy had yet another epiphany. Nicole and Bria were visiting Bubble Hill and Bria was sick; mom was in bed, comforting the child. Murphy peeked out from behind the bathroom door. The fatherless Nativity scene made him realize what the picture was missing.

Nicole remembered how he popped *the* question. "Bria wasn't feeling well, and I was talking to Eddie about her fever. He came out and laid on the bed, and all of a sudden he grabbed my hand. I thought he was looking at my nails. But then he slipped this big rock on my finger and said, 'Let's get married.' I was so happy I couldn't sleep all night." Eddie explained simply, "I had to do the right thing."

Nicole must have felt something coming, because that night she had a gift for Eddie that symbolized her love for him but didn't demand his signature on a wedding license. Her Christmas present for her brand-new fiancé was a gold charm bracelet with small locks and keys "to my heart," a smitten Murphy said, showing off the gift to a *Newsweek* reporter. Also dangling from the trinket were the letters "N" and "B" for the two women who owned the keys to the owner's heart.

A cynical reporter couldn't resist commenting on standup comedy's most famous misogynist's transition to George Bailey's wonderful life. "From the rage of *Raw* to life in Frank Capra's living room—all in only five quick years," *Esquire* dryly noted.

The star didn't deny the metamorphosis. "The Eddie Murphy who was in *Raw* does not exist anymore. It's not like I experienced some epiphany or some shit like that. I just got older. I'm thirty-one years old. I'm a thirty-one-year-old motherfucker."

But even after proposing, Murphy hesitated to set a date. It took more than a year and another child for the reluctant bridegroom to make it to the altar. By the time the couple exchanged vows, there were two offspring at the ceremony. Bria now had a baby brother, Miles Mitchell, born November 7, 1992, and named after jazz legend and Murphy idol Miles Davis. Interestingly, both Bria and her sibling bore Nicole's last name, Mitchell, not their father's.

As they prepared for a spring wedding, Murphy proclaimed himself a happy man. His third music album, *Love's Alright*, after having trouble finding a label willing to distribute it—unheard of for an artist whose previous efforts went gold—came out to glowing reviews. Profits from a single off the album, "Yeah," went to a new foundation to help people "in need from all walks of life." The contribution may have been Murphy's mea culpa for stiffing Michael Jackson and Stevie Wonder on their *We Are the World* album-video in 1984.

Although his two films in 1992 got a critical drubbing, they both turned a profit. Murphy described his happy outlook at the time. "Now I'm as happy as I've ever been. I've got a beautiful chick, a beautiful daughter, a great record, a great movie. But it was a long time coming."

Even those pesky lawsuits couldn't diminish Murphy's euphoria or scare his fiancée away. In 1992, Tamara Hood

sued the *National Enquirer* after it ran a story that said
Murphy had installed Hood in a $376,000 house and set up a
million dollar trust fund for their child, Christian Edward
Murphy. According to the *Enquirer,* Murphy was a very
generous parent, making child-support payments of $2,000 a
month. For a change, Murphy wasn't a party to the suit,
although having the details of his extramarital fatherhood
must have been embarrassing. Nicole, in Kennedy-wife mode
again, never revealed her feelings about the situation. Hood's
suit didn't deny the details in the *Enquirer* story, which for a
change were accurate. She sued under a California statute
that allows noncelebrities to claim invasion of privacy if a
published story about a nonpublic figure is "private, offensive, and not newsworthy." The judge threw out the suit.

The wedding ceremony itself reflected the dynamic between
Eddie and Nicole. Murphy once quoted former friend Stallone's description of his relationships: "It's my way or the
highway." Nicole wanted a private ceremony, but Murphy's
wishes prevailed: he invited five hundred guests to the Grand
Ballroom of the Plaza Hotel in New York. For once, their
host, Donald Trump, engaged in understatement when he
called the gala "one of the most elegant, glamorous, and
classiest weddings."

   The cream of white and black society showed up. Record
and film producer Quincy Jones and his gorgeous significant
other, actress Nastassja Kinski; Bruce Willis; Bill Murray;
Tony-winning actor Charles S. Dutton; Keenen Ivory Wayans;
Sugar Ray Leonard; directors John Singleton and Robert
Townsend; The Marla (still a Maples, although Murphy's
surrender of bachelorhood may have given her ideas about
The Donald); country singer Johnny Gill; comic David Alan
Grier. Even Wayne Newton got an invitation, although he was
the kind of celebrity Murphy would have mercilessly imper-
sonated on *Saturday Night Live*. Another unlikely guest was

Terrie Williams, the personal publicist who had fired the bridegroom.

Arsenio Hall was on hand as best friend and cheerleader. For once, Hall's boosterism wasn't overstated when he said, "This wedding was like a fantasy come true, and there was so much electricity surrounding it. I was with Eddie the night he met Nicole, and I'm so happy because this restores my faith in what the concept of love is really all about." Hall has never married.

The wedding was not only a fantasy come true, but an ultraopulent series of events that an Indian mogul bridegroom might have envied. If there's anything more lavish than first class all the way, Murphy and his planners managed to find it. Eddie stayed in the Presidential Suite on the eighteenth floor of the Plaza. Nicole prepped thirteen floors below in the Vanderbilt Suite, which *Ebony*'s reporter, the only member of the press invited, said cost $3,000 a night. *Ebony* had also negotiated exclusive photo rights for far less than the $200,000 both the *Enquirer* and *Globe* had offered. *Time, Newsweek,* and all four networks volunteered to cover the event gratis. The tabloids underbid. Pirated photos of the wedding and reception sold for $1,000 apiece. Murphy explained why *Ebony* got the exclusive. "I always wanted to have a big, beautiful wedding, and I wanted it to be showcased in *Ebony,*" but not without a lot of haggling by the magazine's publishers. With a level of wrangling usually reserved for nuclear test ban treaties, *Ebony* got its photo and story exclusives only after six months of negotiations with Murphy's publicists. *Ebony*'s efforts paid off. Murphy also persuaded guests Whitney Houston (a former girlfriend) and husband Bobby Brown to grant exclusive interviews for their thoughts on the proceedings. Murphy's fee for the exclusive went to charity.

Nicole, having abandoned all hope of a small-scale bash, went all-out on her trousseau. *Ebony* pronounced her wed-

ding gown "breathtaking," and photos of the tall, slender
model showed that for once the hype wasn't hype. The silk
and satin dress featured lots of décolletage, with French
alençon lace and rosettes, a 12-foot-long Cathedral train, with
matching Cathedral tulle veil edged in Belgian embroidery
and decorated with iridescent Austrian crystals and pearls.
Four-year-old Bria preceded her mother down the aisle sprin-
kling rose petals in her path.

Matrimony hadn't matured Murphy beyond recognition. He entered the ballroom wearing sunglasses and doing
his cheeky impersonation of Stevie Wonder. The only concession to tradition was his tux. The music also wasn't
traditional. "Don't Give Up on Love," a track from *Love's
Alright*, replaced Mendelssohn's "Wedding March."

Murphy hadn't been speaking just for public consumption when he said on several occasions, "I just love the guy,"
referring to his stepfather. Instead of a blackpacker or sibling,
Murphy chose Vernon Lynch Sr., to be his best man.

The Reverend Calvin Butts of Harlem's Abyssinian Bap-
tist Church presided, although the ceremony was non-
denominational. When Reverend Butts asked if anyone knew
why Eddie and Nicole shouldn't be married, Murphy spun
around and pretended to glare at the crowd. After the minister pronounced them husband and wife, Eddie kissed Nicole
repeatedly, then held her in a long embrace. As they left the
ballroom, Murphy picked up Bria and escorted both the
women in his life out.

Post-wedding commentary on the marriage game, Murphy said, "It was important for me to get married now
because I was in love, and I had found someone who loved
me. And we fit. Nicole is intelligent, she's sweet, she's fine,
she's a good mother, and she has a good sense of humor.
There wasn't just one single thing that attracted me to her;
she has a lot of positive attributes."

In the rose-colored glasses of hindsight, Murphy claimed

that he had known all along he would make it down the aisle with Nicole, even though the trip took five years. "The day I laid eyes on Nicole, I *knew* she would be my wife. That's vibe; it wasn't aesthetic. It took this long because I wanted to be sure about everything. And Nicole had to be sure. I'm a romantic," said a man known to propose on a first date, "but I'm a realist, too," the prenuptial-obsessed groom added. "We just did everything slowly."

The reception looked more like a flower show than a post-nuptial blowout. A garden of delights, the two-story-high reception room featured pink rose trees, hundreds of orchids, gardenias, and tulips. The food was equally lavish: jumbo shrimp, Russian blinis and crepes, a "wreath" of lobster with sliced turnips and red bell pepper, California asparagus, squash and mashed potatoes, and tsunamis of Cristal champagne at $60 a bottle. There was even a dish named after the bride, Chicken Nicole with Cognac sauce.

Eddie felt uncomfortable in his tux. For the reception, he did a costume change, slipping into sports jacket and slacks. Nicole followed suit, with a sexy, formfitting white sequined gown. Karyn White sang "Cuteness," a song Murphy had specifically written for his wife, as the newlyweds took to the floor for the first dance of the evening. The dancing went on all night, but Eddie didn't last that long. He said that at this time in his life, it was unusual for him to stay up so late. While he took a break, Nicole led the other partygoers in a funky variation on a conga line called the Electric Slide. Like royalty, Eddie and Nicole kibitzed among the guests, greeting each one personally.

From the dance floor, Arsenio Hall predicted longevity for the couple. "When you're as beautiful as Nicole is, it's hard to have close friends. I think Eddie is her best friend, and if a marriage is to work, you have to be friends."

Ebony proclaimed him at peace with himself, a man who had found the happiness that had proved so elusive up to then. Murphy agreed with this press. "Everything is cool right now. This is the first time in three years when no one is suing me! I have a project I want to do. I'm involved in a relationship that I treasure, and I have beautiful kids. Everything is cool."

The fantasy honeymoon was so lavish it made the Plaza fest seem like a frat party. Murphy rented an entire private island in the Caribbean for their weeklong getaway. They both would have preferred more time in the tropics, but the demands of work and parenting dragged them back to the mainland. It was Eddie's work and Nicole's maternalism that abbreviated the honeymoon. The new Mrs. Murphy had decided to jettison her successful modeling career to spend more time with the kids. Eddie ditched the Caribbean to make a movie. Fatherhood and now married life enriched him, but a wedding ring and adorable kids are rarely enough for an overachiever who got to the top by being work-obsessed. Some ingrained traits don't disappear because of a little thing like happiness and personal contentment. However, Nicole's ongoing project in the nursery would fare much better than her husband's new effort.

Chapter 18

......

Very Strange Bedfellows

ROGER EBERT ONCE TOLD ME, "Everybody has two jobs: what they do for a living and film critic." In Hollywood, everyone moonlights with a third job: show biz analyst. The most unlikely people feel the need to handicap a faltering star's career or decry a bounced executive's golden parachute. Mike Ovitz's departure from Disney got almost as much press as Britain's from Hong Kong.

So it was with the feeling of Alice having fallen through a fun-house mirror that I listened to my urologist in his Beverly Hills office. I was waiting to hear whether my PSA results indicated I had prostate cancer. Dr. Bradley Landis wanted to talk shop.

Director John Landis's first cousin, Dr. Landis, had so many interesting things to say about his famous relative and Eddie Murphy, I stopped worrying if I had a terminal illness (I didn't) and resumed my previous occupation of investigative journalist.

Was it true that his cousin, who the doctor said was a "really nice guy," grabbed Murphy's genitals during an argument on the set of *Coming to America?* And did Murphy respond by choking the director?

Dr. Landis didn't know about any physical confrontations between the two men, but he was privy to information I hadn't heard or read about. The doctor told me, "[Murphy]

213

certainly choked him [Landis] financially. After they had a falling out, John, who's a really sweet guy, found himself blacklisted by Murphy, and he didn't work for some time. John was hurting for a while financially." More likely, a series of film failures rather than badmouthing by the star had made the director unemployable.

Ironically, eight years earlier, Landis had exhibited a paternal concern about the evolution of his protégé's career. In 1986, the director prophetically said, "My only concern about Eddie is that he choose wisely. Ten years from now, I'd hate to see him making *Beverly Hills Cop IX* or something." Landis was off by two years and a few Roman numerals. Back then, Landis would have been horrified had he known he would be making "*Cop IX* or something" with Murphy eight years later. In 1993, the former sparring partners agreed to team on the third installment of Axel Foley's adventures in Beverly Hills.

How did the Tyson and Holyfield of Hollywood end up in the ring again? Waning box office, like politics, makes for strange bedfellows. Both men needed a hit, Landis more than Murphy. Their previous collaborations on *Trading Places* and *Coming to America* had been blockbusters. So what's a little strangulation when career resuscitation is at stake?

It also helped that the star had undergone a personal metamorphosis. Landis said, "Eddie Murphy, regardless of what went on between us, this is a happy guy right now. He is in a very successful marriage with two beautiful children and another on the way." Murphy agreed and labelled his transformation maturity. "We never had one problem on *Beverly Hills Cop III*. I'm a man now."

Eddie was willing to let bygones be bygones, especially since the money was right. At this point in his life, the superstar didn't really need any more of the stuff. *Forbes* had called him the fifth richest entertainer in America. What he needed was a blockbuster that would earn him renewed respect, and the clout to get first look at the best scripts. "First look" is a more valued commodity than a table near the door at Spago. An industry analyst said, "Any one of the brat packers would have been terrific in *Jerry Maguire*, the script was so good. Tom Cruise was just first in line."

Murphy knew his new film wouldn't allow him to cut in line. Going in, he admitted he was making the film to make a buck—fifteen million of them. Even a script he loathed couldn't take his eyes off the bottom line. Eddie found his biggest payday to date irresistible.

"Sometimes the studios offer you a film like *Beverly Hills Cop III*, which you may not want to do, and they say they will give you a certain amount. But when you read the script it looks even worse than you thought. And when you say you don't want to do it, they throw so much money at you that you do it anyway. The only problem is that you have to watch yourself afterwards," Murphy said without explaining why he had to watch his back. Murderous fans? Film connoisseurs turned urban guerrillas?

By now, Murphy was engaging in a bit of revisionist history, blaming all his film missteps on greed. Hopelessly reductionist, his economic theory didn't explain ego-driven vehicles like *Harlem Nights*. "Every bad decision I've made has been based on money. I grew up in the projects, and you don't turn down money there. You take it, because you never know when it's all going to end. I made *Cop III* because they offered me $15 million. That $15 million was worth having Roger Ebert's thumb up my ass."

Paramount provided other perks. Eddie Murphy Productions would receive a fee of $1.65 million—and this time, his ex-managers Wachs and Tienken wouldn't be collecting a usurious fifty percent of the production company's take. Another half a million was thrown in for someone described as his "personal producer," a unique status symbol. Many stars demand a personal hairdresser, trainer, or masseur on

the set, but a personal producer represented a new milestone
in the care and feeding of a superstar. Then there was the $1.5
million that amounted to a tip for various perks like limos,
security, and gofers.

To make the third *Beverly Hills Cop* on the scale of its
successful predecessors would have cost $70 million. Inflated
star salaries and below-the-line costs had outpaced inflation
in the ten years since the first outing of Axel Foley on Rodeo
Drive. Paramount looked at the grosses of his recent films
and finally said no to its tarnished golden boy. When Paramount slashed $30 million from the proposed budget, the
producer-auteurs of the series, Don Simpson and Jerry
Bruckheimer, left the picture and the lot and fled over the hill
to Disney. The producers realized that an action movie had to
have lots of action, like crashing trailer trucks and exploding
skyscrapers. Cop car chases just didn't do it with jaded
audiences demanding more and more spectacle, which costs.
Eddie didn't mind the cutback, because his salary remained
intact.

The reduced budget, however, didn't look good on Eddie's resume. An unnamed studio source felt Paramount's
diminished outlay reflected Murphy's diminished stature at
the box office. "If Paramount made the movie with Harrison
Ford or Tom Cruise, they wouldn't have done the film for less
than the original budget. He was once capable of making
$100 million time after time. Now, he has sort of dropped out
of that league," the source said.

Other handicappers felt Murphy was being held to a
different standard. Schwarzenegger, Julia Roberts, and Mel
Gibson had suffered bigger embarrassments than Murphy
(*Last Action Hero, Dying Young*), but studio chiefs were happy
to keep writing them blank checks for their next extravaganza. Murphy, on the other hand, was being slapped down
because of the sheer number of box-office disappointments
he had made in a row. Gibson and Roberts were getting close

to Murphy's record, but it all revolved around perception and expectation. Schwarzenegger et al. had made films that lost money; Murphy had never had a single film that at the very least didn't make it into the black. John Landis was Murphy's biggest cheerleader for the star's track record. "Eddie hasn't failed yet. Eddie has never been in a flop. All of his movies have made money. What other movie star can claim that?" Well, Tom Cruise, if you don't count the early *Legend*.

Robert Rehme, one of the film's producers, also defended the star as a victim of unrealistic expectations. "It's impossible to expect from someone that they sustain a constant rise in the box-office success of their movies. That is a false guideline, but I understand that is the standard many movie stars are held up to."

The naysayers who always see the glass as half empty— usually unnamed sources in this fearful industry—turned their pessimistic gaze on *Cop III*'s opening weekend. Monotonously by now, Murphy proved he could open a film. This time the take was $20 million. It was well above the average opening of his films, which was $16 million. But armchair demographers claimed that Murphy had lost his crossover appeal to white audiences. An unnamed source—again— said, "There's no question he has lost some of his white audience because otherwise *Beverly Hills Cop III* would have opened to $30 million."

Way back in 1983, amid the box office euphoria of *Trading Places*, the *Chicago Tribune*'s Gene Siskel looked into a very clouded crystal ball and predicted a career evolution that never took place. "In *Trading Places*, I think Murphy shows that he can be a terrific dramatic, as well as comic, actor. His potential is unlimited. He's special." Murphy, however, never grabbed the brass—preferring the crass— ring of comedy.

After *Beverly Hills Cop III* grossed a disappointing $42 million in the U.S. and Canada, Monday morning quarterbacks urged him to take refuge in a low budget, character-driven film. Bruce Willis and Robin Williams do it all the time when they fall in love with an intriguing role, regardless of the remuneration. If the art-house film flops, the money lost is so tiny that, as Murphy might say, "no one freaks." And the critical approbation for a superstar who stretches, however inexpertly (Sharon Stone's *Last Dance*), can make up for an opening weekend of only $75,000 in three theaters. The only problem with little films is that they also pay very little. And Murphy always had those looming projects in Brooklyn looking over his shoulder and examining his net worth.

John Landis didn't feel the fat lady had come anywhere near to singing as far as Murphy's career went. "Do I think he's over? I don't. But a lot depends on his choice of material and who he works with."

Both the material and collaborators on his next film would prove Landis right and suggest a superstar who was out of touch.

Chapter 19

......

Vampire Flick Bites

THE DISAPPOINTING PERFORMANCE of *Beverly Hills Cop III* called for a fall guy, but Murphy had already fired his manager three years earlier. Instead, his agent of fourteen years, Jim Wiatt at ICM, got the pink slip. Murphy moved a few blocks up the street in Beverly Hills to CAA, the hottest agency in the industry. The *Hollywood Reporter* quoted unnamed sources who said Wiatt was the fall guy for the star's decline in popularity. Murphy had long called the shots in script development, and he had no one to blame but himself—and his script readers.

Murphy's slump didn't discourage CAA, which counts Steven Spielberg and Tom Cruise among its stellar stable. CAA was notorious for poaching talent by offering a discount on the standard 15 percent agent's commission. The firm has always denied giving megastars kickbacks. In fact, both CAA's main men, Mike Ovitz and Ron Meyer, were spotted hovering around the set of *Cop III*. If not waiting for the kill, they at least hoped to benefit from the actor's disillusionment with his representation at the time. Ovitz's blandishments included the promise that CAA's entire roster of agents and clients would be his to command. The best writers and directors—CAA trophies like Spielberg, Barry Levinson, and Ron Howard—would recharge his stalled career. Not one but four agents, including Ovitz and Meyer, would commandeer vehicles perfect for their new client. CAA could point to Robert Redford as an example of its thaumaturgy, signing and finding him the hit *Sneakers* after his previous agency had come up with the disastrous *Havana*.

On the face of it, Murphy's move may have reflected desperation, but it seemed like a wise career decision. In the boutique-y world of talent agencies, ICM was Banana Republic; CAA, Bergdorf's. But by the time Murphy ended the relationship only a year later, CAA looked like a wholesale outlet. During its tenure, CAA found Murphy one script that never got made (*Sandblast*), and another that didn't please critics or fans (*Metro*). When he returned to ICM, the agency brought him a script that revived his career.

The *Hollywood Reporter's* unnamed sources turned out to be right about who was ultimately responsible for the star's slump. Murphy did call all the shots, including script selection. His next film, *Vampire in Brooklyn*, had the sad distinction of being the only Eddie Murphy project that failed to show a profit.

A look at the credits says a lot more than who was to blame for his one and only failure. The story credit shows the concept was a family affair, like *Harlem Nights*, but his relatives were beginning to have a Borgia-like effect on his career. His older and younger brothers, Charles Murphy and Vernon Lynch Jr., collaborated with their superstar sibling on the story. That bit of nepotism wasn't necessarily fatal. Anybody can come up with an attractive storyline: shark terrorizes resort community. But getting the script and the shark to float requires a professional. Two professionals, Michael Lucker and Chris Parker, received credit for the screenplay, but so did Charles Murphy. A bit of Screenwriter's Guild minutia: When writers collaborate on a script, their names are linked by an ampersand. When a script has to be rewritten, the original contributor has his name separated from the rewrite men by the conjunction "and." The actual credit listing spoke volumes about nepotism and amateurism without saying anything actionable: "Screenplay by Charles Murphy *and* Michael Lucker & Chris Parker." The backstory, as they say in development meetings, was that Charles turned in the first—unfilmmable—draft, and two "hit men" were called in to polish it, although jettison is probably the more accurate term.

The story and screenplay credits are not the only things that leap out at you when you watch *Vampire in Brooklyn* on video. Murphy, who had worked with A-list directors like Martin Brest and Tony Scott, now teamed with Wes Craven, slasher-auteur of various *Nightmare(s) on Elm Street* and *Swamp Thing.* Where Brest had guided Al Pacino to an Oscar with *Scent of a Woman* and Scott had helped Murphy to the top with *Beverly Hills Cop II* (ditto Tom Cruise in *Top Gun*), Craven's biggest collaborator was Freddy Krueger. (Since then Craven has achieved A-minus status with the sleeper hit *Scream.*)

Although it says more about unemployment among black actresses than it does about the quality of the role, Murphy dipped into the Ivy Leagues for his leading lady, Angela Bassett, an Oscar nominee for Tina Turner's biopic and a graduate of Meryl Streep's alma mater, Yale.

Besides being his one and only flop, *Vampire in Brooklyn* deserves another place in the trivia books. The film was Murphy's only non-comedy, unless you think spitting out a Mafioso's tongue and saying, "I've already eaten—Italian," is funny.

Another item for Trivial Pursuit: Sexy, handsome Eddie is made to look unattractive, and we're not talking about his transformation into a ghoul toward the end of the film. Much was made of the new hairdo for his Cary Grant makeover in *Boomerang.* The hairdresser on *Vampire in Brooklyn* should have been charged with felony wig abuse. Besides an unflattering widow's peak, his 'do has been processed and dips to

his shoulders, thanks to hair extensions. The effect is pim-
pish. His scraggly Van Dyke doesn't help either.

The unintelligible plot revolves around a vampire (Ed)
who leaves home in the Bermuda Triangle and relocates to
Brooklyn in search of the one remaining vampire in the
world (Bassett). If they don't meet and mate within twenty-
four hours, the race will die. The scriptwriters never bother
to explain the conceit, but it does allow one sex scene with
Bassett and Murphy that is more cannibalistic than erotic.
The title character's Caribbean roots call for a Rastafarian
accent, which comes and goes during the film. Amazingly,
the genius mimic, who has done everything from a Boston
Brahmin to a Mandarin Chinese, had trouble with Rasta.

With its state-of-the-art morphing and other special
effects, *Vampire* looks much more expensive than its $20
million budget. Unfortunately, it grossed only $19 million
domestically. At first, Murphy admitted that it was his only
film flop; then he claimed it made a $1 million profit, which
is Mad-Hatter-accounting, since the $20 million figure
doesn't include the cost of marketing and prints.

A real-life tragedy on the set eclipsed amateurish writing
and embarrassing accents. Bassett's stunt double, Sonja
Davis, 26, died on November 3, 1994, while performing
something called a backward high fall from a four-story
building. Davis's family and Wanda Sapp, another stunt
woman who survived, filed suit against the director, the stunt
coordinator, and the star. Murphy must have felt as though he
were starring in nightmarish outtakes from John Landis's
life. Filed in Los Angeles Superior Court on February 7, 1995,
the complaint alleged that the defendants had "failed to
obtain proper safety equipment" for the stunt. The negligence
suit, which asked for $50 million, claimed that Murphy et al.
had "refused to obtain porta-pits" (high tech cushions) to
surround the primary airbag for additional security. Worse,

the suit said the airbag had been "improperly placed." And worst, the defendants had also "recklessly instructed Davis not to use a decelerator," a device that slows a stunt person's fall. Unlike Landis, who had to endure a torturous trial, Murphy was eventually dropped from the suit. Fortunately, unlike writing, directing, and producing, stunt coordination was one messy area the star didn't mess with.

Chapter 20

......

Resurrection

Lᴉᴋᴇ ᴀ ᴘʀᴏᴅɪɢᴀʟ sᴏɴ, Murphy returned to ICM, which didn't kill a fatted calf but gave him a tastier morsel to chew on. Jim Wiatt earned his commission when he suggested a remake of Jerry Lewis's 1963 cult classic, *The Nutty Professor*. The agent realized that his client's previous forays into romantic comedy and Freddy Krueger's turf, and cookie-cutter cop capers didn't let Eddie be Eddie. *The Nutty Professor* would allow Eddie to be Eddie times seven, playing that many characters.

Just how far Murphy had fallen down the Paramountain is exemplified by the hoops the studio behind *The Nutty Professor* made him jump through. Gone were the days when he could summon Paramount's production chief to his office. If Universal had the temerity to tell its dinosaur wrangler he could only have $27 million to make *Schindler's List,* imagine the leverage the boys in the Black Tower had over a fading superstar.

Eddie loved the script's multiple roles so much that when the studio said jump, he said how high? "I've been wanting to do something really funny for a long time," he said. "I have been doing different types of movies and mixing genres, but…I wanted to have some fun again like I did in *Coming to America,* where I did multiple characters. My background on *Saturday Night Live* was…doing voices, impressions, and shit. My nature is to be a bunch of different people in my

224

show. So I'm just doing what I do best in *The Nutty Professor.* It's what people expect from me—to be funny."

To get the gig, he had to suffer a series of humiliations. The studio ordered him to audition for the role(s). He did. Then, it demanded he take a pay cut, down from *Vampire's* $15 million to $12 million. Murphy agreed. And then, Universal's notorious bean counters balked at his plan to play seven different characters, including an octogenarian grandma, because major makeup and special effects cost. You can be sure Murphy didn't charge any filet mignon carryout to Universal's parent, Matsushita. Producer Brian Grazer, back on board despite their disappointing collaboration on *Boomerang,* revealed that the star wanted the job so badly he waived script-and-director approval, unheard of for a star of his stature, however diminished. It was a wise move. Murphy wanted John Landis to direct. The studio looked at Landis's recent filmography and declined. Instead, it tapped director Tom Shadyac and writer Steve Oedekerk, both masters of star-making and resuscitating, having performed similar feats for Jim Carrey with *Ace Ventura* and *his* comeback, *Liar, Liar.* Murphy thanked Grazer for his loyalty by agreeing to make two more films with the producer, best known as Ron Howard's staff consigliere.

Like Weimar Germany, Murphy accepted Universal's *Diktat* unconditionally. "The studio didn't want to do those characters. They were like, 'Too expensive,' and so I had to audition. It was the first time I'd auditioned since I was nineteen, and I actually had to do separate makeup tests for all five, put them on video." The master mimic charmed the accountants and their masters.

Despite the fact that it was a remake, *The Nutty Professor* was autobiographical. The central character, Sherman Klump, is a university scientist—and morbidly obese. Although he had never blimped out to Klump-like dimensions, Murphy had waged his own battle with Entemann's after

Harlem Nights failed to do blockbuster business. "Our movie is about obesity. America is obsessed with weight. You have to look a certain way. Being obese is like having any other kind of handicap." Although he didn't receive a story credit, Murphy claimed it was his decision to turn Jerry Lewis's merely dorky scientist into a Macy's float. "The whole concept of *The Nutty Professor* being done again was tricky to me because that film is such a huge part of the Jerry Lewis iconography, the whole thing with buck teeth and stuff. With something great like that, you don't remake it exactly. My idea was to look at how the American public is obsessed with looking a certain way. That's where I came up with the idea of making the professor fat."

On the set, political correctness became a fetish for the star and producer. Less than a decade earlier, Murphy had told jokes about victims of a terminal disease and his victimization by mercenary girlfriends. This time, the filmmakers didn't want fat people picketing the theaters. The decision to lay off the fat wasn't just political; it was also tactical. Murphy had developed such a sense of delicacy, he refused to even use the "f" word. "I don't think overweight people will object. Heavyset people like this movie. Brian Grazer was on the lookout for that. Anytime he heard a line overweight people wouldn't like, he'd say, 'No. Take that out.' Because the minute the movie starts making fun of Sherman, it stops being funny." Murphy's empathy may also have come from the fact that he himself had fought the battle of the bulge in the late eighties.

Rolling Stone's film critic, Peter Travers, felt it wasn't just the avoirdupois that was autobiographical. Klump's spiritual metamorphosis from fat slob to hot stud imitated the star's career trajectory. "Who isn't fed up with Eddie Murphy? The 35-year-old megastar hasn't made a comedy you could sit through without wincing since Reagan won a second term.

You can't see him under the makeup for many of his characters, but autobiographically he looks exactly like the arrogant, sexist, vulgar Buddy Love. Talk about art imitating
life. *The Nutty Professor* symbolizes the real-life Jekyll-Hyde
battle going on inside Murphy. He began as an underdog in
48 HRS. and *Trading Places* and became a fat cat egomaniac,
faux-hip...*The Nutty Professor* owns up to this 'demon inside'
the devil who made him do it—and to laugh the sucker out of
the business before Murphy's career goes kaput. The new
movie is more than a comeback—it's an exorcism," Travers
wrote, moonlighting in a think piece for *US* magazine.

Professor Klump was a personal showcase. Unrecogniz-
able under layers of latex and padding, Murphy could not rely
on his trademark-swaggering image to coast through yet
another rehash of his greatest hits. Klump's romantic yearn-
ings are especially touching for such an all-out farce. By
film's end, the star accomplishes a feat that is magical: He
makes a grotesque fat man sexy. When the professor's beautiful graduate student says I love you during their climactic
dance, the suspension of disbelief is complete.

But what also helped *The Nutty Professor* gross $200
million worldwide were his other characters, who were
anything but lovable. Start with one named Buddy Love.
When Klump swallows a slimming potion he developed in
the lab, the academic turns into a manic love machine who
looks just like Eddie Murphy, slim and studly with the
feminist consciousness of Henry VIII. Buddy didn't require
anything more elaborate than pancake makeup, which
couldn't be said for his other roles.

Sherman belongs to a monumentally dysfunctional family, all but one played by the star. Grandma likes to describe
her sex life in gross-out detail at the dinner table. Sherman's
father and kid brother engage in farting contests that would
make Jonathan Swift blush. Perhaps his best turn is as

Sherman's mother, a domestic saint with apparently no sense of smell. The warmth of the portrayal may reflect his real-life affection for Mrs. Vernon Lynch, Sr.

Murphy loved the limelight, but he didn't hog it. He rejected plans to play one more role, a vicious stand-up comic who humiliates Sherman with a string of fat jokes at a nightclub. It was a wise move. The comic isn't funny, just cruel. Plus, giving the job to another actor allowed Murphy—as Buddy Love—to beat the hell out of his persecutor in a scene that is both amusing and surprisingly satisfying.

The reviews were orgasmic; ticket sales, volcanic. *The Nutty Professor*'s opening weekend of $30 million proved Murphy could not only open a film he could disembowel the competition. *The Nutty Professor* was the No. 1 comedy of 1996 and, until *Independence Day* made the world safe for Rupert Murdoch, the No. 1 film of the year, period.

Headlines proclaimed him the "comeback kid," a term he rejected tongue-in-cheek. "It's not like I'm coming back. Y'all are coming back to the theaters. I've been there every season—just alone." Curmudgeonly critics sounded like *Tiger Beat* columnists, with some urging an Oscar nomination for the star. (He didn't receive one, which may have been the Academy's payback for his tongue-lashing at the 1988 Oscars.) The star engaged in a little sour grapes when he asked if he envied other actors who commuted from comedy to serious, Oscar-worthy roles. "I make more money than Robin Williams. That's the reality of it. If you ask Nick Nolte or Robin Williams if they'd rather have an Oscar or what I get a picture, they'd take the salary. Or they're nuts." (They're apparently nuts. Robin Williams will often take a juicy cameo or supporting role for scale when artsy filmmakers like Kenneth Branagh or Terry Gilliam call. The biggest names in Hollywood are willing to work for peanuts if Woody Allen or Quentin Tarantino is supplying the peanuts.)

The Oscar snub was an irritant quickly forgotten amid

the ecstasy of financial and critical praise. Murphy described his emotional geography just before the film opened. "Right now, I'm in a really good place."

He planned to stay there. Within three months, he had signed on for a sequel, with Steve Oedekerk and Tom Shadyac back on board, and principal photography set for fall 1997. Ominously, considering Murphy's previous efforts at the word processor, *Variety* reported that the star "will be heavily involved in developing the storyline and characters for a sequel." A chorus of "uh-ohs" could be heard in the executive suites at Universal. With Murphy's clout restored, there'd be no haggling the second time around over auditions or the price of pancake.

While his career went full throttle, his home life purred like an old Mazda rotary engine. "There hasn't been one negative moment—not one. A couple of years ago, I would have thought I would be confined by marriage, but it has been just the opposite." The relationship was strengthened by the birth of another daughter, Shayne, in 1995. Murphy called the child "a miracle baby," because the couple had been practicing birth control when Shayne was conceived. "Several methods," Murphy said, sharing perhaps more than even enquiring minds cared to know.

Shayne was a happy accident. To prevent a tragic one, the solicitous father sold the house in Beverly Hills he had bought from Cher for $6 million in 1989 for the fire sale price of $4 million the same year Shayne was born. Murphy unloaded the property because he feared the baby would fall from its unprotected second-story windows.

Chapter 21

......

Comeback or Fluke?

$\mathbf{I}$F F. SCOTT FITZGERALD had ever sobered up long enough, he would have realized the fatuity of his claim that there are no second acts in American life, a case of projection, if ever there was one. Some stars have had more incarnations than a Hindu avatar—Madonna's *Evita*, Cybill Shepherd's Top 10 sitcom, to name two. If not invented by Hollywood, the term career comeback has been embraced by it.

After *The Nutty Professor*, a national magazine called him the "Comeback Kidder." In fact, the star has had two more acts than Fitzgerald allowed. His first was *Saturday Night Live*. The second lasted almost a decade with his tenure as the No. 1 box-office draw—until he turned into the Burt Reynolds of the nineties. The third act began with *The Nutty Professor*, which one critic proclaimed "the most spectacular comeback since Jesus' tomb was found empty."

Although the film was the No. 1 comedy of the year, wet-blanket pundits wondered if *The Nutty Professor* was a comeback or a fluke. Would the play continue its run, or would the curtain fall on the third act of *The Eddie Murphy Story?* In 1997, the omens weren't good.

As *Nutty*'s numbers came in, a euphoric Eddie said from the San Francisco set of his new movie, *Metro*, "This is a trip. This whole town works on numbers. I feel like a big weight has been lifted off my shoulders. I feel like I'm in school and I got an A."

Entertainment Weekly, which gives movies grades instead of stars, probably would have given *Metro* a C, had the magazine even bothered to review it. Others called the film a clone of *48 HRS.,* except this time Eddie played a wise-cracking hostage negotiator. After *The Nutty Professor* showed the rewards of stretching, Murphy mystifyingly re-lied on a formula that hadn't proved viable since the mid eighties. *Rolling Stone's* Peter Travers nailed the reasoning behind the star's decision perfectly: "Complacency dies hard."

In January 1997, fans of *The Nutty Professor* showed up in large enough numbers for *Metro* to take in $25 million its opening weekend. Word of mouth was garrulous about *Metro's* stale formula, and the film disappeared from theaters after making only $31 million.

Murphy could console himself with another figure, the $17 million 20th Century–Fox was paying him for a remake of the 1967 musical *Dr. Doolittle*—a $5 million-dollar raise from *The Nutty Professor.* Jim Henson's magnificent Creature Shop, which made a pig named Babe seem more human than a lot of actors, signed on to create the animals Dr. Dolittle would talk to. Also encouraging, Betty Thomas, who made two subversive *Brady Bunch* features, agreed to direct. Some wondered why anyone would remake a flop, but then again the original *Nutty Professor* was only a cult classic, not a box office hit—except possibly in France. Fox had faith, if not in the project, at least in its star, because along with Murphy's $17 million fee, the studio budgeted the film at a whopping $70 million. Talk is never cheap when audio-animatronic critters are doing the talking. The film's demographics also raised concerns among box office handicappers. The all-important market of filmgoers aged fourteen to twenty-five make or break a blockbuster. No matter how many ingenious special effects are used, *Dr. Dolittle* will remain a kiddie film, and kiddies, even when accompanied by reluctant parents, can't generate $200 million without the help of their adolescent siblings. Murphy's adventure on Santa Monica Boulevard last spring may also turn off parents who could boycott another Murphy performance, as the voice of a dragon in Disney's animated *Mulan*. As if the Magic Kingdom didn't have enough problems already with Southern Baptistry.

Another project that's a definite go, *Holy Man*, sounds more promising. Murphy will reteam with Brian Grazer and Universal on a satire about the cable home shopping network. Murphy will play the materialistic program director of a shopping channel whose job is jeopardized by falling sales. As a gimmick, he hires a New Age minister to host the show. Satire, George S. Kaufman once remarked, is what closes on opening night, and it will be interesting to see if fans of his broad comedies and action flicks accept Murphy in a Nöel Coward turn. Other A-list talent has flocked back to Murphy like moths to a supernova. Tom Schulman, the Oscar-winning author of *Dead Poet's Society* who helped Robin Williams go from successful clown to respected actor, directs from his script.

The light has also turned green for *Life*, which sounds like a more comfortable fit for Murphy's strengths. The action comedy returns him to the buddy genre and prison, *48 HRS.*'s milieu, except this time Murphy has to break out of the pen.

Although he rejected serious roles in the past because he feared fan backlash, Murphy may finally be worthy of Oscar consideration with a biopic on Stevie Wonder. Maybe *The Nutty Professor*'s serious numbers gave Murphy the courage to tackle a serious role. The project isn't firm, but Brian Grazer has already purchased the rights to Wonder's life story for his main man. Murphy shares Grazer's enthusiasm. "This is for real. This is serious. Stevie's story has everything…a child prodigy at twelve, a black blind man who crossed every barrier. You know I *never* do movies about the 'hood. [But] I like movies about overcoming adversity." In that sense, despite their different socioeconomic backgrounds, Wonder's life will be autobiographical—for Eddie Murphy. And regardless of the final product, it will be fascinating to watch Murphy take a character he mercilessly lampooned on *Saturday Night Live* and give it the reverential treatment typical of black biopics. Industry observers, however, aren't optimistic. They note that the last film about a black entertainer, Tina Turner, failed to find the crucial crossover audience.

Such caveats, however, don't faze the star, whose eyes no longer focus solely on the bottom line. A man who once confessed he made a script he loathed for the bucks (*Beverly Hills Cop III*), the *Forbes's* poster boy nicknamed "Money" by friends doesn't value the stuff quite the same way anymore.

"I'm an artist. If a movie makes ten cents or $300 million, it has nothing to do with my choice of films."

To beat a metaphor about the afterlife to death, while the star's professional life hovers in limbo, his personal life may dwell somewhere in the cantos of *Il Purgatorio*. Did the incident on Santa Monica Boulevard represent a habit rather than an aberration? Is he a regular customer rather than a counselor of male prostitutes? Does his homophobia camouflage latent—or not so latent—homosexuality?

The pioneering sex researcher Alfred Kinsey posited a universe of sexual orientation that existed on a continuum. Sexual identity wasn't an either/or proposition, straight or gay. Those absolutes occupy opposite ends of a spectrum with six points, one being exclusively heterosexual; six, exclusively homosexual. In between fall people who may favor one sex, but like to sample the other to varying degrees or, to use a clinical term, "swing both ways."

If Murphy was buying a male streetwalker dressed as a woman, he may be close to No. 1 on Dr. Kinsey's scale, but not quite there.

Where does all this leave Nicole and the three little Mitchell-Murphys—not to mention kids from other liaisons and lawsuits? During his kid-glove interrogation on *Entertainment Tonight,* post-Santa Monica, Murphy said his wife was "embarrassed" and "heart-broken" that he had stopped to chat with a streetwalker. Mrs. Murphy's distress may have been caused by issues of infidelity or her husband's sexual identity. Or it may have seemed to her a matter of life and death—hers. One wonders how Nicole must have felt when a tabloid alleged an exchange of bodily fluids between her husband and a male porn star who now has AIDS—and the tab has a polygraph test to back up the porn star's story. Murphy can file all the multimillion dollar libel suits he wants, but will they buy Nicole peace of mind or prove anything other than that her husband can afford the services of an excellent tort attorney?

One also wonders if Nicole has made an appointment with a discreet internist or scheduled one for Eddie. Or have they both found peace of mind in anonymous testing?

Ironically, back in 1992, a visitor to Bubble Hill asked Murphy if Magic Johnson's contraction of the AIDS virus worried him. Earlier, *Sports Illustrated* quoted Magic as saying, "There were just some bachelors almost every woman in L.A. wanted to be with: Eddie Murphy, Arsenio Hall, and Magic Johnson." Murphy excused himself from this lethal fraternity. He said, "The Magic situation depressed me. But I know how I live my life. How I've lived my life. It didn't scare me." In light of the Santa Monica Boulevard and other incidents, his Olympian detachment now seems misplaced.

And what about the mental health of Edward Regan Murphy? Revisiting Murphy's formative years allows a biographer to do more than wallow in pop psychodynamics. His childhood may provide an explanation for adult behavior that would otherwise seem inexplicable. Friends and associates describe a man about to blow via self-detonation. Cruising a well-known red light district, they say, was a cry for help. Unfortunately, the whole world was listening. Why does Eddie need help? Without the access of a therapist, we have to rely on autobiographical memories recovered by interviewers with a degree in armchair psychology: his father's murder when Eddie was eight; his mother's year-long hospitalization; foster care by a "black Nazi;" an affectionate but tipsy stepfather who confused Dr. Spock with the Marquess of Queensbury. A tough childhood sometimes creates a tough adult. Others grow into exquisitely sensitive souls who register the slightest pinprick as an outrageous arrow of misfortune. Murphy seems to have evolved into the latter, although one might be excused for mistaking sensitivity for temperament and petulance. Whatever the label, Eddie holds a grudge.

Two celebrity feuds point to an adult with skin as thin as a child's. Interestingly, both incidents involved fellow *Saturday Night Live* alumni, Billy Crystal and David Spade. In a 1988 *Playboy* interview, Crystal disobeyed Hollywood's 11th Commandment: Thou shalt not diss a superstar because you never know when you might want to work with him. "I don't think he's a good comedian," Crystal said about Murphy. "When he came back and hosted *Saturday Night Live* during my season [1984-1985], it was an uncomfortable week. He would come very late to rehearsals or not at all. And never apologize." Crystal was the one apologizing when he realized he had alienated the most powerful actor in the business. But Murphy refused to accept the apology. The superstar's snit didn't end there. He also ditched an *SNL* reunion show in 1989 because of Crystal's participation. That same year, when Eddie hosted a tribute to Sammy Davis Jr., Crystal, who does a dead-on impression of the Candy Man, was pointedly omitted from the guest list. Don't get mad; get even, the creepy tenet of back-stabbing etiquette says. Murphy does both.

Another feud suggests Murphy's emotional fragility. As *SNL's* fey movie reviewer, David Spade once flashed Eddie's picture on the screen and said, "Look, kids, a falling star," when Murphy's career was becalmed in box-office doldrums. Murphy's protégé, *SNL's* Chris Rock, later told Spade, "Eddie's got his biggest movie in ten years, a beautiful wife, and he still can't shake the fact that you took a swipe at him." Spade replied, "Tell him three words that'll change his life: *Let it go.*"

That of course begs the real question. What is Eddie Murphy holding on to?

THE FILMS OF EDDIE MURPHY

· · · · · ·

IT'S HARD TO NAME a superstar who's had more dramatic ups and downs in his career than Eddie Murphy. The No. 1 box-office attraction of the eighties, he became the butt of jokes on TV and in clubs during the following decade. (Particularly galling, his artistic birthplace, *Saturday Night Live,* seemed to keep a running tab on his career downturns and private peccadilloes.)

During the eighties, Murphy could do no wrong—on-screen at least. Even his less satisfying movies in this era were critic-proof. Unfortunately, there was no such thing as "audience proof." In the nineties, fans joined the critical consensus and ignored his efforts to stretch as a romantic leading man and nice guy. But he prevailed and continued to test himself with offbeat roles until the audience came back by the millions to his comeback film, *The Nutty Professor.* Murphy ignored high-priced counsel to replicate his street-smart tough guy, and instead played a fat man in love. The audience fell in love with him all over again. Today the happy workaholic has half a dozen film projects in various stages of development and a fee of $20 million per film.

48 HRS., 1982

Murphy's film debut turned him into a major star. A success with the public and critics, who predicted a long

237

career for the twenty-one-year-old actor, *48 HRS.* cast Murphy in a role he came to own, the lovable con man. In this cops 'n' robber barons adventure, Murphy is a con man and a con, let out of prison for the title's two days to help a San Francisco police detective (Nick Nolte) track down murderous drug dealers. Most memorable scene: Murphy, impersonating a cop, rousts a bar full of rednecks with the taunt, "I'm your worst fucking nightmare. A nigger with a badge."

Trading Places, 1983

Murphy's second film was an even bigger hit. Playing a con man again, he starts out as a homeless beggar taken under the wing of two corrupt stockbrokers who make a wager they can turn Murphy into a successful businessman. To that end, they cheat stockbroker Dan Aykroyd out of his home and job and give them to Murphy, who suddenly finds himself living in Aykroyd's posh townhouse and driving his car—even bedding his girlfriend. When Murphy learns about Aykroyd's misfortune, they team up to turn the tables on the evil execs. Most memorable scene: Homeless, Murphy pretends to be a double amputee with his legs hidden under a blanket. When a passerby expresses disgust at this panhandling ploy, he asks on his knees, "What's the matter? Ain't you seen *Porgy and Bess?*"

Best Defense, 1984

Billed as a "strategic guest star," Murphy spent only twenty minutes on screen as a whacked-out military advisor in Kuwait. The film was actually a vehicle for Dudley Moore, and the two men didn't appear together in a single frame. Audiences, expecting an Eddie Murphy movie, boycotted the comedy, while the, uh, strategic star later admitted he only did it for the money, $1 million, his biggest payday to date. Most memorable scene: None.

Beverly Hills Cop, 1984

His first film made him a star, his fourth, a superstar. As a tough Detroit cop who tracks down his best friend's murderers in Beverly Hills. Murphy's Axel Foley created another trademark persona, the fish out of water. The culture clash between a street-smart cop from the inner city and his lame Beverly Hills counterparts made this generic action film a comedy classic. Most memorable scene of many: Eddie bluffs his way into an exclusive, members-only club by telling the maitre d' he has to tell his "gay lover," a gangster dining at a nearby table, that he's given him herpes. Trivia note: Murphy rewrote most of his dialogue, deleting white concepts of black slang like "jive turkey" and "sucka." Bonus trivia: Sylvester Stallone and John Travolta both passed on this career-making role.

The Golden Child, 1986

Murphy plays a fish out of water again, this time way out of the water and in Tibet, as a social worker who must rescue a child reincarnation of the Buddha or the world will come to an end. Mel Gibson rejected the script, and Murphy didn't like the dialogue either, so he ad-libbed most of his lines. The critics loathed this slight action comedy, but its unlikely commercial success made Murphy "bankable," i.e., his name attached to any project would get instant financing. Murphy could name his price and picture. His next choice was a mixed blessing. Trivia note: Murphy's first love scene on-screen with off-screen girlfriend Charlotte Lewis ended up on the cutting room floor.

Eddie Murphy Raw, 1987

The most successful concert film of all time. *Raw* was shot during his stand-up act at New York's Felt Forum. The star had just broken up with his girlfriend, and he seemed to be projecting his anger toward her onto the entire opposite sex. For sheer misogyny, *Raw*, is one for the time capsule. During his ninety-minute set, he also managed to offend gays, Asians, Italian-Americans, and even blacks. One critic said of his unfunny anger, "To review *Raw* was to leave the domain of criticism for psychiatry."

Beverly Hills Cop II, 1987

A sequel to 1984's biggest hit was inevitable, and Axel Foley's second trip to L.A.'s gilded suburb became the No. 1 film of 1987. By now the fish-out-of-water conceit seemed as fresh as day-old trout. Murphy again battled drug dealers, but the film contained an original twist—the bad guy was actually a bad girl, Danish model Brigitte Nielsen, Mrs. Sylvester Stallone at the time. Most memorable, albeit chauvinistic line: A comment on one woman's talents—"She could suck a golf ball out of a garden hose."

Coming to America, 1988

This time Eddie is a fish out of Africa, Prince Akeem of the mythical kingdom of Zamunda, who comes to America in search of a sophisticated bride. Industry observers speculated that, as the poor little rich prince, Murphy was trying to soften his *Raw* screen image. The hugely successful comedy contained some noticeable firsts: Best buddy Arsenio Hall's first major film role. Eddie's first on-screen romance. His first film with an almost all-black cast. And the first to showcase his protean talents in multiple roles. Most memorable scene: As Murphy soaks in a swimming pool-sized bathtub at the palace, a handmaiden rises from below the water and announces, "The royal penis has been cleaned, Your Highness."

Harlem Nights, 1989

Murphy produced, directed, co-wrote and starred in this vanity production, which marked the beginning of his near decade-long decline at the box office. Murphy and his idol, Richard Pryor, play the super suave owners of a nightclub in Depression-era Harlem who foil a white mob's efforts to take over their business. Its derivative flavor had one critic derisively call it *"The Sting* in blackface," but *Harlem Nights* didn't come anywhere near that classic's box office or critical acclaim. In fact, the reviews were so lacerating Murphy went on an eating binge and gained fifteen pounds. Most memorable scene: Eddie challenges rival club owner Della Reese to a fist fight, and she whups his butt.

Another 48 HRS., 1990

After the public humiliation of *Harlem Nights,* Murphy returned to what he thought was a tried-and-true formula: The wise-aleck street persona of his film debut. Murphy and Nolte re-team to catch a drug dealer in a storyline that was such a Xerox of the original, a film encyclopedia called it a "virtual remake." Unfortunately, it didn't make the original's money.

Boomerang, 1992

Murphy tried romantic comedy again with this tale of a male chauvinist buppie (black urban professional) who falls for his boss (Robin Givens), an advertising executive as sexist as he is. Soon, the former lover-and-leave-'em has become a whimpering codependent, whining to Givens, "Why haven't you called me?" Most memorable scene: Eartha Kitt, as a nymphomaniac senior citizen, practically date-rapes Eddie after promising him a promotion at her ad agency.

The Distinguished Gentleman, 1992

The public rejected his efforts to become a "black Cary Grant," according to one critic, so he reverted to the kind of role that made him a star, the lovable con man. The improbable plot had Murphy playing a small-time hustler who hits it big when he tricks Florida voters into electing him to Congress. Congressional lobbyists represent multimillion-dollar marks to the con man, but the love of a beautiful lobbyist reforms Eddie. The cynical pol turns into Jimmy Stewart in *Mr. Smith Goes to Washington,* exposing corrupt politicians and the special interest groups that control them. Most memorable scene: To extort hush money, Murphy shows up at a glitzy political fund-raiser with a sleazy phone sex operator whose services the fat cat host has enjoyed and embarrasses the man in front of his high society friends until he pays Murphy to leave.

Beverly Hills Cop III, 1994

By now, Murphy was desperate for a hit, so he returned to the scene of his greatest box-office triumphs, the world of Rodeo Drive. Yet another excuse was found to get Murphy out of Detroit and back in Beverly Hills, but no one, it seemed, wanted to make a third trip with him. The $50 million film cost more than it made in the U.S. The novelty of Eddie making fools out of white cops was ten years old, and fans obviously wanted something new. Eddie would try to give them that in his next effort.

Vampire in Brooklyn, 1995

This ultraviolent bloodsucker has the sad distinction of being the only Murphy film that didn't turn a profit. (All of his other so-called "flops" made back their money overseas). Perhaps the only truly scary thing in this horror film was the opening credits, which listed Murphy's brothers, Vernon and Charles, both amateurs, as creator of the story and screenwriter, respectively. Murphy plays a Rastafarian vampire who travels to New York to mate with the only other living vampire before their race dies out. Murphy has his work cut out for him, because the hair, makeup, and wardrobe people seemed to have gone out of their way to make the sexy star look unattractive. (This is even before he morphs into a ghoul.) Murphy here seems more Hannibal Lecter than Bela Lugosi, eating his victims rather than draining their blood. Least memorable scene: Murphy spits out the tongue of a Mafioso and says, "I've already eaten—Italian."

The Nutty Professor, 1996

Murphy's big comeback, the year's No. 1 comedy. (Only *Independence Day* kept it from becoming the No. 1 film.) In this vague remake of the 1963 Jerry Lewis cult classic, Murphy isn't "nutty," he's obese. As a university researcher who discovers a slimming potion, Murphy's awkward Prof. Sherman Klump metamorphoses into stud Buddy Love, who romances the grad student the fat Klump secretly pines for. Thanks to multimillion-dollar prosthetics and makeup, Murphy also plays four members of his hilariously dysfunctional family, who raise flatulence at the dinner table to a lower art form. The film's quarter-billion-dollar gross had one magazine hailing him as the "Comeback Kidder." His next film generated another headline: "Comeback or Fluke?"

Metro, 1997

The tepid box-office of this formulaic action flick suggested that "fluke" rather than "comeback" applied to *The Nutty Professor*. After his magnificent stretches in that film, Murphy inexplicably returned to stale form, a wise-cracking officer of the law. At least this time, he changed jobs and played a hostage negotiator instead of a cop. Murphy later said *Metro*'s disappointing box office didn't matter; his wife and kids made him happy. (Apparently, not happy enough. See Preface.)

Dr. Dolittle, Spring 1998

Question: Why would 20th Century–Fox spend $70 million to remake a musical flop from the sixties? Answer:

Because the star of *The Nutty Professor* agreed to play the title's veterinarian. Murphy's singing efforts on three albums were largely dismissed by critics, so it's not surprising this will be a non-musical remake. Insiders say the remake improves on the gimmick of the 1967 original that had the doctor speaking animal Esperanto. In the new version, Murphy uses ESP to communicate with his verbally-challenged patients. On the plus side, Jim Henson's magical Creature Shop, which turned a pig named Babe into Chatty Cathy, will try to work similar magic on this one. But the spring rather than summer or Christmas release, when kids are out of school, suggests the studio isn't bullish on its animal movie.

INDEX

......

245